D0982967

The Collected Poems of Philip Lamantia

The Collected Poems of Philip Lamantia

EDITED BY Garrett Caples, Andrew Joron, and Nancy Joyce Peters
FOREWORD BY Lawrence Ferlinghetti
BIBLIOGRAPHY BY Steven Fama

 University of California Press   Berkeley Los Angeles London

University of California Press, one of the most distinguished university presses in the United States, enriches lives around the world by advancing scholarship in the humanities, social sciences, and natural sciences. Its activities are supported by the UC Press Foundation and by philanthropic contributions from individuals and institutions. For more information, visit www.ucpress.edu.

University of California Press
Berkeley and Los Angeles, California

University of California Press, Ltd.
London, England

LIBRARY OF CONGRESS CATALOGING-IN-PUBLICATION DATA

Lamantia, Philip, 1927–2005.
 [Poems]
 The collected poems of Philip Lamantia / edited by Garrett Caples, Andrew Joron, and Nancy Joyce Peters ; foreword by Lawrence Ferlinghetti.
   pages   cm.
 The first collected edition of this poet's work, including poems that have been out of print for more than forty years.
 Includes bibliographical references and index of titles and first lines.
 ISBN 978-0-520-26972-9 (cloth : alk. paper)
 I. Caples, Garrett T., editor of compilation.   II. Joron, Andrew, editor of compilation.   III. Peters, Nancy J. (Nancy Joyce), editor of compilation.   IV. Title.
 PS3562.A42   2013
 811'.54—dc23   2012050020

Manufactured in the United States of America

22   21   20   19   18   17   16   15   14   13
10   9   8   7   6   5   4   3   2   1

In keeping with a commitment to support environmentally responsible and sustainable printing practices, UC Press has printed this book on Rolland Enviro100, a 100% post-consumer fiber paper that is FSC certified, deinked, processed chlorine-free, and manufactured with renewable biogas energy. It is acid-free and EcoLogo certified.

Contents

Foreword

I first saw the young Philip Lamantia sometime in about 1954 at one of Kenneth Rexroth's Friday night soirées in his big old flat above Jack's Record Cellar at 250 Scott Street in the old Fillmore district when it was still largely a black ghetto. Local and itinerant poets and other flickering literary lights would show up, usually loaded in more ways than one but mainly with the latest poetry. Rexroth, with his book review program on KPFA radio, was the reigning avant-garde arbiter of all things radically poetic. He was an anarchist and libertarian in those days when libertarians weren't followers of Ayn Rand but were philosophical anarchists and pacifists, as were many of the poets.

As a recent, unpublished, and totally straight arrival from New York, I didn't dare open my mouth at these far-out gatherings but sat as far back as possible, imbibing the dago red and listening to the likes of Lamantia and Robert Duncan carrying on brilliant stream-of-consciousness discourses that flew over my head like exotic birds making letters with their legs. They were passionate, erudite, disputative conversationalists. One word might send them off in opposite directions, with sentences that might run from Foucault's pendulum or the size of Flaubert's penis to a mad disquisition on phallic symbols in general.

However, having opened with Peter D. Martin a one-room bookstore in North Beach called City Lights, and having the idea of publishing an international poetry series, I realized that I had fallen into a veritable quicksilver mine where local poets of the so-called San Francisco Poetry Renaissance met up with the first Beat poets, those wild-ass carpetbaggers from Back East like Allen Ginsberg who proceeded to take over the scene.

It was ten years since the war in Europe had ended. Military service had uprooted so many Americans, many of whom returned home briefly but didn't stay long. And a great migration of my generation began. It was as if the whole continent had tilted, and the population slid westward. It took a whole decade for the disparate elements of postwar America to coalesce in a radically new culture. And it was happening in San Francisco and in places like 250 Scott Street and North Beach. San Francisco was still a last frontier where a new world was aborning.

Philip Lamantia's voice was the most distinctive poetic sound I had ever heard.

In New York after the war, at the Tate Gallery I had heard T.S. Eliot's dry St. Louis accent with a *placage* of Bloomsbury over it. (He tried so hard to be British!) But Lamantia's voice was Something Else. It was a sensual voice (with a kind of mid-Atlantic accent)—ecstatic and visionary. Reading his poetry on the silent printed page, I can still hear the emotive sound of it. Lamantia, both in his person and in his poetry, bridged the gap between European Surrealism and the radical American cultural revolution begun by the Beats. As such, Lamantia was just what was needed for a City Lights Pocket Poets Series with its aim of creating an international, dissident, insurgent ferment. And so it was that City Lights ended up publishing four of Philip's books over the years. And the rest is history . . .

Lawrence Ferlinghetti

Acknowledgments

First and foremost, this book would not have been possible without the efforts of Philip Lamantia's friend and bibliographer Steven Fama, who provided materials he had painstakingly collected over decades, including unpublished poems found in Lamantia's correspondence and other work published in rare and ephemeral journals. In particular, we owe him a debt of gratitude for tracking down Lamantia's first published poem, "Ages in the Wind," from a 1943 high school poetry anthology, *The Young West Speaks,* whose title not even Lamantia himself could recall.

We would also like to thank Anthony Bliss and the entire staff at The Bancroft Library at the University of California, Berkeley, which houses Lamantia's papers. Most especially, we are grateful to Dean Smith, who was most helpful in locating missing documents.

Special thanks are also due to Michael McClure for his insights into Lamantia's life and work during the mid- to late 1950s. McClure shed valuable light on Lamantia's concept of "weir."

We thank Lawrence Ferlinghetti, Elaine Katzenberger, and the staff at City Lights Books, the original publisher of several of Lamantia's books, for their support of this project.

We are also deeply grateful to our original editor at the University of California Press, Rachel Berchten, whose patience and enthusiasm were essential to bringing this project to fruition. Grateful acknowledgment is also made to Kim Hogeland and Mary Francis for seeing this book through its final stages, and to Caroline Knapp for her skillful copyediting.

Robert Kaufman and Joseph Donahue put in a good word for this book in its earliest stage, for which we extend our thanks.

This book has benefited from several conversations and correspondences. Dave Haselwood, the publisher of Auerhahn Press, provided a helpful clue or two regarding the Lamantia books he published. Poet and filmmaker Richard O. Moore lent his insights into Lamantia's participation in Rexroth's Libertarian Circle. John Suiter deserves special mention for his invaluable interview with Lamantia, a transcript of which is housed with Lamantia's papers in The Bancroft Library. Peter Conners provided what scant information exists on Lamantia's visit to Tim Leary in 1962.

David Meltzer shared with us his own experiences with Lamantia over the years; their interview in Meltzer's anthology, *San Francisco Beat,* is one of the vital sources of biographical information on Lamantia.

And finally, Garrett Caples and Andrew Joron would like to thank surrealist poet Will Alexander for having personally introduced us to Philip Lamantia all those years ago. Thanks, Will.

High Poet: The Life and Work of Philip Lamantia

Late in life, Philip Lamantia drafted fragments of a memoir under the working title *High Poet*. He regarded himself as a "high poet" in more than one sense: he was a visionary poet who ascended the heights of pure imagination, one who sought both intellectual understanding and spiritual transcendence. He was also a poet of vast erudition, one for whom learning was equivalent to gnosis; in his wide-ranging reading, he drew out the poetic essence of the sciences, philosophy, and history, which he then infused into his own writing. He welcomed (and sometimes provoked) visions, through such vehicles as meditation, religious ceremony, and psychotropic substances. His quest led outward as well as inward: in 1944, at age sixteen, Lamantia left high school in his native San Francisco to join the company of war-exiled Parisian surrealists in New York; and through the 1950s and 1960s, he lived and wrote in Mexico, Morocco, France, Italy, Spain, and Greece.

Throughout his poetic itinerary, Lamantia would traverse the ecstatic space between writing poetry and religious mysticism, at times rejecting both, then discovering aspects of one within the other—until finally, in the last decade of his life, arriving at a synthesis of scholarly erudition and spiritual discernment. Lamantia's high aspiration as a poet is evident in his desire—stated in a late interview—to achieve a "*miracle in words.*"[1]

In tandem with an alternation between the polarities of poetry and mysticism, Lamantia struggled with a lifelong manic-depressive condition. Bipolar episodes, which could take the form of spiritual crises, led him to withdraw from society for long periods, to suppress his own work from publication, and even, on occasion, to destroy it. As a result, Lamantia maintained a hermetic presence in American poetry, even as he played a seminal role in some of its most innovative developments, both through his participation in mentor Kenneth Rexroth's anarchist Libertarian Circle of poets and scholars, subsequently a major component of the San Francisco Renaissance, and through his later involvement with the Beat Generation. As Rexroth would later write, "a great deal of what has happened since in poetry was anticipated in the poetry Lamantia wrote before he was 21."[2]

Even the barest summary of Lamantia's subsequent life bristles with incident. In the mid-1950s, he partook in rituals with the Washoe Indians at Lake Tahoe,

Nevada, and with the Cora Indians (Nayarit) in Mexico. In 1955, between stays in Mexico, Lamantia participated in the famous Six Gallery reading in San Francisco where Allen Ginsberg first read "Howl." Two years later, shortly after the publication of Jack Kerouac's *On the Road* (1957), Lamantia gave what are widely considered to be the first public jazz poetry readings, with Kerouac, Howard Hart, and musician David Amram. Yet by 1960, even as he was featured in Donald Allen's groundbreaking anthology, *New American Poetry: 1945–1960*, Lamantia had renounced poetry, burning most—though not all—of his unpublished work. In late 1962, he left America for Europe, devoting himself to the study of Egyptian symbology and Renaissance hermetic traditions—yet in 1965, after meeting his future wife, Nancy Peters, he dramatically returned to both poetry and surrealism, beginning his long association with City Lights Books with the 1967 publication of his *Selected Poems: 1943–1966*. In the early '70s, after returning to San Francisco, he affiliated himself with the Chicago Surrealist Group, led by Franklin and Penelope Rosemont, contributing to its journal *Arsenal* while remaining aloof from both mainstream literary culture and the constructivist aesthetics of language poetry. The 1980s would reveal an increasing ecological consciousness in his poetry, manifesting itself through his exploration of the Pacific Coast wilderness, ornithology, and Native American cultures. His ongoing interest in Egypt culminated in a long poem of that title, inspired by his 1989 visit to the monuments at Luxor.

By the mid-'90s, Lamantia had largely fallen silent due to severe depression, though he would reemerge after the publication of *Bed of Sphinxes: New and Selected Poems 1943–1993* in 1997 and a brief return to Catholicism following a 1998 vision in the National Shrine of Saint Francis of Assisi in San Francisco's North Beach. This final burst of poetic activity resulted in a handful of published poems before he fell silent once again, in late 2001. He spent the rest of his life withdrawn from the world. On his death in 2005, the *New York Times* acknowledged Lamantia's vital contribution to twentieth-century poetry by quoting French literary critic Yves le Pellec, who once identified him as "a living link between French surrealism and the American counterculture at its beginnings."[3]

EARLY LIFE

Philip Nunzio Lamantia was born at home, at 1715 Sanchez Street, in San Francisco, on October 23, 1927, the only child of Sicilian immigrants Nunzio and Mary Lamantia. His paternal grandmother, Mattea, also lived with the family, and among Philip's earliest memories were the Sicilian folktales she told him in her backyard rose garden. Nunzio had immigrated from Palermo to the United States in his late teens and had served in the American army in World War I. Mary (née Tarantino) came from a large, impoverished family from the tiny Sicilian island of Ustica; her oldest brother, Paul Tarantino, a produce distributor, served as the head of the family. After the war,

Nunzio was hired by Tarantino as a produce broker, becoming known in the trade by the Anglicized name "Nelson." Nunzio became successful enough to buy a house on Russia Avenue in San Francisco's Excelsior district, then on the outskirts of the city, where Philip spent most of his childhood.

Throughout his childhood, Lamantia was drawn to what the surrealists called "the marvelous"—manifestations of the uncanny, the sublime, or the impossible, that resist or exceed rationalization. On the one hand, this is perfectly ordinary, insofar as surrealism associates the ability to perceive the marvelous with the unfettered imagination of childhood. On the other hand, Lamantia's childhood taste for the marvelous—insofar as it can be known—is remarkably consistent with his adult purchase on the topic. Among his papers, for example, are two scrapbooks containing newspaper comics depicting scenes from exotic cultures as well as illustrations from *Ripley's Believe It or Not,* asserting the marvelous as fact. As noted in his essay "Radio Voices: A Child's Bed of Sirens," Lamantia also gravitated toward what he calls "mystery fantasies," whose characters powerfully resonated in all media: comics, movies, and radio.[4] "I can trace a profound awakening of the poetic sense of life and language directly to the exemplary magical myth of *The Shadow.*"[5] "On the poetic plane," he continues, "*The Shadow* and *Mandrake* are paragons of hermetic knowledge: modern forms, respectively, of the fairy tale wonder-worker and the sorcerer."[6]

That these uncanny, fantastic elements of pop culture influenced the poetics of the precocious Lamantia is evident from his earliest days as a poet. Lamantia first began writing poetry in middle school, under the tutelage of a flaming-haired Irish immigrant named Griffin, whose English classes consisted purely of the reading and discussion of poetry and whose standing policy was that anyone who wrote a poem didn't have to do that evening's homework. Lamantia's choice to embark on an orientalist fantasia modeled on Edward FitzGerald's *Rubaiyat of Omar Khayyam* already seems characteristic of his prior interest in the marvelous (even as its inherently open-ended nature allowed him to avoid homework indefinitely). From the *Rubaiyat,* Lamantia would move on to Edgar Allan Poe, thus placing himself directly in touch with one of surrealism's earliest acknowledged forebears. "Poe," André Breton writes in the first "Manifesto of Surrealism" (1924), "is surrealist in adventure," consonant with Lamantia's poetic reading of "night-beings" like the Shadow.[7]

Nothing from Lamantia's *Rubaiyat* survives; nonetheless, the poem impressed the adults in his life with its level of accomplishment, leading to his own self-identification as a poet by age fourteen. According to his autobiographical notes, his poetic vocation came to him on the top of San Bruno Mountain, after observing the weird effects of the winds and fog banks that surrounded it, evidence of his response to the marvels of the natural world.[8] There, in the center of a "classic grove of trees," he heard "an inner voice declaring me a poet." Lamantia noted that "it was there on that mountain that I wrote my first modernist poem 'Paranoid Dream.'" This poem was not preserved, though another from this time, "Ages in the Wind," survives, due to its appearance in the 1943 installment of *The Young West Sings: Anthology of California High School Poetry*—his first publication. With its reference to the "dark cultures and ages" and "the Nile," "Ages in the Wind" appears to allude to Lamantia's burgeoning interest in the mysteries of past civilizations, fueled in part by a visit around this time to the library of the Philosophical Research Society, established by Manly P. Hall in 1936, in Los Angeles.

ENCOUNTER WITH SURREALISM

"Paranoid Dream" seems to reflect (or even to anticipate) the young poet's encounter with the "paranoia-critical method" of renegade surrealist Salvador Dalí, whose paintings were exhibited in a retrospective at the San Francisco Palace of the Legion of Honor in the spring of the year that this poem was written, 1942.[9] The Dalí exhibition, along with a nearly concomitant retrospective of the works of Joan Miró at the San Francisco Museum of Art, brought surrealism to the attention of the teenaged Lamantia with all the force of a revelation. Here was a worldview and a practice that could accommodate the unsettling modes of consciousness that were already flowering in him. Lamantia would reiterate, throughout his life, the lessons learned from these two exhibitions: that surrealism is not a *style* (as demonstrated by the contrast between Dalí's classical figuration and Miró's semiabstraction) but a transmogrification of art—and ultimately of reality itself—into something *other*. Moreover, the citations from surrealist texts that accompanied the paintings were electrifying in their own right. These texts seemed, as Lamantia later attested, to flow into the paintings themselves, aspiring toward the *supreme point* (posited by André Breton) where conventional categories—between word and image, sleep and waking, reason and madness, life and death—are abolished.

After viewing these examples of surrealist *painting*, Lamantia resolved to practice surrealist *writing*—seized with the notion, as he explained many years later in his lectures at the San Francisco Art Institute, that paintings and poems were interchangeable manifestations of the same unsayable, unpictureable sur-reality.[10] Following his visits to these exhibitions, Lamantia scoured the San Francisco Public Library for materials relating to surrealism and came up with only a handful of books, among them David Gascoyne's *A Short Survey of Surrealism* (1935), Julien Levy's *Surrealism* (1936), and Georges Lemaître's *From Cubism to Surrealism in French Literature* (1941). On newsstands, Lamantia found issues of *View*, a glossy, New York–based avant-garde magazine that often featured surrealist art and writing; he immediately ordered the surrealist books advertised in its pages. Lastly, in the library of the San Francisco Museum of Art, Lamantia discovered two issues of the lavishly produced *VVV*, a magazine emanating from the New York circle of European surrealists in exile during World War II.

Thus inspired, Lamantia, by his own account, "in no time had a dozen poems ready," which he ventured to submit to the editors of *View* magazine.[11] Five of these—"I Am Coming," "Apparition of Charles Baudelaire," "The Ruins," "By the Curtain of Architecture," and "There Are Many Pathways to the Garden"—were accepted for publication in the June 1943 issue, and another poem, "Automatic World," appeared in the subsequent (October) issue. The power and originality of these works—written by a fifteen-year-old—caused Lamantia to be hailed by the New York avant-garde as a kind of American Rimbaud. A flurry of correspondence ensued between Lamantia and *View* editors Charles Henri Ford and Parker Tyler. After his subsequent discovery of *VVV*, the young poet wrote directly to surrealist leader André Breton and enclosed some poems for his consideration.

Breton at that time was much concerned with the survival of the surrealist project, which was facing, in the midst of the wartime dispersal of its key practitioners, increasingly hostile criticism declaring the movement to be irrelevant and outmoded. Not long before Lamantia's emergence on the scene, Breton had given a lecture at Yale University on "The Situation of Surrealism between the Two Wars" in which he emphasized, with an eye toward the next generation, that surrealism "was born of a limitless affirmation of faith in the *genius* of youth." He therefore welcomed the advent of a young American poet of genius, accepting three of Lamantia's poems— "The Islands of Africa" (dedicated to Rimbaud), "The Touch of the Marvelous," and "Plumage of Recognition"—for publication in *VVV* and praising him as "a voice that rises once in a hundred years." Breton also asked Lamantia to compose a statement clarifying his relation to surrealism; this statement—"Surrealism in 1943"—appeared in the final double issue of *VVV* alongside Lamantia's poems.

In this brief statement, Lamantia brought everything he had learned about surrealism in the previous year into focus, and especially made a point of citing Breton's *Second Manifesto*. "Surrealism," Lamantia wrote, "is fundamentally a philosophy endeavoring to form a unity between particular opposite forces.... Surrealism carries this dialectic process to one of its farthest points." He fully embraced the role that he sensed Breton wanted him to fill, that of a bringer of youthful vitality to the movement, proclaiming that "the voice of Lautréamont, pure, young and feeding the fire that has begun to issue from my depths, is again heard." Lamantia added the proviso that, since he was "only fifteen years old," his opinions would "inevitably change to a certain extent." It would turn out to be a prescient comment: by the end of the following year, he would renounce his adherence to surrealism. Lamantia would wrestle—as in a "dialectic process"—with many other visionary and esoteric worldviews before finally formulating his own version of surrealism in later life.

For the moment, however, the young poet was still flushed with the excitement of his recognition by the surrealists in New York. In contrast to his literary success, he had been experiencing difficulties at home and at school, mostly due to his precocious intelligence and rebellious behavior. In early 1944, Lamantia and his father were called into a meeting with the principal of Balboa High School, who, attempting to get Philip to conform to school regulations, invoked the Depression-era phrase

First author photo, San Francisco, 1943. Courtesy of The Bancroft Library, University of California, Berkeley.

"the common man." To the principal's consternation, the young poet shot to his feet and declared, "I am *not* the common man!" While it resulted in expulsion from Balboa, this display of defiance won the respect of Nunzio Lamantia, who was otherwise mystified by his son's strange pursuits. In April 1944, on the basis of an offer from the editors of *View* of an editorial assistant position and with the approval of his parents, the sixteen-year-old poet boarded a "gaslit wartime priority train," bound for New York City.[12]

Lamantia thus became known as a poet in New York some time before he participated in the literary scene of his native San Francisco. Nonetheless, soon after his debut in *View,* Lamantia was contacted by Berkeley-based poet/editor George Leite, who would shortly launch his own magazine, *Circle.* Leite would publish Lamantia in *Circle* alongside such international literary figures as Henry Miller, Anaïs Nin, and

Yvan Goll. More important, on the night before Lamantia's departure for New York, Leite invited him to dinner to meet anarchist-pacifist poet Kenneth Rexroth, thus preparing the way for his entry into the San Francisco milieu of oppositional writers, artists, and intellectuals upon his return to the Bay Area. In *An Autobiographical Novel* (first published in 1964, revised in 1991), perhaps wishing to claim discovery of the teenage poet, Rexroth presents a highly fictionalized account of their initial meeting that writes Leite out of the picture:

> One day I got a telephone call from someone I didn't know who was an English teacher in a high school. . . .
> He said, "I am sending you over a student in whom I think you would be interested and who you might be able to help. He is a poet with immense talent."
> In a few days, we got a phone call from Philip Lamantia. We asked him to dinner that night. It was an amazing experience. He was about sixteen years old and extremely hand-some—a small Italian lad who seemed already to have read most avant-garde literature and who, again, was already the best of the third generation of surrealists. . . . I have never known anyone else who started out, without preliminaries, with no five-finger exercises or scales, as an achieved poet.[13]

Having published three books of poetry by that time, Rexroth was well versed in avant-garde literature and active in radical politics; he had visited Paris in the twenties, when surrealism was at its height of influence, and even claimed to have met some of the group's members. He had also resided in New York, but ended up rejecting that city's intellectual culture as "too European." Rexroth, robust in body and spirit, was attracted to what he perceived as the wilder side of the American continent, taking up residence in San Francisco in 1927. His influence on the young Lamantia would prove to be both deep and lasting.

As soon as he arrived in Manhattan, Lamantia was plunged into an exhilarat-ing—but at first, undoubtedly bewildering—milieu where he encountered many of the famous surrealists whose work he had studied in the past year. He took up his post as an editorial assistant at *View,* "mostly rejecting the daily deluge of unsolicited manuscripts." As Lamantia recalled in a 1998 interview with David Meltzer,

> My milieu was mainly among the many English-speaking French and other European painters and intellectuals: Max Ernst, Duchamp, Yves Tanguy, Nicolas Calas, Kurt Seligmann, Pavel Tchelitchew, André Masson, the critic Leon Kochnitsky—and their American counterparts, the writers Harold Rosenberg, Lionel Abel, Parker Tyler, the painter William Baziotes, and Paul Bowles, who introduced me to world music [and, as Lamantia notes elsewhere, to modern jazz, especially bebop]. There were weekly gal-lery openings, jazz on Fifty-Second Street, endless parties, and almost daily invitations to lunch and dinner.[14]

Lamantia found Breton himself to be less accessible than he may have hoped, partly because of the language barrier (Breton spoke only French), and partly because, as

Lamantia jotted in his autobiographical notes, Breton was "not social, and didn't go to galleries." Their first encounter occurred by chance, when Breton came by the *View* offices at 1 East Fifty-Third Street to sign the contract for a bilingual selection of his poems, *Young Cherry Trees Secured against Hares,* which View Editions would publish in 1946. This encounter was brief, with Charles Henri Ford acting as translator, but Breton would soon arrange for a more formal and substantial meeting between himself and *"le jeune poète américain"* at Del Pezzo's Restaurant, where they dined alone, save for the presence of art and music critic Leon Kochnitzky, who translated between the two as they discussed surrealism.[15]

The significance of this dinner—as well as the special introduction to Lamantia's poems in *VVV*—can be gauged by Breton's oft-criticized aloofness from the New York art milieu. The introduction to an anthology of *View,* for example, cites Edouard Roditi, the polyglot poet and translator of *Young Cherry Trees*: "Surrealism proper, Roditi reminds us, was a closed society. 'One must be invited to join, and we never sought admission.'"[16] While Breton usually withheld his endorsement of their work as surrealist, the New York avant-gardists attracted to European surrealism maintained a sense of independence, refusing to pledge their allegiance to Bretonian principles as Lamantia had. This was especially true of Charles Henri Ford and Parker Tyler, editors of *View*; while surrealism remained central to their concerns, they sometimes featured material from the wider avant-garde scene. Their "Americana Fantastica" issue, in particular, was intended to showcase the art and writing of a homegrown imagination complementary with, but not beholden to, European surrealism. As Tyler pointedly stated in that issue, the fantastic, "having no home but its own . . . cannot be transplanted."[17]

Although his encounters with Breton were infrequent, Lamantia met with the Swiss artist Kurt Seligmann on a weekly basis. Seligmann spoke English fluently and shared his knowledge of magical lore, "graciously" allowing Lamantia to peruse his vast collection of alchemical texts.[18] Edouard Roditi became a good friend; the two would reunite in San Francisco the following year, when Roditi was working at the United Nations Charter Conference. Lamantia also was introduced to the surrealist-influenced American filmmaker Maya Deren, who was sufficiently impressed that she gave him a brief role in her film *At Land* (1944), which also includes appearances by Gregory Bateson, John Cage, and Parker Tyler. Lamantia and Tyler would stay in touch until Tyler's death in 1974.

As the war came to an end, the European refugees began to return home, and their American counterparts appeared either uninterested in or incapable of perpetuating surrealism in its original form. The transplantation of surrealism to the United States had indeed failed. Moreover, Lamantia had, as he put it, "a fight with Ford" and resigned from *View*.[19] Filled with bitterness and disappointment, Lamantia decided to return to San Francisco. At that point, he hadn't seen Breton for some time; indeed, his last encounter with Breton—by chance, in the company of Yves

Tanguy, at the corner of Fifth Avenue and Fifty-Seventh—was one of the experiences he treasured most from the half-year or so he had spent in New York.

Having witnessed infighting and further examples of aversive behavior among the New York surrealists, followed by the breakup of the scene at war's end, Lamantia was alienated and disillusioned—and for the moment, ready to renounce surrealism. He boarded a train back to San Francisco in late 1944.

KENNETH REXROTH AND
THE SAN FRANCISCO RENAISSANCE

In San Francisco, Lamantia enrolled in the Bates School for a year in order to obtain his high school diploma. "But my real education," he stated in his interview with Meltzer, "came from and through the great Rexroth," with whom he renewed his association upon his return from New York. "I saw a great deal of him for a couple of years. Above all, I was attracted by his inexhaustible and encyclopedic way of conversing. I'd visit him once a week. . . . Sometimes we'd talk a whole weekend."[20] Rexroth's mentorship was a decisive influence, for he provided Lamantia's first serious exposure to the historical depth and geographical breadth of poetry, while encouraging his protégé to pursue religious and political studies. He also afforded Lamantia much practical assistance in obtaining Conscientious Objector status, after turning eighteen in October 1945, in order to register a pacifist refusal to go to war. In terms of his own poetry, Lamantia would frequently refer to this period as his "naturalistic" phase, implying a rejection of the original sources of his inspiration in the unconscious and automatic writing. The poems he wrote at this time comprise the first section of his first book, *Erotic Poems* (1946), published by George Leite's friend and collaborator Bern Porter, whose eponymous imprint had previously published books by Henry Miller, as well as Parker Tyler's *The Granite Butterfly* (1945), a poem dedicated to Lamantia. The second half of *Erotic Poems* contains the earlier surrealist poetry published in *View, VVV,* and elsewhere.[21] *Erotic Poems* was introduced by Rexroth, who also suggested its title. In his introduction, Rexroth downplays the distinction between the two sections, and notably, Lamantia would reprint some of the poems from the "naturalistic" section in the first edition of his retrospective gathering of his early surrealist work, *Touch of the Marvelous* (1966). Generally speaking, the naturalistic poems are more measured in tone and pace than the earlier work, but lines like "You flee into a corridor of stars. / You sleep in a bleeding tree, / And awaken upon the body of trance" suggest that the "naturalism" of this period is highly relative.

In the late 1940s, Lamantia was an active participant in the San Francisco Libertarian Circle, a Wednesday-night discussion group that formed around Rexroth, concomitant with his famous Friday-night at-home salons. "Poets associated with the Rexroth circle," as Michael Davidson notes, "included Robert Duncan, Philip Lamantia, Jack Spicer, William Everson, James Broughton, Thomas Parkinson,

Madeline Gleason, and Richard Moore."[22] In short, the meetings were the beginning of the pre-Beat-era San Francisco Renaissance, yet they were by no means restricted to poets and artists; Lamantia estimated that the participants eventually numbered over a hundred.[23] The subject matter of these meetings was as various as Rexroth's protean interests—Lamantia once lectured on the theories of Wilhelm Reich—but appears to have largely focused on philosophical and political anarchism, with participants reading the works of such writers as Peter Kropotkin, Enrico Malatesta, Emma Goldman, Martin Buber, and Nikolai Berdyaev. During this period, along with fellow poets Sanders Russell and Robert Stock, Lamantia also edited a magazine, *The Ark,* intended as a more politically oriented companion to *Circle,* though disagreements among the three editors halted its publication after the first issue in spring 1947.

In addition to these activities, between 1947 and 1949, Lamantia audited a number of classes at the University of California, Berkeley, though he never formally enrolled. While he sat in on poetry lectures by Josephine Miles—mentor to Duncan and Spicer, among others—Lamantia primarily attended classes in comparative religion and medieval history. He was deeply influenced by the lectures of Leonardo Olschki and Ernst Kantorowicz. Olschki taught a course that formed the basis of his later book, *Marco Polo's Asia: Introduction to His "Description of the World" Called "Il Milione"* (1960). His lecture on "The Assassins" sparked Lamantia's interest in Islam, leading him to study the Koran and retain a lasting sympathy for that religion. Kantorowicz, an expert on medieval political and intellectual history, specialized in Frederick II of Sicily, the thirteenth-century Holy Roman emperor whose religious tolerance, polymath erudition, and patronage of poetry had a lifelong appeal for Lamantia and awakened his interest in his own ethnic heritage. Kantorowicz's 1947 lectures titled "The King's Two Bodies"—the basis of his 1957 book of that name—were attended by Duncan, Spicer, Moore, and Lamantia of the Rexroth group. For a time, Lamantia even roomed in the same Berkeley boardinghouse as Duncan and Spicer, at 2018 McKinley.[24]

It was also in Berkeley that he met the linguist Jaime de Angulo, whose work would inspire Lamantia's investigations into Native American cultures. Mention must also be made here of the eccentric ethnomusicologist, painter, and filmmaker Harry Smith, whom Lamantia met in 1948 and with whom he would further develop his interest in modern jazz and the newly emerging rhythm and blues. In addition to their frequent attendance at small after-hours clubs throughout San Francisco's Fillmore district, as well as downtown Oakland, the two shared a fascination with alchemy, aided and abetted by Smith's knack for obtaining rare alchemical texts.[25]

Apart from Rexroth, Lamantia's most important friendship during this period was with John Hoffman. Born in Menlo Park, California, in 1928, Hoffman was a thin, bespectacled poet with long blond hair and a small beard, the very image of the subsequent "beatnik" stereotype in American culture. He and Lamantia met in San

Francisco around 1947 after a poetry reading. Hoffman was already familiar with his new friend's poetry, for, when they repaired to Hoffman's cheap hotel to smoke marijuana, Lamantia noted "there were only two books in his room: a bound copy of the poems of St. John of the Cross—a rare book even then—and a copy of my first book, *Erotic Poems*."[26] The pair became fast friends, even sharing an apartment together in Berkeley for a time, and Lamantia would later describe their relationship as "the deepest friendship I've ever had with another male in my life."[27] "John was a very religious person," Lamantia recalled, suggesting their mutual interest in the spiritual life was one of the bases of their bond.[28]

BEAT GENERATION

The appearance of Hoffman might be considered a sign of Lamantia's transition into the "Beat" phase of his life. For whereas Lamantia's precocious rise to avant-garde prominence in the 1940s meant that his first colleagues had often been considerably older, he now began to associate with poets and artists approximately his own age; "the best minds of his generation," as it were, were catching up with him. At the same time, the 1950s would prove to be one of the most difficult periods of his life—one he often referred to as a period of "eclipse"—marked by poetic restlessness, intense spiritual and physical wandering, and drug addiction.[29] In late 1949, Hoffman went to New York City, where Lamantia joined him shortly afterward. By the time Lamantia arrived, Hoffman had already begun intravenous use of heroin, and he immediately introduced his friend to the drug. Lamantia would struggle with heroin addiction throughout the 1950s. In New York they also met Jack Kerouac, Allen Ginsberg, and other key figures of the Beat Generation. Indeed, according to Kerouac, aspects of Lamantia and Hoffman are "condensed" into the generalized portrait of junkie squatters in *The Subterraneans* (1958), while Hoffman is mentioned in William Burroughs's first novel, *Junky* (1953).[30]

Lamantia's travels, drug use, rebellious attitude, interest in jazz and spiritual exploration, and friendships with Kerouac, Ginsberg, and others seem to mark him as a Beat poet. Certainly his poetry developed a more vernacular diction during this period. Yet there were notable differences between Lamantia and the Beats. The Beats were in the ascendant, loudly laying claim to their own space within culture, confidant of the authenticity of their own voices. Lamantia, in contrast, was at this time unsure of his identity and direction as a writer. Moreover, Lamantia's focus on esotericism set him apart from the Beats, who were more interested in immediate reality. As Nancy Joyce Peters observed in her biographical essay on Lamantia, "While much Beat writing was spontaneous reportage and meditation on daily life, Lamantia concentrated on hermetic, symbolic, and magical themes."[31] This observation is echoed by one of Ginsberg's biographers, Bill Morgan, who wrote, "Allen thought that Lamantia's writing was too focused on cabalistic themes. Deep down

Allen felt Philip was not an ignu (a special honorary term he and Kerouac had coined to apply to like-minded people)."[32]

In 1950, Lamantia made his first trip to Mexico, accompanied by another friend, the poet, avant-garde filmmaker, and editor of *Contour,* Christopher Maclaine. Very little is known about this particular trip. According to an unpublished interview with John Suiter—used as source material for Suiter's book *Poets on the Peaks: Gary Snyder, Philip Whalen & Jack Kerouac in the North Cascades* (2002)—Lamantia had read Antonin Artaud's *Voyage to the Land of the Tarahumara* (written in 1936, published in 1945) "by 1949," and, though the two poets didn't visit these remote people, it seems likely that Artaud's account of the psychotropic effects of the peyote cactus at least partially motivated their visit.[33] Whether or not they obtained peyote on this trip, Lamantia soon learned he could order dried peyote buttons through the mail, from various seed catalogs. It's no exaggeration to claim, as Suiter does, that Lamantia introduced peyote into the Bay Area literary scene, over a decade and a half before San Francisco's late '60s psychedelic heyday.[34] "As early as 1951," Suiter writes in *Poets on the Peaks,* Lamantia "and a half dozen friends had 'a sort of little Berkeley peyotl cult of our own . . . taking peyote weekly for several months.'"[35] During this time, Lamantia was living with others in one of two Maybeck-designed houses in the Berkeley Hills owned by Jaime de Angulo's widow, Kathleen Freeman.[36] The house in which he lived contained de Angulo's library of ethnographic and anthropological books, among them Carl Lumholtz's *Unknown Mexico* (1902), in which Lamantia read of the three indigenous Mexican peoples with peyote rituals: the Tarahumara, the Huichole, and the Cora.

Also at this house, in early 1952, Lamantia would receive a visit from Kerouac and Neal Cassady, turning them both on to peyote, though Kerouac would famously fall asleep and experience none of the plant's hallucinatory effects.[37] Still, Kerouac would report on his continuing fascination with Lamantia's poetry, personality, and peyote experiences in a letter to Ginsberg that year, describing the de Angulo house as a "stone small castle overlooking Berkeley Calif." Lamantia, "reclined in a sumptuous couch," was reading the *Tibetan Book of the Dead* and speaking in arcane terms about his peyote visions. Kerouac wrote Ginsberg that the visit precipitated the first quarrel between himself and Cassady, inasmuch as the latter objected to Lamantia's esoteric behavior and conversation. According to Kerouac, "I was disappointed in Neal that night for not at least digging" what Lamantia had to say. "This made Neal mad, and the next night, for the first time in our lives, we had a fight—he refused to drive me to Lamantia, outright."[38]

That Lamantia and Cassady failed to connect is perhaps unsurprising. The "barbaric yawp" of the Beats exemplified by Cassady contrasted with what many of them, including Kerouac, perceived as Lamantia's hieratic manner. In Kerouac's novel *Desolation Angels,* Lamantia (as "David D'Angeli") is described "lying elegantly on a white fur cover on a bed, with a black cat, reading the Egyptian Book of the Dead

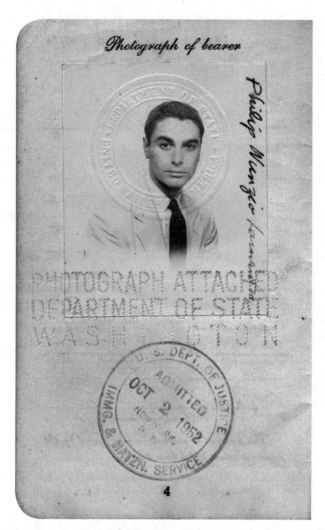

Passport photo, 1952. Courtesy of The Bancroft Library,
University of California, Berkeley.

and passing joints around, talking strangely . . . holding out his thin white delicate priest-hand to gesture." Kerouac was especially struck by Lamantia's unusual speech pattern: "that accent he talks in I do not know where he picked it up—It's like a Moor educated at Oxford . . . it's a distinctly flavored accent made up of (apparently) American Italian second-generation but with strong Britishified overlays upon his Mediterranean elegance, which creates an excellent and strange new form of English I've never heard anywhere."[39]

In the summer of '52, Lamantia traveled to Europe for the first time, visiting

Paris though not making contact with the surrealist group, then on to Morocco, where he lived for six months and renewed his friendship with Paul Bowles. By 1953, Lamantia had returned to San Francisco, taking a room in a neglected mansion on Franklin Street known as the "Ghost House," which also housed Robert Duncan and Jess Collins, Chris Maclaine, and others. In the spring of that year, Lamantia met Goldian "Gogo" Nesbit, a photographer and poet whom he would marry not long afterward. Their relationship heralded one of the most visionary periods of his life, beginning with an "out of body" experience Lamantia had that Allen Ginsberg would later celebrate in line 5 of "Howl": "who bared their brains to Heaven under the El and saw Mohammedan angels staggering on tenement roofs illuminated."[40] Although Ginsberg took the poetic license of setting the scene in New York, the actual incident took place in an apartment on Polk Street in San Francisco. Lamantia would later recount the vision for the 1986 annotated edition of *Howl*:

> 1953, Spring, aged 25, reading the Koran on a couch, one night I was suddenly physically laid out by a powerful force beyond my volition, which rendered me almost comatose: suddenly, consciousness was contracted to a single point at the top of my head through which I was "siphoned" beyond the room, space and time into *another* state of awareness that seemed utterly beyond any other state before or since experienced. I floated toward an endless-looking universe of misty, lighted color forms: green, red, blue and silver, which circulated around me accompanied by such bliss that the one dominant thought was: This is it; I never want to return to anywhere but this *place*—i.e., I wanted to remain in this Ineffable Blissful Realm and explore it forever—since I felt a radiance beyond even further within it and so, suddenly the outline of a benign bearded Face appeared to whom I addressed my desire to remain in this marvel—and who calmly replied: "You can return, after you complete your work."[41]

Ginsberg, who had moved to San Francisco that same year, first heard this story after one of Rexroth's Friday night gatherings, which he had begun to attend with Lamantia. As Morgan writes in his biography of Ginsberg, "After a party at Rexroth's, Allen and Philip Lamantia spent the night in a cafeteria talking about Lamantia's own visions. . . . Allen was envious of Philip's mystical experiences, which reminded him of his Harlem epiphanies of nearly a decade earlier."[42] This vision—like Ginsberg's epiphanies, unaided by hallucinogens—had a profound impact on Lamantia. During this period he also began writing the poems he would collect as *Tau,* the only complete but unpublished manuscript found among his papers. In contrast to the baroque quality of Lamantia's radiant vision, the poems of *Tau* are frequently spare and meditative, seemingly related to his esoteric researches at the time though frequently opaque in regard to their subject matter.

Another manuscript from this period that didn't survive was called *Expel the Green Pain,* announced in Lamantia's biographical note in James Laughlin's annual *New Directions in Prose & Poetry* 14 (1953). This book was to have concerned Lamantia's experiences on peyote, and it's unclear whether he retained any of these poems. In any case, his most significant peyote adventure was yet to come, for in 1954, accompanied by his wife and George Leite, who arranged the visit, Lamantia went to Woodfords, California, to participate in the Washoe Indians' peyote ceremony. This ceremony took place at night in a large tipi, specifically erected for this purpose, with "about forty or fifty people" seated in a circle around a fire, accompanied by drumming and singing.[43] The content of Lamantia's peyote-induced visions hasn't been recorded, beyond such synesthetic statements as "The sky tasted like crystal star meat" in an unpublished notebook "memorial" of the event, but it seems clear that the ritual helped foster his attraction to communal religious experience.

Later in 1954, Lamantia and Nesbit moved to Mexico, where he would live for extended periods over the next several years. He immersed himself in its history and cultures, and formed friendships with surrealist painter Leonora Carrington and poets Homero Aridjis and Ernesto Cardenal. Lamantia was drawn to the distinctly baroque character of Mexican Catholicism, with its marvelous churches and its idiosyncratic iconography, rites, and penances. His solitary visions continued, including what he described as a thirty-second "Christic" revelation later that year. Yet the increasing intensity of Lamantia's mysticism appears to have put a strain on his marriage, and in early 1955, the couple would split up; Goldian became involved with a friend of theirs in Mexico City, André VandenBroeck, whom she would later marry, while Lamantia set out on a perilous journey to visit the Cora Indians, about whom he'd read in *Unknown Mexico* and who lived in Sierra Madre mountains of Nayarit.

Although he stayed with the Cora Indians for two months, Lamantia never took peyote with them; as he told John Suiter, there were "something like thirty secret rituals in the course of a year . . . but I was there in early spring, and the peyote rite didn't come on until Easter."[44] Instead it was the season for *yahnah*, an extremely potent black tobacco the Cora cultivated whose effects Lamantia described as "narcotic." The yahnah ceremony took place at night in a Jesuit missionary church, as did a Cora funeral he witnessed on first arriving. What struck him forcefully was that the Cora's indigenous beliefs and Catholic practice existed side by side in this remote mountain village, and seemed equally real embodiments of the human aspiration to union with the Divine. This insight was amplified by another incident occurring prior to the yahnah ceremony, when Lamantia was stung by a scorpion and nearly died; in his pain, he spontaneously cried out to the "Madonna"—that is, the Blessed Virgin Mary—to save his life. The combination of these events led to Lamantia's subsequent fervent embrace of the religion into which he was born; this had serious implications for his poetry, as he began to view his preconversion writings as blasphemous.

SIX GALLERY

In 1953, when the owner of San Francisco's Six Gallery, an old garage that had been converted into an art gallery and performance space, offered to host a group reading,

Kenneth Rexroth and Allen Ginsberg drew up a list of five younger poets—Ginsberg himself, Lamantia, Gary Snyder, Michael McClure, and Philip Whalen—whom they considered most representative of the new, antiestablishment poetics at that time. Rexroth would act as master of ceremonies. Ginsberg also wanted to include Kerouac on the bill; at Ginsberg's urging, Kerouac returned from Mexico to participate in the event, but subsequently declined to read.

Lamantia also was reluctant to present his own work at the Six Gallery reading. His engagement with Catholicism reached its greatest intensity in 1955, just around the time of the reading. As Lamantia recalled in an interview, "I was going through a crisis of conversion and I couldn't write and I didn't want to read my old poems—I didn't want to publish my old poems, I ceased to publish, I wanted to withdraw."[45] Lamantia had, in fact, withdrawn, six months before the reading, to a Trappist monastery in Oregon for a retreat, and had also pulled the manuscript of his poem-cycle *Tau* from the publisher Bern Porter just as the book was about to go into production.[46] At the persistent urging of Rexroth and Ginsberg, Lamantia finally agreed to read, not from his own work, but from that of his friend John Hoffman, whose death in 1952 under mysterious circumstances in Mexico affected Lamantia greatly. A collection of Hoffman's poems, *Journey to the End,* was scheduled for publication by Bern Porter around the same time as Porter was to have published Lamantia's *Tau.* This reading would be a memorial tribute to his friend.

The Six Gallery reading took place on October 7, 1955, before a large and enthusiastic crowd. Lamantia was first to read, and made his entrance, according to Kerouac's mildly fictionalized account in *The Dharma Bums,* looking like "a young priest." As Kerouac noted, it was "the night of the birth of the San Francisco Poetry Renaissance.... It was a great night. Delicate Francis DaPavia [Philip Lamantia] read, from delicate onionskin yellow pages, or pink, which he kept flipping carefully with long white fingers, the poems of his dead chum Altman [Hoffman] ... and read them in a delicate Englishy voice that had me crying inside with laughter though I later got to know Francis and liked him."[47] According to Michael McClure, Lamantia's reading of Hoffman's "beautiful prose poems ... left orange stripes and colored visions in the air."[48] As is well known, the pivotal moment of the event occurred when Ginsberg read from his long poem "Howl." The founder of City Lights Books, Lawrence Ferlinghetti, was in the audience and was moved, upon hearing "Howl," to offer Ginsberg a book contract. Yet, after the Six Gallery reading, when, in Kerouac's words, "all the poems were read and everybody was milling around wondering what had happened and what would come next in American poetry," Hoffman's poems slipped from sight and would not be published until the next century, when Hoffman's *Journey to the End* and Lamantia's *Tau* were issued in the same volume by City Lights (2008).

Of all the younger poets on the bill, Lamantia was the best known at that time;

the others had yet to publish their first books. There is some irony in this, for the other Six Gallery readers would, in less than a decade, achieve much wider recognition than Lamantia. When the reading was restaged five months later in Berkeley—mostly for the benefit of the media—Lamantia was the only member of the original lineup who did not participate, having returned for another visit to the Trappist monastery in Oregon. For the next few years, Lamantia's fervent Catholic devotion seemed to inhibit his poetic practice, or, at least, his confidence in its results. Perhaps surprisingly—in view of his amusement at the more baroque features of Lamantia's persona—one of Lamantia's closest friends during this period was Jack Kerouac. Immediately following the Six Gallery reading, Kerouac and Lamantia stayed a few weeks at Lamantia's mother's home in San Francisco, where the two resumed their ongoing dialogue on comparative religion.[49] Kerouac had been looking beyond the doctrines of his own French-American Catholicism—which prioritized the culpability of the individual ego in relation to God—toward the "ego-less" doctrines of Buddhism that, by defining suffering as merely an illusion of the ego, seemed to offer greater consolation, while Lamantia pointed out the inherent "emptiness" and "negativity" of Buddhism and tried to lead Kerouac back to the Catholic faith. As Kerouac confessed in *Desolation Angels,* Lamantia "really dented my brain with his enthusiastic, passionate and brilliant expositions of the Universal Orthodoxy."[50] Recalling these discussions many years later, Lamantia said that he believed Kerouac "in his heart had remained a Catholic, all right."[51] Nonetheless, Lamantia credited his friendship with Kerouac, as a Catholic whose faith accommodated an enthusiastic interest in and practice of various tenets of Buddhism, with helping him relax his quite possibly self-destructive level of rigor in the immediate aftermath of his first conversion.

In the three years that followed the Six Gallery reading, Lamantia frequently went on the road—partly as an attempt to stave off the cycles of depression that plagued him—traveling between Mexico and New York in hope of finding sources of ecstatic experience. In New York in late 1957, he reunited with Kerouac, and the two joined forces with the Beat poet Howard Hart and David Amram, a composer and pioneer jazz French horn player, to stage what has been recognized as the "first jazz-poetry reading" at the Brata Art Gallery in Greenwich Village, followed by performances at Circle in the Square.[52] It is likely that Lamantia read passages from *Tau* at these events in the Village. The manuscript of *Tau* that has been preserved among Lamantia's papers is marked with musical notations that may have been intended as performance cues. The fact that Lamantia chose to read poems from *Tau* in New York, after suppressing these poems at the Six Gallery reading three years earlier in San Francisco, gives some indication that he was relaxing—undoubtedly with Kerouac's encouragement—the strictures that he had imposed on himself at the height of his "fervent" Catholicism.

New York City, 1950s. Courtesy of The Bancroft Library, University of California, Berkeley.

During this period of jazz and mysticism, Lamantia had one of his more singular experiences as a "spokesperson" for the Beat Generation when he and Kerouac were each interviewed by TV personality Mike Wallace for his daily column in the *New York Post*. After quoting the last section of Lamantia's poem "Binoculars"—"COME / HOLY GHOST / for we can rise / out / of this jazz"—Wallace questions Lamantia on the connection between jazz and God. Lamantia answers, "throughout the ages, mankind has been searching for some kind of ecstasy, some marvelous vision of God, you know. That's why we smoke marijuana, or listen to jive. It's all just a way to ecstasy."[53] *Time* magazine would publish a rather flip encapsulation of the two interviews under the heading "Beat Mystics," accompanied by fragmentary excerpts, two weeks later.[54] But this was mild compared to the treatment they would receive the following year in *Life* magazine's Beat Generation attack piece, "The Only Rebellion Around," which also offers caustic appraisals of Ginsberg, Corso, McClure, Burroughs, Ferlinghetti, and Bob Kaufman. Under the heading "A Fix at the Altar," Lamantia is derided as "a Catholic and impassioned student of theology who has convinced himself that the use of drugs to obtain visions does not conflict with the canons of the Church."[55] Ironically, it seems that Lamantia's religious belief most offends *Life's* conformist critique of the Beat Generation.

By 1958, Lamantia had returned to Mexico City, where he met Lucile Dejardin—a Frenchwoman working in the theater as a costume designer—whom he would marry two years later. Not much is known of this marriage, as Lamantia seldom spoke of it after it ended in divorce in 1964. The fact that, as two Roman Catholics, their marriage was not merely civil but sacramental exacerbated his sense of failure when their relationship ended.[56] Manic depression also contributed to the breakup; when they met, Lamantia was in a stable phase of his cycle, and Dejardin was understandably unprepared for the intense manic episodes when they inevitably returned. The separations and reunions that occurred throughout their relationship were compounded, moreover, by legal difficulties, for Lamantia was expelled from Mexico in 1959 due to his association with a known drug dealer, and was subsequently arrested on his arrival in Texas, spending approximately two months in jail.[57] He reentered Mexico illegally in 1961, and soon after had one of his most elaborate visionary experiences, when he and the painter Aymon de Sales were driven off the Pyramid of the Sun at Teotihuacan by "hundreds" of "Black Shapes" that the two considered to be "demons."[58] His presence in Mexico came to the attention of governmental authorities, however, and he was deported again in 1962, losing many valuable papers in the process, including the letter he had received from André Breton back in 1943.

Nonetheless, the period was a productive one for Lamantia, at least in terms of publishing. In 1959, some thirteen years after *Erotic Poems,* he finally published a second book of poems, *Ekstasis,* with Dave Haselwood's Auerhahn Press. A member of the Wichita Beat vortex that produced Bruce Conner and Michael McClure, Haselwood would publish some of the most significant books of this period of San Francisco poetry, including John Wiener's *The Hotel Wentley Poems* (1958), McClure's *Hymns to St. Geryon* (1959), Philip Whalen's *Memoirs of an Interglacial Age* (1960), and Jack Spicer's *The Heads of the Town up to the Aether* (1962), among many others. According to its brief prefatory note, *Ekstasis* contains poems written between 1948 and 1958, presented in reverse chronological order.[59] Much of *Ekstasis* is religious in nature, such as the prayer "Ah Blessed Virgin Mary" or the hermetic lyric "Mysterium Mysticus Ecclesia." Influenced by his reading of Welsh metaphysical poet and priest George Herbert (1593–1633), Lamantia also expressed his devotion through concrete or "pattern" poems: "Christ" (in the shape of a cross), "In a grove" (a vortex and triangle), and "What gift to bring" (a cross-topped dome). Three poems from the *Tau* manuscript— "Man is in pain," "Terror Conduction," and "Intersection"—appear in *Ekstasis,* indicating he had come to terms with them, and even a few earlier preconversion poems, after their initial suppression. Moreover, the book's third and thus comparatively recent poem, "Interior Suck of the Night," has no overtly religious theme, but rather concerns a visionary experience smoking opium. This poem most explicitly links the mysticism of *Ekstasis* to the other Lamantia title issued by Auerhahn that year, *Narcotica.*

Announced in *Ekstasis* under its original title, *A Demand for Extinction of Laws Prohibiting Narcotic Drugs, Narcotica* is at once Lamantia's most notorious and iconic publication and the one toward which he felt the most ambivalence. Its notoriety partly stems from its cover photographs, by *Semina* creator Wallace Berman, depicting Lamantia shooting up. As Lamantia told it, he didn't authorize the appearance of these photos, claiming the cover was to be all text; indeed, the pamphlet-sized book seems to have two covers, the photographic wrap with four images of Lamantia, and a sheet of red cardstock with a variant of the original title, *I Demand Extinction of Laws Prohibiting Narcotic Drugs*, printed in pyramid form. Lamantia was dismayed by the images for reasons both personal—not wanting his family to see and fearing the very real possibility of arrest—and philosophical, for he felt they sensationalized the text, undermining the seriousness of its purpose. Notably he would never reprint any of *Narcotica*, his misgivings compounded by the feeling the text was no longer "accurate" in terms of the evolving political discourse around drugs in the United States.

A hybrid text, *Narcotica* consists of four poems by Lamantia, his translation of a poem by Giocomo Leopardi, and the prose "Demand" of its alternate title, plus two texts by Artaud concerning opium, translated by Lucile Dejardin. While his enduring anarchist political orientation is evident throughout the text—particularly in his assertion that "It is I WHO AM THE LAW!"—Lamantia felt *Narcotica* was misinterpreted, writing in an undated typewritten note: "any creep who got the impression I was recommending the taking of narcotics—addictive or not—doesn't understand THE NATURAL RIGHT OF THE POET TO SPEAK TRUTH AS HE SEES IT." Much of *Narcòtica*, including Artaud's two texts, "A Letter to the Legislator of the Law on Narcotics" and "General Security—The Liquidation of Opium," concerns the psychic pain motivating drug addiction, which, in Lamantia's case, was rooted in his still-undiagnosed manic depression. While it has ecstatic moments—notably the ode to hashish, "Memoria"—generally speaking, *Narcotica* is concerned with the political and psychiatric aspects of illegal drugs, while moments of *ekstasis* are reserved for the book of that title, hence the inclusion of "Interior Suck of the Night" there. The division between *Ekstasis* and *Narcotica*, in other words, isn't between religious and drug experience but rather between mystical and political experience.

Of particular note in Lamantia's Auerhahn period is the emergence of a concept he christens "weir." This is not to be confused with the contemporary English word "weir," a type of dam, but instead is a variant on the word "weird" that Lamantia derived from his researches into Anglo-Saxon. Perhaps the most widely read elaboration of the concept comes not from Lamantia but rather from Michael McClure, whom Philip had known since the mid-1950s but who became a close friend around this time. In "Phi Upsilon Kappa," the first essay in the second edition of his book *Meat Science Essays* (1963, 1966), McClure cites Lamantia's concept as he describes the visionary state induced by peyote: "Philip Lamantia and I had spoken many times. He had mentioned his concept of Weir to me. Now I knew the phenomena I had seen with my still peyoted eyes—the chill luminescence—and the aelf-scin of the Anglo Saxons were the same radiance and halo. I saw that the aelf-scin was much the same light illuminating what Philip called Weir. Weir is a solid spectral reality of light on particular objects in special moments of vision."[60] To this we might add Lamantia's own dictionary-style definition, drawn from an ambitious, heavily worked, but ultimately abandoned text, "Weir-o-Rama": "weir: anglosaxon: 'weird,' from Latin & Greek: TO SEE in a certain 'light.'" This too suggests the visionary state, and while clearly engendered by Lamantia's experiences with hallucinogens—in a handwritten poem of the early '60s, he will write: "My land of Weir, that is, sight of LSD light"—weir would seem to be an attempt to correlate his experiences of mystical, drug-induced, and poetic vision under one heading. This is a singular instance in his poetics, for Lamantia was by nature a seeker, researching a wide variety of extant knowledge, rather than a synthesizer or developer of original concepts. There's some indication he found this task uncongenial, given his inability to complete "Weir-o-Rama" and the existence of several unpublished poems relating to weir. Nonetheless, the concept persists in Lamantia's work for nearly a decade, beginning with the word's appearance in *Ekstasis* (in "Fragments from an Aeroplane" and "Ball") and *Narcotica* (in "Opium   Cocaine   Hemp") through its final manifestation in "Gork!" in his 1967 *Selected Poems*.

But the weir concept probably exerts its greatest influence on Lamantia's third Auerhahn title, *Destroyed Works* (1962), which ends with the following "Note on DESTROYED WORKS and *later*":[61]

For me it is the Vision in its density and the truth of what I see
the breath is in the Vision and I come to the rhythms it is above
all a question of MY VISION thru which the images are focused,
the beat in the activation of this energy field, hence the density,
that the Being of poetry erupts out of nerves emotions skeleton
muscles tongues eyes spirits beasts birds rockets typewriters
into my head and I *see*, the weir pivot, at that point all is
Evidence Clarity Incomprehension Flame of Perfect Form and Chaos.
     October 20, 1960

From this statement, it isn't difficult to see weir as a conceptual bridge out of Lamantia's Catholic phase and back to surrealism, for weir has gone beyond passive experience of "the Vision" to become a poetic practice—an eruption—not unlike surrealist automatism. Indeed, despite his disavowal at the time, surrealism continued to exert its influence on Lamantia, manifested through his inclusion of a dissident surrealist like Artaud in *Narcotica* or by his remark in *Ekstasis* that "Christ IS the marvellous," prefiguring his surrealist Catholic period of the late '90s. Notably, in any case, the concept of weir will disappear not long after he formally returns to surrealism in 1965.

The title of *Destroyed Works* refers to one of the signal events of Lamantia's artistic life: the burning of most of the poetry he'd written but not published since *Erotic Poems*. The exact circumstances and sequence of events around this act aren't fully known, but it was a deliberate, premeditated renunciation of his life as a poet, a continuation and amplification of the spiritual crisis begun on his conversion and compelling him to suppress his own work at the Six Gallery reading. The immediate catalyst may have been a deep depression over the deterioration of his relationship with Lucile, aggravated by his deportation and arrest. Prior to destroying these poems, however, Lamantia created a twenty-five-page typescript titled "Destroyed Works," made up of forty-one numbered sections; these sections contain fragments from longer works as well as some complete poems, such as number 36, "Cora," about his experiences with the tribe, and number 38, "Sphinx or Cat," dedicated to Leonora Carrington, whom he'd first met in Mexico in 1954. That the contents of this typescript go back at least as far as the beginning of the '50s is evident from number 5, a variant of which was recorded by John Hoffman in one of his notebooks and credited as "Philip Lamantia, 1950."[62] The quantity of work Lamantia destroyed is unknown, and he didn't destroy everything, as evidenced by the survival of the *Tau* manuscript and other stray poems. Nonetheless, almost nothing from the late 1940s appears to survive, while most of the remaining poems from the 1950s tend to be from late in the decade.

Oddly enough, nothing from the "Destroyed Works" typescript appears in *Destroyed Works*. Judging from both stylistic and internal evidence, moreover, the majority of *Destroyed Works* consists of poems written between 1958 and 1960, thus making its contents roughly contemporary with its publication.[63] The title refers to the event itself, in other words, rather than the actual poems in the book. Lamantia seemingly used the "Destroyed Work" typescript as a model—using bullet points rather than numbers to separate the various poems—but filling this structure with more recent content. Unlike the typescript, the book is divided into four suites of poems: "Hypodermic Light," "Mantic Notebook," "Still Poems," and "Spansule." Stylistically, *Destroyed Works* grows out of the manic denunciations of *Narcotica*, continuing that volume's emphatic use of capital letters and tending toward long lines and prose poems. While the Catholic content of *Ekstasis* remains, its quiet, reverential tone has disappeared in favor of fervent but unorthodox pronouncements like "Christ is a rocket ship."[64] Notably, the book's cover is a photograph of Bruce Conner's assemblage "Superhuman Devotion," which itself had been destroyed by the time the book was printed. Conner and Lamantia met as early as 1955 in San Francisco and continued their friendship in Mexico City, when Conner moved there in the early 1960s.

Lamantia's second deportation from Mexico, in 1962, effectively put an end to his

Tangiers, Morocco, 1964. Courtesy of The Bancroft Library, University of California, Berkeley.

relationship with Lucile, who would initiate divorce proceedings the following year. It also seemingly coincided with Lamantia's leaving the Catholic Church, though exactly when this occurred is unknown. His intention to renounce poetry remained, yet though he withdrew from publishing, he never seems to have entirely stopped writing. At the invitation of his ex-wife Goldian Nesbit, Lamantia decided to relocate to Nerja, Spain, where she and André VandenBroeck were living. Since they had left Mexico, VandenBroeck and Nesbit had fallen under the influence of the "sacred science" of Egyptologist R. A. Schwaller de Lubicz, whose chief work, *Le Temple de l'homme* (1958), was an exigesis of ancient Egyptian philosophy, mathematics, and science as embodied in the symbology of the Temple of Luxor. Through VandenBroeck, Lamantia hoped to gain an understanding of "sacred geometry," conceiving that he would thenceforth devote himself to philosophy instead of poetry.

Before undertaking such a journey, however, Lamantia needed to break his heroin addiction, having fallen into a period of heavy use in the wake of his failed marriage. He accomplished this in late 1962 in Newton, Massachusetts, through LSD therapy guided by Timothy Leary, whose early research into hallucinogens included their use in the treatment of alcoholism. "Phil Lamantia was up for a week," Leary wrote to Allen Ginsberg. "He's going through a death-rebirth sequence. Painful but he's great."[65] Following this cure, Lamantia left for Europe, arriving in Nerja, Spain, in February 1963 and renting a small house down the street from the VandenBroecks. Lamantia would remain there for six months, studying Schwaller de Lubicz with VandenBroeck, but he found himself more interested in Egyptian myth and symbol than in sacred geometry. Lamantia grew frustrated, moreover, with VandenBroeck, whose initial enthusiasm had waned somewhat, though he would later write both a study, *Philosophical Geometry* (1972), and a memoir, *Al-Kemi: Occult, Political, and Private Aspects of R. A. Schwaller de Lubicz* (1987), as well as translate, with Nesbit, Schwaller de Lubicz's own writings. In any case, the VandenBroecks went to the Aurobindo ashram in Pondicherry, and by July 1963, Lamantia had resumed his travels in Europe, including a period in Italy, before arriving in Tangiers, Morocco in 1964, where he studied music with his old friend Paul Bowles. At the end of May of that year, however, he was arrested for possession of kif and imprisoned for five days, before being deported from the country.

RETURN TO SURREALISM

Lamantia's return to surrealism coincided with a reawakening of his poetic powers after three years of silence, a period which he later described as his "season in hell."[66] Certainly, he had always drawn upon his surrealist roots, writing under the sign of a transgressive and transformative imagination. Nonetheless, he had distanced himself from the movement since the late forties; and when he was in Paris in the fifties, he had not bothered to seek out members of the surrealist circle there. By 1960, after an often tortuous itinerary through the cultural landscape of the post–World War II era, Lamantia may have felt that if, as he had phrased it in the title of one of his earliest poems, "There Are Many Pathways to the Garden," he now had no sense of where his next path would take him.

After he left Morocco, Lamantia went to Athens, where he made contact with the circle of the Greek surrealist poet Nanos Valaoritis and American surrealist artist Marie Wilson. Their circle served at that time as a way station for European and American youths and intellectuals going on the road to seek enlightenment in the Middle East and India. Here, Lamantia encountered a number of past acquaintances, including Charles Henri Ford and Harold Norse. And it was here, as a result of the stimulus of this scene, and also of the fact the he was beginning to emerge from a cycle of depression, that Lamantia composed the first poem that pleased him, at least a little, since his renunciation of poetry three years earlier.[67] The poem was entitled "Blue Grace," an exuberant hymn to the "resurrection" of his "muse" in the guise of the "prophetess," Blue Grace.

It was also in Athens a few months later that Lamantia met the American poet Nancy Joyce Peters—a woman who appeared to him as the very embodiment of his muse. Peters had just arrived in Athens from a sojourn in Egypt. Not only was she a participant in the Valaoritis-Wilson scene but she happened to be staying in the same hotel as Lamantia: their courtship began when Lamantia sent her a note, asking her to tell him everything she knew about the moon.[68] Falling in love, the pair left Athens to visit the site of the Delphic oracle. Their travels took them to the Greek islands and Crete and eventually to Paris; here, Lamantia reunited briefly with Lawrence Ferlinghetti, who was reading at the International Festival of Free Expression. This meeting was not without consequence: later that year, Ferlinghetti would offer to publish a volume of Lamantia's poetry in the City Lights Pocket Poets Series. For the time being, Lamantia and Peters left France and, after a stay in Segovia, settled on the southern coast of Spain, residing a year in Málaga and then in Nerja, the fishing village where Lamantia had lived near the VandenBroecks.

In Spain, Lamantia resumed his study of Egyptian architecture and symbols with Peters, utilizing Peters's knowledge of French to make reading translations of Schwaller de Lubicz's writings. They made new friends, traveled throughout Andalusia, enjoyed gypsy *juergas,* and spent time in Alhaurín el Grande, visiting Gerald Brenan, whose books on the Spanish Civil War and on Spanish literature Lamantia had admired. Now in a relaxed and joyous relationship with Peters, Lamantia began writing poetry again in earnest. As the title of his first collection, *Erotic Poems,* indicates, Lamantia had always derived poetic inspiration from the power of Eros; in Málaga, he composed a series of poems—notably, "She Speaks the Morning's Filigree"—giving evidence of Peters's restorative effect on his imagination. Peters was impressed with all of Lamantia's work, but especially charmed by his early surrealist poems, with their fresh vision and imaginative freedom. Recognizing that Lamantia was attempting to overcome his poetic self-destruction, she encouraged him to reconnect with the forces that had sustained his first flowering as a surrealist poet.

Peters, it turned out, was not alone in favoring Lamantia's early work: Oyez Press and City Lights almost simultaneously contacted Lamantia in Málaga, each offering to publish a collection of poems from his surrealist period. Both presses stood at the forefront of the burgeoning literary scene in the San Francisco Bay Area; while City Lights was well established, Robert Hawley's Oyez Press had just begun to attract notice with a small list of finely printed titles by innovative poets. In consultation with Peters—who now acted as both Lamantia's muse and his literary adviser, a role she would continue to fill for the rest of his life—Lamantia decided to give Oyez the collected poems of his first surrealist phase, and to turn the City Lights book into a selected poems volume covering his entire career up to that point.

Thus, there was some overlap between the contents of the Oyez book, which was entitled *Touch of the Marvelous* and released in 1966, and the first section— "Revelations of a Surreal Youth"—of the *Selected Poems* from City Lights, released in 1967 as Pocket Poets Number Twenty. The second section of the *Selected Poems*—

"Trance Ports"—represented the poems of his Catholic/Beat phase; and the final section—"Secret Freedom"—contained new poems representing his return to surrealism. Lamantia's *Selected Poems* therefore described not a circle, but a Hegelian spiral: a return to the point of origin, but at a higher level. On the back cover, supportive comments were provided by Parker Tyler, associate of Lamantia's first surrealist phase, as well as by Allen Ginsberg, associate of Lamantia's "transitional" period; also included was Lamantia's own declaration: "I'm returning to my initial sources—like an act of nature."[69]

Lamantia's return to these roots was motivated, no doubt, by subjective processes, but it occurred within the context of an objective sociocultural shift at the beginning of the sixties—a shift that resulted in a worldwide renewal of surrealist thought and practice. The French surrealist José Pierre periodized the fortunes of surrealism during the fifties and sixties as follows: "The Traversal of the Desert," 1952–58; "The Resurgence," 1959–65; and "The Hour of the Phoenix," 1966–69.[70] These periods roughly correlate with Lamantia's self-described "eclipse" during the fifties and his own surrealist resurgence in the sixties.[71] Thus, the two books announcing Lamantia's return to surrealism appeared as part of a rising wave of interest in surrealism in the United States and elsewhere.

Prominent among the new magazines and presses explicitly devoted to surrealism were the publications of the Chicago Surrealist Group, organized by Franklin and Penelope Rosemont in 1966. The Rosemonts had traveled to Paris in 1965 to meet with André Breton and others in the Paris group. Breton welcomed them into the movement; shortly thereafter, the Rosemonts launched an ambitious publishing program that brought many of the seminal works of French surrealism into English translation for the first time.[72]

Certainly, the upwelling of oppositional activity in the sixties promoted a "return to surrealism" within the larger culture. The Situationists and other radical groups explicitly cited surrealism; its influence seemed to expand in proportion to the intensity of the struggle against imperialist war and the one-dimensionality of capitalist society (the slogans of the May '68 revolt in Paris, such as *"L'imagination prend le pouvoir," "Je prends mes désirs pour des réalités car je crois à la réalité de mes désirs," "Explorons le hasard,"* recall passages from the surrealist manifestos). The mystical, apocalyptic, and psychedelic tendencies of sixties counterculture also mingled with political currents, adding momentum to the surrealist surge. By the end of the sixties, surrealist groups and publications were flourishing not only in Western Europe and the United States, but in Eastern Europe and Latin America as well. There was some cause to celebrate the phoenix-like rebirth of surrealism, even at the hour of Breton's death (which occurred in 1966).

The reawakening of interest in surrealism also provided a wider context for the reception of Lamantia's work; by the end of the decade, his *Selected Poems* from City Lights had sold fifteen thousand copies. In the wake of its publication, Lamantia and

Peters decided to return to the United States to live. She relocated to Seattle in 1967 to earn a degree in library science from the University of Washington; Lamantia joined her there the following year, taking a steamer across the Atlantic and then a train across the Canadian Rockies. On the steamer, Lamantia wrote a prose poem, "The Romantic Movement" dedicated to Peters, looking forward to their reunion ("The boat tilts on your image on the waves . . . ") and invoking "Chief Seattle's lost medicine pouch." In Seattle, Lamantia and Peters lived together for six months while Peters finished her degree; Lamantia wrote some of the poems that would form part of his next book, *The Blood of the Air*.

Upon graduation, Peters was offered an excellent position as a librarian at the Library of Congress in Washington, D.C., and Lamantia returned to San Francisco. By that time, San Francisco had become a mecca for the youth movement, which had massively infused fresh energy into the city's long-standing—but marginal—countercultural tradition. Alternative lifestyles, radical politics, and experimental music and art were flowering madly—no longer, as in the fifties, on the margins, but in almost every aspect of the city's life. After spending the better part of a decade away from his hometown, Lamantia was returning to a different San Francisco. He found a inexpensive apartment at 30 Genoa Place in North Beach. Besides reconnecting with family and friends, he began to associate with a number of the young, self-styled surrealists now active in the city, and collaborated in the production of the tabloid-sized magazines, *Octopus Typewriter* and *Anti-Narcissus*.

Similar small surrealist groups were arising at many points throughout the United States at this time; in 1970, an effort was undertaken by the largest of them, the Chicago Surrealist Group, to organize their activity at a national level. The resultant organization would be called the "Surrealist Movement in the United States." In keeping with the revolutionary ferment of the period, the movement circulated fiery manifestos and staged political protests and happenings that incorporated art and dance. Its main vehicle was the anthology series entitled *Arsenal: Surrealist Subversion*, issued by the Chicago Group itself.[73] After seeing the first volume (whose format and typography was modeled on French surrealist periodicals of the thirties), Lamantia decided to make common cause with the group. Indeed, Lamantia was eventually recruited to serve on the editorial board of *Arsenal*; its subsequent three volumes featured not only his poetry but also some of his most important prose statements and essays.[74]

In the same year that the Surrealist Movement in the United States was launched, Lamantia's first all-new collection of poems following his return to surrealism, *The Blood of the Air*, was published in San Francisco by Donald Allen's Four Seasons Foundation.[75] To make no mistake about the author's surrealist orientation, an extensive quote from André Breton was placed at the beginning of the book; in addition, a frontispiece drawing was provided by Marie Wilson.[76] The collection—dedicated to Nancy Joyce Peters, "at the secrets / of the marvelous"—opens with "I Touch You,"

At home in San Francisco, 1970. Photo by Nancy Joyce Peters.
Courtesy of The Bancroft Library, University of California,
Berkeley.

perhaps Lamantia's most ardent love poem. Despite its brevity, the book as a whole
projects—in contrast to the work of Lamantia's earlier, self-destructive phase—a
sense of self-confidence, a reclamation of poetic powers, with the poet-magus once
more in command of "the coiled element, the supreme root of fire."

In 1971, Peters moved permanently to San Francisco to look for a position as a
librarian, after she and Lamantia decided that San Francisco suited them better than
D.C. Peters worked briefly for editor and publisher Donald Allen, who was then edit-
ing Frank O'Hara's *Collected Poems* for Knopf; not long after, she joined Ferlinghetti
at the editorial offices of City Lights. (Peters would remain at City Lights for the
next four decades, becoming its executive director in 1982, as well as a co-owner of
the enterprise.) Around this time, Peters and Lamantia, together with Donald Allen,
traveled by car through the American Southwest, visiting Hopi pueblos and other
Native American sites. Such excursions to explore the West, its natural beauty and
complex history, continued for the next twenty-five years, becoming an increasingly
important source of inspiration for Lamantia's poetic thought and practice.

In the fall of 1971, Lamantia taught a course on poetics for one term at San Francisco State University at the invitation of Nanos Valaoritis (who, along with his wife, Marie Wilson, had recently relocated to California from Greece). Thanks to Valaoritis's presence on the SF State faculty, literary surrealism had gained an academic foothold in the Bay Area. Valaoritis, who held his position at San Francisco State for many years, was a popular and influential teacher, yet certain members of the decidedly antiacademic Surrealist Movement in the United States became suspicious of what they regarded as Valaoritis's "revisionist" tendencies. Both Valaoritis and Sotère Torregian, an Armenian-American surrealist poet and friend of Lamantia, were criticized by the group for failing to adhere to Breton's allegedly "simple" definition of surrealism as "pure psychic automatism."[77] Lamantia himself never came under such criticism, despite the fact that he had called for surrealism to reinvent itself in the very pages of the group's publication *Arsenal*. In its second volume, published in 1973, Lamantia defined post-Bretonian surrealist poetry as "a rigorous reconstruction *against* the past, an adamant refusal to be entangled in previously conquered areas of association.... [W]e can all the more happily trace our inspirations from ... Breton and Péret ... *without literally re-tracing in one's own poetic praxis their inimitable movements* [emphasis added]." Nonetheless, besides contributing to *Arsenal,* Lamantia supported the activities of the group in many ways during this period, from collaborating with them in editing a surrealist section of the 1974 *City Lights Anthology* to cosigning many of their collective declarations.

In 1976, Lamantia and Peters traveled to Chicago for the World Surrealist Exhibition organized by the Surrealist Movement in the United States. The show featured "over 600 surrealist works—paintings, drawings, photographs, lithographs, collages, sculptures and objects—by nearly 150 active surrealists from 31 countries."[78] Here, Lamantia enjoyed stimulating encounters with older surrealists Leonora Carrington, Gerome Kamrowski, E. F. Granell, Mário Cesariny, and Clarence John Laughlin; and here he met Penelope and Franklin Rosemont and their young Chicago associates for the first time. The Rosemonts, who had been labor organizers in their youth, remained intent on putting surrealism in the service of social revolution, which meant, in their view, building a revolutionary organization. Lamantia was always too self-absorbed for such work, too attentive to his inner transformations: for him, the surrealist revolution was first and foremost a "revolution of the mind."[79] The two faces of global surrealism—one looking exoterically outward to political and cultural revolution, the other looking inward to spiritual revelation— were reflected in the Rosemonts' and Lamantia's respective approaches. In politics, Franklin Rosemont then argued for a more orthodox Marxism, and Lamantia took a utopian anarchist position. In spite of their sometimes differing ideas about social organization and surrealist tactics, they were in full agreement about incorporating the "marvelous" into daily life. They were nourished by their many communications, and were to remain lifelong friends.

Lamantia's long poem "Redwood Highway" from this period gives a clear indication of the direction of his interests: the poem concatenates the European hermetic tradition and Native American thought with Lamantia's new awareness (developed under Peters's guidance) of the deep ecologies of the West Coast. Lamantia now understood nature itself as a magically potent sign system that could both activate and be activated by the poetic imagination. In the notes to another poem from the seventies, "Oraibi" (a Hopi village), the poet refers to the *cabala* of nature as a "universal unspoken language, easily understood by all." Through Peters's encouragement, Lamantia, an urbanite who was unfamiliar with wilderness, was learning to enjoy hiking and exploring the wild. Lamantia and Peters were married in 1978 in Nevada, during a trip in which they explored bioregions from the Southwest deserts to the mountains and forests of British Columbia.

Lamantia would gather his poems of the seventies—many of them marked by his newly emerging bioregional sensibility—into a second collection for City Lights, *Becoming Visible,* published in 1981. The book's title was partly a reference to the becoming-visible of heretofore hidden magical signs in the poet's experience of nature, but it was also partly a reference to the poet's own becoming-visible—that is, to his renewed prominence and participation, following years of hermetic withdrawal, in the local and national poetry community. From 1978 to 1982, Lamantia, at the invitation of the San Francisco Art Institute, taught a well-received course on The Poetic Imagination. He found teaching to be very stimulating, just as he had at San Francisco State. He enjoyed contact with his students and appeared at ease in the classroom, carrying on a wide-ranging discussion of the sources of creativity. During the eighties, Lamantia also engaged more frequently in public readings of his work. In 1980, at the International Poetry Festival in San Francisco, Lamantia shared the stage with his old mentor Rexroth for the last time. Rexroth, whose health was visibly failing (he would die two years later), read from his translations of Japanese poetry, while Lamantia read from the manuscript of *Becoming Visible.* Although his relationship with Rexroth had been strained at times, Lamantia, in the years following Rexroth's death, always spoke of his old mentor with the greatest respect.[80]

In one sense, Lamantia's earliest mentor had been Edgar Allan Poe; in later years, he enjoyed reading Poe's twentieth-century inheritors, the fantasy-horror writers, among them Fritz Leiber, with whom Lamantia met occasionally in San Francisco, and Clark Ashton Smith, perhaps the most gifted member of a group of Symbolist poets led by George Sterling in World War I–era San Francisco. Around 1980, Peters introduced him to Donald Sidney-Fryer, the executor of Smith's estate.[81] In 1985, Fryer asked him to speak at the dedication of a Clark Ashton Smith plaque in Auburn, California; Lamantia remarked that Smith was a writer who (much like Lamantia himself) "followed his poetic genius to reveal the heights and depths of a rich cosmic revery."[82] The mid-eighties were also marked by occasional readings in small venues, and, in 1987, Lamantia and Peters read at the Santa Barbara Poetry

Festival, organized by his friend Daniel (Abdl-Hayy) Moore, the creator of the Floating Lotus Magic Opera Company, a spectacular ritual theater group in the Bay Area.

A significant turning point for Lamantia during the eighties was his engagement with birding and bird lore, an extension of his ongoing studies of the cabala of the Western biosphere. Lamantia accepted an invitation to read (with Robert Duncan and Susan Griffin) at the 1983 Bisbee Poetry Festival in Arizona so that he could use the occasion to visit a nearby hummingbird refuge. Through binoculars, Lamantia observed, in an epiphanic moment, the dartings of hundreds of hummingbirds: the becoming-visible of the secret, sacred text of nature. One of the festival organizers then led him on a vigorous hike along the San Pedro River, where he was overwhelmed by the sight of so many rare and colorful birds. Lamantia's fascination with what he perceived as their magic potencies and role in culture—manifested in their plumage, their behavior, their songs—continued for the rest of his life.

Whenever possible during this period, Lamantia and Peters sojourned up and down the West Coast, with Lamantia attentive not only to bird life but to all aspects of what, in a poem called "America in the Age of Gold," he termed "mystic geography." This concept he derived from his reading of Native Californian legends in anthropologist and linguist Samuel A. Barrett's *Pomo Myths* (1933), a book that became as important to Lamantia as Schwaller de Lubicz's *Le Temple de l'homme*. The exploration of locations crucial to Pomo Indian mythology, such as Clear Lake (including Daladano and Mount Konocti) and Fort Bragg (site of the creation of the world), formed the basis of Lamantia's "many centers of mystic geography," invoking "the time of joy with the supernatural beings" in the pre-Columbian world. Lamantia was fascinated with the extraordinarily poetic metaphysics of Pomo culture, as well as its ethical system, as embodied in the marvelous actions of characters such as Coyote, the creative spirit Madumda, Resin Man, Obsidian Man, and the Squirrel Girls, to name a few that are referenced in his poems. As in Egypt, every animal and stone and imaginal spirit-being had specific meanings, which interrelated in sometimes astonishing ways. But unlike the system of Egyptian symbols, where meanings were recorded on man-made artifacts, in Pomo thought, meanings were embodied in features of the physical world and expressed in a complex and imaginative oral literature. This revelation led to his and Peters's involvement with green politics and bioregionalism, and their friendships with figures in this movement such as Peter Berg and Judy Goldhaft, directors of Planet Drum Foundation.

These influences resulted in Lamantia's final full-length collection of new poems, *Meadowlark West* (City Lights, 1986), a startling mix of environmentalist agitation and Native American lore with old-world hermeticism and modernist metropolitan sensibilities. Exemplary of his approach is a poem he devoted to "Mt. Shasta," a dormant volcano in Northern California venerated by Native American tribes and surrounded by singular wind and weather patterns; for Lamantia, the mountain was a "locus of dream" aligned with other mythical loci such as Lemuria and the "Whirlpool of Ys." Other poems, such as "Wilderness Sacred Wilderness," pursue a similar practice of reading the book of nature for revelatory insights, even as such unlikely protagonists as Nietzsche, Simon Rodia, Man Ray, and Buffalo Bill people the landscape. In keeping with Lamantia's conception of poetry as gnosis, *Meadowlark West* is dense with reference to his readings in Amerindian myth, Egyptology, alchemy, ornithology, and surrealism—a concise, left-wing riposte to Pound's *Cantos*. A synthesis and apotheosis of new and lifelong interests, *Meadowlark West* is, in many ways, Lamantia's most original book.

"EGYPT," *BED OF SPHINXES*, AND *SYMBOLON*

In 1981, Lamantia had undergone surgery for cancer of the mouth; in 1986, the cancer returned in a metastatic form, necessitating more serious surgery and radiation treatment. After his recovery, he and Peters traveled to New Orleans—where he wrote his contribution to the *Annotated Howl*—and then along the Gulf Coast. Unfortunately, following this trip, his bipolar illness began to grow much worse. Yet in 1989 he was able to make one final trip abroad, traveling with Nancy to Egypt, where he would experience firsthand the breathtaking iconography that had inspired him for so long: the temples of Luxor and Karnak, the tombs in the Valley of the Kings, and other significant monuments. While in Cairo, he connected with Egyptian writers and also paid a visit to the Mosque of Al-Haqim, the Ismaili imam and teacher of the inner meanings of the Koran. This trip would inspire one of Lamantia's major late poems, "Egypt," which he sometimes considered his masterpiece. Yet this triumph was mitigated by increasing health problems. By 1990 he was suffering periods of prolonged and incapacitating depression, punctuated by disruptive manic episodes, a state of affairs that would endure through mid-decade.

In 1997, however, City Lights released a new selection of his work, *Bed of Sphinxes: New and Selected Poems 1943–1993*, which gathered a small number of important uncollected pieces including "Egypt," "Poem for André Breton," "Diana Green," and "Passionate Ornithology Is Another Form of Yoga." Yet even as it looked back at fifty years of poetry, *Bed of Sphinxes* would herald Lamantia's emergence from his state of depression into a new flurry of poetic activity.

This emergence was precipitated by a mystical vision Lamantia had at the National Shrine of St. Francis in North Beach, San Francisco, where in 1998 holy relics of St. Francis and St. Clare were put on display.[83] As he writes in a third-person note among his papers: "August 15, 1998: While on a casual visit to the newly designated (now National) Shrine Church of St. Francis of Assisi, poet Philip Lamantia experienced an unprecedented sense of unity with *the-divine-in-the-human*, renewing his Catholic Christian practice, inspirational source for his subsequent poetry." During this vision, as he related to Nancy, the shrine became suffused with bright

At Mount Shasta, California, 1986. Author photo by Nancy Joyce Peters for Lamantia's *Meadowlark West.* Courtesy of The Bancroft Library, University of California, Berkeley.

light, and Lamantia was convinced the experience emanated from the relics. In the immediate aftermath of this experience, Lamantia was stricken with a terrifying and uncontrollable manic episode. Once he became more stable, he found refuge in the ritual of the Mass, and also broke his long poetic silence, writing poetry once again. Unsurprisingly, these final poems of Lamantia's are frequently religious and devotional in nature.

As he accumulated poems, Lamantia began to contemplate a new collection to be called *Symbolon,* the Greek word σύμβολον from which the English word *symbol* derives, composed from the root words σύν- (*sym-*), "together," and βολη (*bolé*), "a throw," thus, "thrown together." For Lamantia, *symbolon* was a multifaceted concept, reaching into the very mechanism of language itself, as he writes in "Theoria": "words are eidetic / perceptions of a synthesis / of symbolons—'*things*' / thrown together." On an esoteric level, symbolon evoked the "symbolique" of Schwaller de Lubicz. "The symbolique includes imaged writing as well as gestures and colors, all aimed at transcribing in a functional manner the esoteric significance of a teaching whose inner meaning remains inexpressible by any other form," Schwaller de Lubicz writes in *Sacred Science,* citing by way of example the Catholic symbolization of the concept of the "divine Trinity" as a triangle. "Here there is symbolique," he continues. "It pertains to an unobjectifiable fact and a creative function at the same time.... [T]he symbolique is the means of evoking the intuition of a function which eludes rationalization; it therefore applies only to theogony, to theology, to sacred science, in fine, to knowledge of a world of causes."[84] From here it is not difficult to link this "function which eludes rationalization" to surrealism, for notably, during this final poetic phase, Lamantia found himself able to synthesize his experiences as a Catholic and as a surrealist, even asserting, in one of the last poems he wrote, that "God is a surrealist / in the union of opposites."

During this brief period of activity, from late 1998 through late 2001, Lamantia published three new poems, "Ultimate Zone," "Seraphim City," and "Triple V: The day non-surrealism became surrealist," and gave readings in New York City, Los Angeles, and San Francisco. His last major public event occurred at City Lights on September 20, 2001, at which he read once again the poems of John Hoffman, as well as a handful of his own. Yet before the end of the year, he would once again fall victim to depression. The Mass was no longer a conduit for revelation, and he was increasingly disappointed in the church, which was not moving toward liberation theology, the "civilization of love" he had hoped for. He ceased to write, see friends, or appear publicly. During the next few years of seclusion, however, he gave more thought to his *Symbolon* project. Reviewing crucial touchstones of his long poetic and spiritual journey, he was finding compelling relationships among all his diverse paths to transcendent understanding, and he envisioned writing a long poem that would be an inclusive synthesis. However, he wrote down only a few rough notes and some fragments of poetry, and did not live to create this work, dying suddenly of heart failure on March 7, 2005.

CONCLUSION

Although his hermetic nature has sometimes obscured his role in literary history, Philip Lamantia was one of the most significant American poets of the twentieth century. Quite aside from his status as a child prodigy and as the only American poet welcomed into the surrealist movement during André Breton's exile in New York City, he arrived as a truly singular, romantic figure in 1940s American poetry, at a time when the high modernism of the 1910s through the 1930s was being repudiated or tamed by academic poetry as embodied by the New Criticism. As we have seen Rexroth observe, Lamantia's work pointed the way to the future new American poetry of the 1950s and beyond. And, along with Yves le Pellec, we can justifiably assert that Lamantia and his work constituted a direct and important link between the radical culture of European modernism in the first half of the century and the radical American counterculture of the second.

As those who knew him can attest, Philip Lamantia was an extraordinary person. When not disabled by depression, he was a magnetic presence, both charismatic

At the Temple of Luxor, 1989. Photo by Nancy Joyce Peters. Courtesy of The Bancroft Library, University of California, Berkeley.

At home in San Francisco, December 2000. Photo by John Suiter. © John Suiter. Courtesy of The Bancroft Library, University of California, Berkeley.

and charming. While his formal education ended with his high school diploma, the breadth and depth of his erudition, as well as his recall, were astonishing, and he could discourse freely on a bewildering variety of topics, from art, music, and literature, to utopian, anarchist, and Marxist thought, to world religions, renaissance hermeticism, medieval alchemy, and Egyptology, to ornithology, California natural history, and Native American culture, to surrealism, of course, and, most fundamentally, to poetry. His discourses weren't so much linear as spiral, taking so circuitous a route through history and geography you'd forget what he was talking about until you were suddenly struck by an unexpected return to the subject from whence he'd begun—a process that sometimes took hours. Although he could discourse cogently, as a writer he conducted his intellectual life almost exclusively through poetry, manifesting the fruit of his knowledge in the poem itself.

Poetry for Lamantia was both an expression and a form of gnosis. The esoteric nature of his researches makes some of his poetry difficult, much as it does with, say, Yeats, from whom Lamantia borrowed the title phrase of his book *The Blood of the Air*. The phrase is significant, for it hints at the vitality that runs through even the most opaque poems of both these poets. In *Whitman's Wild Children*, Neeli Cherkovski makes a telling observation when he writes: "Breton, Péret, Rimbaud, Lautréamont . . . they didn't exist in history for Lamantia; they were contemporaries. He brings them alive in his small, crowded studio just as he does in his poetry."[85] Cherkovski might have easily said Nicholas Flamel, Teresa of Ávila, Frederick II of Sicily, or Apollonius of Tyana—and by "bringing them alive" he doesn't mean *portray*, for the history and ideas of such figures were relevant to Philip's everyday life, inasmuch as his life was a continual search for enlightenment. Ancient ideas were as alive to him as contemporary matters. He was essentially a mystic, concerned with the eternal rather than the ephemeral, to the occasional detriment of practical, daily existence.

Lamantia's way of being—his wants and needs, his conversation and demeanor— was as tumultuously imaginative as his poetry. He was one of those rare poets who dwelled perpetually within the Poem, whose life was coterminous with *poiesis*. This places him and his work in opposition to the two dominant paradigms of American poetics that view poetic practice either as a personal expression (the mainstream model) or as a critique of socially constructed meaning (the avant-garde model). Lamantia's work—in all phases of its development, as the poems collected here demonstrate—both achieves these aims and goes beyond them. For Lamantia, the poetic Word was transcendent, exceeding the limits of self and society to participate in a cosmic and even divine order. He fulfilled the definition of the poet, handed down from antiquity, as one possessed by "divine madness." His work points the way to the future of poetry as a medium once more integrated with the very sources of being, as the earthly manifestation of an inexhaustible Mystery.

NOTES

1. David Meltzer, ed., *San Francisco Beat: Talking with the Poets* (San Francisco: City Lights, 2001), 142.

2. Kenneth Rexroth, *American Poetry in the Twentieth Century* (New York: Herder and Herder, 1971), 165.

3. Christopher Lehmann-Haupt, "Philip Lamantia, 77, Surrealist Poet, Is Dead," March 21, 2005, www.nytimes.com/2005/03/21/arts/21lamantia.html, accessed November 29, 2012.

4. Philip Lamantia, "Radio Voices: A Child's Bed of Sirens," in "Surrealism & Its Popular Accomplices," *Cultural Correspondence* 10–11 (Fall 1979): 25–31.

5. Ibid., 25.

6. Ibid., 26.

7. André Breton, *Manifestoes of Surrealism,* trans. Richard Seaver and Helen R. Lane (Ann Arbor: University of Michigan Press, 1972), 27.

8. He refers to the visual effects of advection fog, common to the southern neighborhoods of the city.

9. There is an exact resonance between Lamantia's title "Paranoid Dream" and a phrase attributed to Dalí—"a dreamed itinerary of new paranoic phenomena"—that appears in Gascoyne's *Short Survey of Surrealism,* a book that exercised a great influence on the young Lamantia.

10. Indeed, Lamantia had brought a set of colored pencils with him to San Bruno Mountain, perhaps intending to sketch, and instead ended up using the pencils to write his first original poem.

11. Meltzer, *San Francisco Beat,* 135.

12. Nancy Joyce Peters, "Philip Lamantia," in *Dictionary of Literary Biography* (Detroit: Gale Research, 1982), 330.

13. Kenneth Rexroth, *An Autobiographical Novel* (New York: New Directions, 1991), 510.

14. Meltzer, *San Francisco Beat,* 135–36.

15. See Garrett Caples, "André Breton and Philip Lamantia," in *Titanic Operas, Folio III: Poetries and New Materialities II,* ed. Joseph Donahue, http://archive.emilydickinson.org/titanic/material/three/caples.html, accessed January 9, 2013.

16. Catrina Neiman, "Introduction," in *View: Parade of the Avant-Garde,* ed. Charles Henri Ford (New York: Thunder's Mouth, 1991), xii.

17. Cited in Dickran Tashjian, *A Boatload of Madmen: Surrealism and the American Avant-Garde 1920–1950* (New York: Thames and Hudson, 1995), 254.

18. Tashjian, *Boatload of Madmen,* 137.

19. Though he quit the editorial staff, Lamantia would remain a "Contributing Editor" on the masthead of *View* until his definitive break with Charles Henri Ford in March 1946 over what he saw as the magazine's increasing sensationalism.

20. Meltzer, *San Francisco Beat,* 136.

21. As early as its December 1943 issue (no. 4, series III), *View* had announced the projected publication of Lamantia's surrealist poems under its new View Editions imprint, which in 1946 would issue the first single-volume English translation of André Breton's poetry, *Young Cherry Trees Secured against Hares,* with a cover by Marcel Duchamp. Lamantia's book was to have been titled

First Poems, with a cover by Max Ernst, but this plan was complicated by tensions between Ernst and Breton and ultimately scuttled by Lamantia's 1946 break with Charles Henri Ford and *View.*

22. Michael Davidson, *The San Francisco Renaissance: Poetics and Community at Mid-century* (Cambridge: Cambridge University Press, 1989), 38.

23. Meltzer, *San Francisco Beat,* 139.

24. See Lewis Ellingham and Kevin Killian, *Poet Be Like God: Jack Spicer and the San Francisco Renaissance* (Hanover, NH: Wesleyan, 1998), 21. Ellingham and Killian identify this address as McKinley Street, though it's actually McKinley Avenue.

25. In an autobiographical note among his papers, under the heading "1948," Lamantia writes: "Discovery of R&B 'Little Harlem' later described in Kerouac's *On the Road* as one of two SF sites of jazz and R.B. musical culture. Important contacts with genius Harry Smith, painter & ethnomusicologist—very important exchanges between us re magic, gnosis, & music—Nights of 'Jackson's Nook' & Jimbo's Bop City within Fillmore, & Post & Buchanan."

26. Philip Lamantia and John Hoffman, *Tau* and *Journey to the End* (San Francisco: City Lights, 2008), 58.

27. Ibid., 59.

28. Ibid., 59–60.

29. Peters, "Philip Lamantia," 331.

30. *Tau* and *Journey to the End,* 64.

31. Peters, "Philip Lamantia," 332.

32. Bill Morgan, *I Celebrate Myself: The Somewhat Private Life of Allen Ginsberg* (New York: Viking, 2006), 152.

33. John Suiter, "Philip Lamantia Interview, North Beach, December 11, 2000," Carton 21, Folder 23 of the Philip Lamantia Papers, 1944–2005 (BANC MSS 2006/179) at The Bancroft Library at the University of California, Berkeley), p. 6.

34. John Suiter, *Poets on the Peaks: Gary Snyder, Philip Whalen and Jack Kerouac in the North Cascades* (Washington, D.C.: Counterpoint, 2002), 114.

35. Suiter, *Poets on the Peaks,* 114.

36. Suiter, "Philip Lamantia Interview," 2. De Angulo had died in 1950.

37. Suiter, *Poets on the Peaks,* 115–16.

38. Jack Kerouac, *Selected Letters, 1940–1956* (New York: Penguin, 1995), 349–50.

39. Jack Kerouac, *Desolation Angels* (New York: Riverhead Books, 1995), 206–8.

40. Allen Ginsberg, *Howl and Other Poems* (San Francisco: City Lights, 1956), 9.

41. Allen Ginsberg, *Howl: Original Draft Facsimile, Transcript and Variant Versions, Fully Annotated by Author, with Contemporaneous Correspondence, Account of First Public Reading, Legal Skirmishes, Precursor Texts and Bibliography,* ed. Barry Miles (New York: HarperPerennial, 1986), 124. Another account of this incident appears in Lamantia's uncollected 1961 poem "Visions."

42. Morgan, *I Celebrate Myself,* 202.

43. Suiter, "Philip Lamantia Interview," 16.

44. Ibid., 23.

45. Ibid., 42.

46. It is likely that Lamantia would have destroyed the manuscript of *Tau,* as he had done with many of his other writings, if not for the intercession of his first wife, Goldian Nesbit, who implored him to preserve "this beautiful manuscript." See Garrett Caples, "A Note on *Tau,*" in the Pocket Poets edition of *Tau* (San Francisco: City Lights, 2008), 7.

47. Jack Kerouac, *The Dharma Bums* (New York: Penguin, 2006), 10.

48. Michael McClure, *Scratching the Beat Surface* (New York: Penguin, 1994), 12.

49. As Lamantia told Suiter in their interview, "I really got to know Jack after the Howl reading and then when he came to stay with me, which was not long after." Lamantia insisted, too, that Kerouac "was virtually in the Church when he spent those few weeks with me when I was very fervent." Suiter, "Philip Lamantia Interview," 35–36.

50. Ibid., 209.

51. Interview with Lamantia in Meltzer, *San Francisco Beat,* 140.

52. *Tau* and *Journey to the End,* 12.

53. *New York Post,* January 22, 1958. Thanks to Steven Fama for providing this citation.

54. "Beat Mystics," *Time,* February 3, 1958.

55. Paul O'Neil, "The Only Rebellion in Town," *Life,* November 30, 1959, 123.

56. In fact, they were married twice, in a civil ceremony in Crawford, Texas, in 1960, and then in a Catholic rite in Mexico in 1961.

57. This circumstance is referred to in "Peroxide Subway" in *Destroyed Works* (San Francisco: Auerhahn, 1961): "66 days in Huntsville Prison." According to Lamantia, he was searched and busted merely for a stray marijuana seed that was found in his one of his pant cuffs.

58. This incident is documented in Lamantia's previously uncollected poem, "Ceylonese Tea Candor (Pyramid Scene)," from which the quoted terms are drawn.

59. This is broadly but not strictly true, as the final poem of the volume, "Binoculars," refers to people like Gregory Corso, whom Lamantia met sometime after the Six Gallery reading.

60. Michael McClure, *Meat Science Essays,* 2nd ed. (San Francisco: City Lights, 1966), 10. The essay "Phi Upsilon Kappa" originally appeared in *Kulchur* 8 (Winter 1962), but didn't appear in *Meat Science* until the decision in *Grove Press Inc. v. Gerstein* (1964) lessened the potential to prosecute literary publishers on obscenity grounds. (The essay is partly devoted to the word "Fuck.") McClure, who found the word *aelf-scin,* meaning "shining like an elf," in an Anglo-Saxon dictionary, likens this to Lamantia's weir.

61. This book, for example, includes "Deamin," whose original title was simply "Weir."

62. *Tau* and *Journey to the End,* 123.

63. It appears Lamantia sent the manuscript to Auerhahn in late 1960—hence the date of his "Note on *Destroyed Works*"—though the book wouldn't be printed until 1962.

64. Lamantia's Auerhahn books are unpaginated, but this poem is the sixth section of the opening suite, "Hypodermic Light."

65. Peter Conners, *The White Hand Society: The Psychedelic Partnership of Timothy Leary and Allen Ginsberg* (San Francisco: City Lights, 2010), 154.

66. Autobiographical notes, Carton 11, Folder 11, of the Philip Lamantia Papers, 1944–2005 (BANC MSS 2006/179) at The Bancroft Library at the University of California, Berkeley.

67. Previously, during the period of his ostensible silence, Lamantia had written a longer poem, "Kosmos," relating to his LSD experiences, but deemed it unworthy of publication.

68. Nancy Joyce Peters, address at the memorial for Philip Lamantia, San Francisco, March 31, 2005.

69. The back-cover copy further stated that, after Lamantia was "welcomed by André Breton into the Surrealist movement," there "followed a long, transitional period of mystical orientations & silences."

70. José Pierre, *Tracts surréalistes et déclarations collectives* (Paris: Terrain Vague, 1982).

71. In his 1973 prose statement "Between the Gulfs," Lamantia wrote: "From having initially found the key (the road opening, 1943–1946) to having lost the key (the road closed down, 1946–1966) and since rediscovering the key (the road re-opening in 1967), my solidarity with the surrealist movement . . . re-invents itself without the slightest ambiguity." *Arsenal* 2, no. 2 (1973): 32.

72. See Andrew Joron, *Neo-Surrealism; Or, The Sun at Night: Transformations of Surrealism in American Poetry 1966–1999* (Oakland, CA: Kolourmeim, 2010).

73. See Ron Sakolsky, ed., *Surrealist Subversions: Rants, Writings and Images by the Surrealist Movement in the United States* (Brooklyn, NY: Autonomedia, 2002).

74. Lamantia's long essay "Poetic Matters," published in *Arsenal* 3 (1976): 6–10, stands as one of the clearest statements of his own poetics while offering a sustained critique of the American poetry scene in the midseventies.

75. A decade earlier, Donald Allen had included selections from Lamantia's work in the landmark anthology *The New American Poetry: 1945–1960* (Grove Press: New York, 1960).

76. The book's epigraph gives a definition of "Lamantines" as a species of "mermaid-like mammals native to Africa. . . . They play, in West-African myth, a role similar to that of the Sirens in Europe." It is telling that the listing of previous books by Lamantia on the copyright page of *The Blood of the Air* includes only the two published after his return to surrealism in the midsixties.

77. See Pete Winslow, "What American Surrealism Is Fanatical About," in *The Forecast Is Hot: Tracts and Other Collective Declarations of the Surrealist Movement in the United States 1966–1976* (Evanston, IL: Black Swan Press, 1997), 111.

78. Ron Sakolsky, "Surrealist Subversion in Chicago," in *Surrealist Subversions*, 79.

79. This phrase occurs in Breton's *Second Manifesto of Surrealism*, written in the wake of the Paris group's failed attempt to join forces with the Communist Party.

80. Lamantia attempted in 1999 to write a poem, entitled "Mentor," about his relationship to Rexroth (the poem begins: "An old mentor mourned / many a night you opened / with the ancient learning we / met eternity at its only juncture / for the living"), but left it unfinished.

81. Peters had contacted Sidney-Fryer in the course of writing, with Lawrence Ferlinghetti, *Literary San Francisco* (San Francisco: City Lights / Harper & Row, 1980).

82. "Clark Ashton Smith Plaque Dedication," in Philip Lamantia papers, 1944–2005, The Bancroft Library, BANC MSS 2006/179, Carton 17, Folder 38.

83. "A Short History of Saint Francis of Assisi Church," www.shrinesf.org/history.html, accessed November 29, 2012.

84. R. A. Schwaller de Lubicz, *Sacred Science: The King of the Pharaonic Theocracy* (1961), trans. André and Goldian VandenBroeck (Rochester, VT: Inner Traditions, 1988), 120.

85. Neeli Cherkovski, *Whitman's Wild Children* (South Royalton, VT: Steerforth Press, 1999), 128.

Editorial Note

Organizing Lamantia's collected poems presents a set of challenges that, while not unique to this poet, are by no means typical. Strict chronology won't do, either in terms of composition, which is impossible to determine for most individual poems, or in terms of publication, which would yield unsatisfactory results, for example, in the case of *Tau*, which was published over fifty years after its composition. That said, the order of presentation in this book is broadly chronological based on the periods during which the poems were composed. Within this chronological scheme, wherever practicable, first priority has been given to individual integral volumes as they appeared on publication. This accounts for *Ekstasis, Destroyed Works, The Blood of the Air, Becoming Visible,* and *Meadowlark West.*

Even here, however, we might note that *Ekstasis* is drawn from a ten-year period (1948–1958), making some of it older than *Tau*, which precedes it here. Similarly, the sections from the "Destroyed Works" typescript are drawn from the same ten-year range. The most convenient location for these poems is the date when the typescript was created, roughly 1960. As we suggest in the introduction, this typescript seems to have served as the model for the book *Destroyed Works*; hence it immediately precedes the latter.

The chief difficulty lay in the early work, for Lamantia disavowed the mixed arrangement of his first book, *Erotic Poems*—whose first section reproduced his then-most recent poems, which he often referred to as his "naturalistic" work, and whose second section consisted of his earliest, surrealist poems—in favor of a "definitive" gathering of the surrealist work called *Touch of the Marvelous.* This volume went through two editions (1966 and 1974) that vary considerably. The 1974 edition deletes several poems included in the 1966 edition, adds three poems from the late 1940s, and almost entirely rearranges the sequence. The "Touch of the Marvelous" section of his second selected poems, *Bed of Sphinxes* (1997), again mixes the order, despite Lamantia's desire to make the 1974 *Touch* the poems' definitive arrangement. His first *Selected Poems* (1967) features yet another order of presentation. (Both volumes of selected poems, moreover, contain sections of new work, and so must remain in some capacity as "books," even as the majority of the poems are redistributed to their respective volumes or periods of origin.)

Bearing in mind Lamantia's intention to group his early surrealist work, we've preserved *Touch of the Marvelous* as a section, though the order and contents are a rationalization of the two editions and the *Bed of Sphinxes* section. Those poems unique to *Erotic Poems* are preserved as "From *Erotic Poems*." This is followed by a section of uncollected work appearing under the heading "Poems 1943–1953." The remaining sections follow this pattern. Uncollected and unpublished work appears as "Poems," followed by the dates from which the poems are drawn. Significant groupings from books that overlap with other books, such as *Erotic Poems* and *Selected Poems,* or poems from the hybrid, multiauthor *Narcotica,* are designated as "from" a given title. When faced with a decision like where to place the three poems from *Tau*—a complete but unpublished manuscript—which later appear in *Ekstasis,* we have in all cases favored those books that Lamantia himself published.

Lastly, there is a section of work from *Symbolon,* a projected final book, which Lamantia grew too ill to complete before his death and which contains his last published poems as well as unpublished ones.

TOUCH OF THE MARVELOUS

1943–1949

The Touch of the Marvelous

The mermaids have come to the desert
they are setting up a boudoir next to the camel
who lies at their feet of roses

A wall of alabaster is drawn over our heads
by four rainbow men
whose naked figures give off a light
that slowly wriggles upon the sands

I am touched by the marvelous
as the mermaids' nimble fingers
go through my hair
that has come down forever from my head
to cover my body
the savage fruit of lunacy

Behold the boudoir is flying away
and I am holding onto the leg of the lovely one
called beneath the sea
BIANCA
She is turning
with the charm of a bird
into two giant lips
and I am now falling into the goblet of suicide

She is the angelic doll turned black
she is the child of broken elevators
she is the curtain of holes
that you never want to throw away

she is the first woman and first man
and I am lost in the search to have her

I am hungry for the secrets of the sadistic fish
I am plunging into the sea

I am looking for the region
where the smoke of your hair is thick
where you are again climbing over the white wall
where your eardrums play music

to the cat that crawls in my eyes ·
I am recalling memories of you BIANCA

I am looking beyond the hour and the day
to find you BIANCA

Plumage of Recognition

A soul drenched in the milk of marble
goes through the floor of an evening
that rides lost on a naked virgin
It gains power over the dull man:
it is a soul sucked by lepers

What liquid hour shall rivet
its song on my cat
with the neck of all space?

Morning and I may lose
the terrible coat of ill feeling
that has curled me into a chained dragon
the flower bursting with eyelids

Ah! a fever the skeleton of arson!
comes to rest on the citadel of the immortals;
the diadem flickers and dies away
while running toward the vat of salted babies

They are creeping upon the wall my dagger
they are bulging with cradles
the era of the lunatic birds has arrived!
They have come to rape the town
infested with iron-blood clerks
and to send the hairless priests
to the pool of deadly anchors

Parades are the enchantment of a brain
piled-up like the water of an ocean
I enjoy the creation of a human table
to be in the center of the delirious crowd

There are birds perched on my bones
that will soon flood the avenues
with their serpent-like feathers
I am at a house built by Gaudi
"May I come in?"

The Islands of Africa

to Rimbaud

Two pages to a grape fable
dangles the swan of samite blood
shaping sand from thistle covered fog
Over sacred lakes of fever
(polished mouths of the vegetable frog
rolling to my iron venus)
I drop the chiseled pear
Standing in smoke filled valleys
(great domains of wingless flight
and the angel's fleshy gun)
I stamp the houses of withering wax
Bells of siren-teeth (singing to our tomb
refusal's last becoming)
await the approach of the incendiary children
lighting the moon-shaped beast

Every twisted river pulls down my torn-out hair
to ratless columns by the pyramid's ghost
(watered basin of the temple stink)
and all the mud clocks in haste
draw their mermaid-feather swords
(wrapped by Dust) to nail them
into the tears of the sea-gull child
The winter web minute
flutters beneath the spider's goblet
and the whores of all the fathers
bleed for my delight

I Am Coming

I am following her to the wavering moon
to a bridge by the long waterfront
to valleys of beautiful arson
to flowers dead in a mirror of love
to men eating wild minutes from a clock
to hands playing in celestial pockets
and to that dark room beside a castle
of youthful voices singing to the moon.

When the sun comes up she will live at a sky
covered with sparrow's blood
and wrapped in robes of lost decay.

But I am coming to the moon,
and she will be there in a musical night,
in a night of burning laughter
burning like a road of my brain
pouring its arm into the lunar lake.

Apparition of Charles Baudelaire

When an ocean of pain moves rivers and bridges
and black eyes flash in grave dust, then
the rapture of Baudelaire strikes a flaming note.

By the blood of somber countenance
hang all fifty chambers of voluptuous girls,
entranced by the poet's pulsating gleam
that nails love only onto his giant queen
sifting in the rays of forgotten children.

Over the laughing brothel and pale garden,
he sings on the pipe of languor
and prays on a flying altar
drowning with every touch of the sun.

The Ruins

Falling from tear-drops of time,
the well of hidden dreams
seems like broken ice over the sun.

Beneath its feathered mirror
love is lying, a wounded flavor
never again to steal,
when ragged for plastic honey,
the moon's long frigid kiss.

Here is a hot wind of knives
cutting my breath for sport,
and leaving behind a limpid song
heard by a million murdered stars.

Balls of arson charge a flood of rats
going down to pray with the blizzard bone
and the sound burns through a tower,
the highest light of forbidden magic.

By the Curtain of Architecture

To all religions that never began, but had to sleep
in the fountain of forgotten engineers; they have come
to the altar of a new history . . .

Over the banners of Oedipus flies the deluge,
a tower of chafed metaphors,
miles of antique lamps,
incantations of a soiled planet
and the weary litanies of drunken dust.

A saint pauses, reads the fire
and nails his heart on the laughing altar.

Somewhere beside child-like hands on a cross
two men meet to bleed their bones of furniture
to preach a sermon in the halls of Africa

to raise their arms to a glass heaven
resting in the jellied clock of Diogenes
to voice a music from the ruins of cities
laid dry upon ages of ritual
and to serve an idea of marble
rolling over the clown's pre-historic martyrdoms
continually breathing a shadow of decayed pianos.

There Are Many Pathways to the Garden

If you are bound for the sun's empty plum
there is no need to mock the wine tongue
but if you are going to a rage of pennies
over a stevedore's wax ocean
then, remember: all long pajamas are frozen dust
unless an axe cuts my flaming grotto.

You are one for colonial lizards
and over bathhouses of your ear
skulls shall whisper
of a love for a crab's rude whip
and the rimless island of refusal shall seat itself
beside the corpse of a dog
that always beats a hurricane
in the mad run for Apollo's boxing glove.

As your fingers melt a desert
an attempt is made to marry the lily-and-fig-foot dragon
mermaids wander and play with a living cross
a child invents a sublime bucket of eyes
and I set free the dawn of your desires.

The crash of your heart
beating its way through a fever of fish
is heard in every crowd of that thirsty tomorrow
and your trip ends in the mask of my candle-lit hair.

Automatic World

The sun has drowned
virgins are no more
there is no need for understanding
but there is so much to see

So come with me
down the boulevard
of crawling veins
Don't be afraid
blood is cheap!

A paradise song?
A dirty story?
A love sonnet?
Scream it out!
Then we'll have the human walls
tumbling down to meet our march
into the raw-meat city!

The velvet robes are strewn
across the landscape
We step upon the sidewalk
that goes up and down
up to the clouds
down to the starving people
Don't ask me what to do!
Keep on going
we'll end up somewhere fast
on the moon perhaps!

Rainbow guns are dancing
in front of the movie queens
Everyone is laughing
flying dying
never knowing when to rest
never knowing when to eat

And the fountains come falling
out of her thistle-covered breasts
and the dogs are happy

and the clowns are knifing
and the ballerinas are eating stone

O the mirror-like dirt
of freshly spilt blood
trickling down the walls
the walls that reach the stars!

O the flock of sheep
breaking their flesh open
with bones sucked
from the brothels!

O the grave of bats
sailing through shops
with the violent hands!

When will these come?
When will these go?

The sun is riding into your eye
virgins are bursting
from under my flaming palms
and we are slowly floating away

Hermetic Bird

This sky is to be opened
this plundered body to be loved
this lantern to be tied
around the fangs of your heart

Lost on a bridge
going across oceans of tragedy
across islands of inflammable virgins
I stand
with my feathers entangled in your navel
with my wings opalescent in the night
and shout words heard tomorrow
in a little peasant cart
of the seventeenth century

Breath by breath
the vase in the tomb
breaks to give birth to a roving Sphinx
Tremble, sweet bird, sweet lion
hunger for you
hunger for your mother

The children in the lamps
play with our hair
swinging over the void

Here is a landscape on fire
Here are horses wet by the sour fluid of women

On the pillars of nicotine
the word *pleasure* is erased by a dog's tongue
On the pillars the bodies are opened by keys
the keys are nailed to my bed
to be touched at dawn
to be used in a dream

If one more sound is heard
the children will come out to murder
at the bottom of the lake
at the bottom of the lake

If the children murder
the owls will bleed
the wanton humans
who parade in basements of the sun

When the columns fall into the sea
with a crash involving prophecies and madmen
together in a little cradle
lifted into the robes of desire
and with our mouths opened for the stars
howling for the castles to melt at our feet
you and I
will ride over the breasts of our mother
who knows no one
who was born from unknown birds
forever in silence
forever in dreams
forever in the sweat of fire

Moments of Exile

This is the air that will not allow us to breathe.
This is the sea that will not allow us to swim.

But we shall spin wildly in the air
we shall go far out to sea.

Knives that cross and recross our bodies
hidden wounds
lust to love
image before me:
heart of hearts
so rich and yet raped by horses
in the athlete's tower of estrangement.

We sleep.

Tonight heated by mist
growing in rabid flesh,
a cloud to the wind:
murdered in darkness
ankle upon ankle
we sleep
as thrust below the sand
your delicate hands cry out to be cut.

Love wanders over the hair of your mouth,
lustful child,
toy circling in the constellations of the heart
surprising the quick gaze of the moon with your caprice
rounding the velvet eye
that is hidden from light

as your blood rushes down to the sea
flows gently over the water
to the fish, luminous,
fins knotted,
their eyes inflamed, burning deeply into our hearts,
their heads breaking the mist,
their tails flashing like diamonds.

Released, they linger in silence
as we do in this moment; inflamed in sleep
with our eyes thrown like dice upon the sand
rolling toward the rocks

over them and into the sky,
shining, waiting for the clouds to take them:
to breathe, to sigh, to swim
into hidden caverns, to be loved.

But as quickly as we came we are sucked away.
We are not asleep now
there is no knife to cut constantly into our hearts
no comb to unknot our venomous hair.

Awakened now, imprisoned in the deep well of longing,
we can see through the green moss
the air that will not allow us to breathe,
the sea that will not allow us to swim.

∎ ∎ ∎

Beneath this bed the caverns gather me like water
to throw me upon moth-eaten women
who sleep violently
in a knot of newly born suns

The arrows that protrude from drunken animals
are swept away to the bottom of the sea
where the most handsome men stand barefoot
over their lovers' bodies rent by young witches
whose hands are in gloves of stone

Sweet renegade, I am before you with burnt flesh
with a heart that wears only a mask born in great storms
to rest in your closet of pain
where a child's body lies open to the hatchets of love

. . .

I am a criminal when your body is bare upon the universe
I am there to steal your amorous fangs abandoned before me

Between the thick folds of a tropical bed
bullets into tears fall swiftly upon your wounded hands:
eyes secreting poisons
over forgotten testaments written by me
in days when I saw your double in a dream

I open a seashell and find your heart
which returns to the *storm of storms*, Desire's mate
raging on the desolate beach of our bed

The hanged girl in my mirror watches with horror
as I exchange my eyes for yours
But, too late
I pull the gun's trigger
and the mirror shatters

Our images multiply and the earth turns into a midget
as arrows are shot into my eyes at dawn

A Civil World

In a moment their faces will be visible.

You shall see the women who walk in a night of offensive sunlight that cuts through their cardboard thighs.

As the street is cleaned by the presidents of the nation, I can see the bowlegged men moving over to copulate with the maniacs.

As a rose runs down an alley, a purple nugget, giving off some blood, is suspended in air.

The children who are ten feet tall are wet.

Their faces are scorched, their eyes cut by glass.

They play their games as a steeple topples, as a clown's laugh is heard in church.

Quietly the mothers are killing their sons; quietly the fathers are raping their daughters.

But the women.

The eye wanders to a garden in the middle of the street.

There are poets dipping their diamond-like heads in the luminous fountain. There are grandmothers playing with the delicate toys of the chimera. There are perfumes being spilt on the garbage. There is a drunken nun flying out of a brothel.

The women are all colors.

Their breasts open like flowers, their flesh spreads over the park like a blanket. Their hair is soaked in the blood of their lovers, those who are the mirrors of this night.

The naked lovers! All of them, fifteen years old! One can still see their hair growing! They come from the mountains, from the stars even, with their handsome eyes of stone. Ah, these somnambulistic lovers, with their bellies full of arrows!

After the street has recaptured its loneliness, a precious stone casts its light on the perambulator I am to enter. One perambulator in the center of a world. A poet—far away in the mountains—can be heard chanting like an ape. I wonder when he will stop?

Invisible

The day announces a bather
slipping under the white plumes of a bird
too much in love with its own image to murder its mate

A day forgotten in swimming pools
where a nude girl repairs revolvers
for her criminal midget

But the day has its little white breasts
of the sadistic virgins from the font
They are caught up by a rose
black and trailing its eye down the street

The brutal clouds meet us on our way
and almost strangle us with their arms and legs
that disappear too quickly for us to see them

And the flags with holes in them
larger than those in the sky
come flowing over me
and singe my hair with invisible flames
The flags have written over them
death is a pearl in the seashell of love

Now the flags are turning into faces
and the words are gone like smoke

A fist, bruised and holding the sun,
opens for night to unfold its assassin
going out to meet his laughing lion
far away where death is extinguished with a sigh

The burning manes of the midnight jungle
announce sleep coming on the fatal horses
of love
an explosive pearl in the seashell of sleep

The Enormous Window

Within closets filled with nebulae
the blood shot eyes
swim upward for the sun

This world of serpents and weeping women
is crushed in the violence
of a swamp large enough to contain
the enormous razorblade of the night

> *In the tropics*
> *the doctors prescribe*
> *sand for the heart*

> *Ad astra*
> *Ad astra*

With fire spitting across the horizon
and like a little flake of flesh
bashed against our heads
midnight seeps through the marigolds
in the garden no longer quiet
as corpses float through its arbor of palm trees

Neurasthenics
with young blood
ride to the stars
with horses from Peru

Tomorrow evangelists
the following day toys fall in love
the last moment brings rabid boys
beating their fathers with lightning rods—

Ad Astra
Ad Astra

In the sea the clown of windows
encounters swift rocks
climbing upon his body
to rub against his wooden anus

As the jungle disappears
one theatre of war gives birth to another
The bleeding eyes of murder
fall into the sea of this night

The performance begins
in the palm of your hand
where the swords mark the spot
where your eardrums take wings
to gather strength between two girls
raped at sunrise

Through the ceiling I can see beggars
walking on hands and knees
to reach a pyramid flung into the storm
where serpents drink champagne
and wash their women with the blood of prophets

The stars are wet tonight
the naked schoolmasters
are no longer in the gardens of childhood
and the sea has been heated for lions

And now you can bleed fire from statues
and the lower you descend into this bottomless pit
the higher will you rise
beyond the raped girls
beyond the wounded boys
trapped in the labyrinth
of their mother's hair
        beyond the soiled curtain of space

Mirror and Heart

The teacups shattered upon the legs of ancient lovers
become a statue in Rome before you
my embittered gypsy

Pluck your feathers
stain the wings that carry your heart among assassins
Watch through the boudoir the satin shirts of drunken men
who have seen their poisoned hair scattered in fire
watch and regret nothing

Your fate is to follow the sleeping women
in the castle of memory with its smoked oceanic rocks
covered by blood and snow

Your body reclaiming the stars
lifts itself in a wooden frame
to be seen in boulevards
that twist themselves at dawn into my room

Advance with caution
as with locust in your belly
make a window that will follow the trees into a lake

Each bridegroom shall inherit a laugh of childhood
that will announce the coming of my felons
soft with murder
soft with your feathers growing upon their hands

The noiseless girl who places the eyes of her lover
in a glass of wine
is only a flower set between the oars of a boat
to petrify and to be sucked for blood

Don't be frightened my dark one
this dream that winds its way
against a mask worn by the first suicide
will fade away into another's fury
when the morning wears your torn dress

Awakened at the side of this hunted slave
your hands will whisper my name into the sands.

As your lips raise water from the mist
an apparition of your mirror
takes you within its warmth
reflecting black wounds set open by the fingernail of the dumb

Solitude is your violence

Your burnt face is fading into the dream

My love
my gypsy
among the fallen you are luminous
You wander with those who are mystery
with a naked heart upon your breast

Infernal Landscape

A window that never ends
where infant eyes are unhooked
from the paper clown
who stands on a shattered mirror
picking rocks from his heart

In the absence of light
pulled through mist
my eyes are imprisoned
And the sun has regained its lions
whose flesh covers the earth
who know solitude is a flavor
of the polar night

But it is a criminal hand
that obscures the shadow of clowns
and the skeleton of solitude
It is this hand hiding in smoke
of burnt flesh
kissed and rekissed, sucked of flames
that is consumed in lust
A hand that grows of its own accord
giving thunder to sleep

as moonlight like a sword cuts through
its bracelet of animal entrails

Eyelids open as mouths
nourishing the criminal hand
Its fingers play upon water from thighs
whose serpents plunge into my body

Sand passes in the heart of the hand
as diamonds in a lake

A Winter Day

In the rose creeping into the tower of exiles
when the buffet is laden with jewels
when the night is filled with hate
when the womb of Eros is deserted
when the sleeping men are awakened
when the old lovers are no longer frightened
—my heart

The old women come down playing on the lawns
of the intangible murderers
the women are mine
Your eye is so smooth in the sunlight
you are no longer a child
you are old
spider of the blind
insolent mother
Do you care for my young hair
I want to lay the fibers of my heart over your face

It is a strange moment
as we tear ourselves apart in the silence
of this landscape
of this whole world
that seems to go beyond its own existence

You roll so beautifully over my bones
that have shaken off the flesh of their youth

My nakedness is never alarming
it is this way I adore you

Your hands with crystals shining into the night
pass through my blood
sever the hands of my eyes

We have come to a place where the nightingales sleep
We are filling up the oceans and the plains
with the old images of our phosphorescent bones

Awakened from Sleep

Swept from the clouds
We are among gardens under the sea.
Flaming white windows
From which nightingales flaunt in the sun.

Have we come from the cities of the plain
Or the moon's lake of demons?

Your whole body is a wing,
Daughter of half-seen worlds;
Together we fly to rocks of flesh
Beneath the ashes of ancient lovers.

There is no rule here,
No seasons and no misery;
There are only our desires
Revealed in the mist.
Here ghosts are reborn every moment
In the spider webs of your face.

Your hair is mingled with little children
Laughing in the moonlight;
Butterflies have come to rest upon your lips
Whose words clothe the dancing stars
Falling lightly to earth.

You have become so monumental,
And I so sleepy.

Water is trickling down your lucid breasts.
In a minute you'll be a shadow
And I a flame in sleep.

We'll meet,
Corridors will open,
The rain will come in,
The hot bite of dogs will be upon us.
And drifting with a marvelous touch
Of all the moons of space,
      Will be the lovers,
Diffusing their blood
In the secret passageways of the heart.

The Diabolic Condition

As the women who live within each other's bodies
descend from their polar regions
to the circle of demons
I become ready to offer myself to the smooth red snakes entwined in the heads of
    sorcerers

Between the black arms coming over the swamp
rushing to embrace me
and the distant sun in which abide the men who hold within their fists the Evil Eyes
between the tombs and beds of boneless magicians
who have worked in the secrecy of abandoned towers
despite my body flying away
despite the lizards who crawl into the altars where the potents are being prepared
despite the intrusion of doctor's maids and egyptologists
despite the old Doric temple carried in by the art lovers
despite the nest of mad beggars
the chant is heard
and the words of the chant are written in oceanic gardens

The flat walls are singing good-bye
we have entered the city where the dead masters speak to us of catacombs and the
    horned enchantress of Africa

The incantation is following us into the streets
and into the sky
We are ascending to the limitless cosmos of architecture
we are crawling backward to enormous hearts
that leap over the snow to climb into our bodies

Come my ritual wax and circles
my rose spitting blood
When the day is lit up by our magic candles
and the hours yell their sadistic songs and suck hard
into the night when the cats invade our skulls
then we will know the destructive ones have gone
out into the world to watch the cataclysm begin
as the final wave of fire pours out from their hearts

Celestial Estrangement

We have been carried here against our will

Burnt stars
Oceanic gardens
where the clouds are soaked into my eyes

How much sand floats in the teacup of your dreams
The rivers you perceive are those of horses
they carry red water
the odor of imperishable sweat
putrescent human bellies stuffed with revolvers and nuns

At the top of the tower
where hounds part with a pool of water
where one comes only with a flaming lance
where there is no escaping the pain of a horse's kick
where toy dolls are nailed to the beds
where lovers suck their bodies dry
as harp strings are plucked away
in this hermit world of old gunny sacks and broken heads

we encounter tons of wingless birds

Submarine Languor

You are the paper in the sky
the enchantress of the winged whales

Celestial
apocalyptic
There are words written on your forehead
the forehead soaked in the sweat of my bowels
As it is midnight beneath the sea
with the wounds of the fish opened for my entrance
do away with me
do away with my sweet pain
my quarrelsome statues

Your song
for the iridescent fauns of the clouds
for female demons
for my raw bleeding flesh
for hearts
for love
Ragged
rampant
you are in the center of a storm
the automobiles are glued to your tail

I hear the stories of the embittered fish
who watch the fire of your entrails

You and I Have Nothing to Fear

Listen
you may hear the ten may poles
out of a womb
pulled through the child's stupefying algebra
of sound
but only if you dip bracelets
in your blood
scratch out the eyes set in my ruby
that is

in turn
set in the sun
washed and preserved
for the rays of urine

    There are more invisibilities
    to be attained

Heavy as the convulsive murderers
hanged at midnight
—somewhere north of our pathways—
swinging over cold islands
in the bowels of the city
As heavy as I have said
you appear with a diamond hatchet
floating over our bodies
whose toads bathe in the eloquent lakes
that no one will ever see again
whose radiant blue columns
spit sperm over the city

On the dogs whispers pop-off
to become songs in the sky
infested with elegance
an elegance which no one has the right to understand
just as no one has the right to understand
why you were born in a house of cigarettes
or I in a howling star

But hold your basket of berries
don't let them fall into the sky-rocketing bones
You may regret having these little cards
with the numbers written over them
but you'll want to hold them close to you
when the flowers come back to the mummies

Rest In Peace
Over the night these words scatter themselves
And as I say this
bloodless nuns pass with lanterns
in their withering hands
They shall kneel until mid-day
forms a dagger for their hearts

Rest assured
we have not been uttering a word
against the master
His leafy ears heal too quickly
and besides the stars have crossed over
our tight embrace
You and I have nothing to fear
not even the bloody sunrise
as it invades the fog
lifting the turbulent aura to our faces

The Image of Ardor

for Parker Tyler

In the tropical islands
that cut through hearts,
beasts, ogres, — the wounded children
separate, become machines of wonder,
follow their thorned fathers
whose mouths contain lakes,
sweet scented cascades,
murdered girls with the eyes of zebras;
follow them to the lamps of flesh
that burn through our diamonds
that draw sweat from the trees of blue iron.

The heavy submarine women
pass over the bodies of wanton youths
who search for ravens lost in swamps,
who roll their eyes in heated bottles,
pursue their lovers with flaming torches
and carry their priceless mirrors
within a network of navel strings.

These painted faces watch only the incomparable,
love only the unopposed flowers of desire.
The lions that issue from lava
claim them, embrace their naked bodies.

They live within wild birds
swiftly ascending mountains of flame.
Their pride is kept within a perfumed box
that sails in a sea of hair,
to land on this island
and be sold to many men
who dwell beneath heated jewels,
beneath the secret idols of love.

Hidden in rocks, in grass of blood,
the youth has grown enormous wings.
He dreams of black chimeras
and wonders about the huge pair of breasts
that sink into the sea.

To You Henry Miller of the Orchestra the Mirror the Revolver and of the Stars of Stars

On entering the house
on the street suffering from heartaches
I encounter you
a little to the right of the parasol
a little over the phonograph record with yellow fans
a little like two dice and a hatchet
you mingle with women who have lost their wombs in the smoke

Insidiously walking down the spacious hallway
where red bandanas wave hello
my sweet bucket of excrement crisscrosses you all the way

Under my foot at noon
when we have bitten glass walls
just when my head is swimming in a pyramid in Mexico
just at that time you crawl forth
reading a parable
for no reason at all

But pass away
the iron rust of your face wants love only love
not a smell of infested testicles

O what is this host of children anyway
it interrupts our hunting
the old women who are producing altars of morphine
So forever the windows shine at the top of your head
forever the madmen are excused from the dinner table

Wave goodbye
your friend is waiting for you
he is secreting a blue fluid from his ear
which spells out in the sky "es—o—ter—ic buddhism"

Don't worry rats hide in the night soil
where old men's beards grow as strong as a priest in the sun
with his cleanshaven face in gasoline

Forget me forget me tomorrow
the virgin will prove wholesome under the sea
Rain on her all the gorgeous animals
have them nestle close to her hymen

What I have related is written on the wall
you talk from the depths of this drunken vocabulary
What does this mean
what does anything mean

It is worth beating the floor of the palace
with your muscles
Oiled and soaked in the magic wines
your body will be preserved for the hawks
who love you dearly
from morning to midnight they remember you
and shower you with scented vapours

But until you regard yourself with suspicion
your attacks on the aerial child will not end
and dung will continue to fall over the child's lips

But wash your thighs
priceless in the prison cell
when you squeeze out the liquids of horses

A little too dry you cling to the building
and watch the mist shooting balls into the sky

But don't let the amphibious wife strangle you without a nightgown
The police might suspect her of hiding in the thunder
where the gulls ride over the silk stockings you stole in Paris ten years ago

To raise a beard on your ear will take centuries
so release the wristwatch from your matchbox
and enter the plate where women ask no questions

The umbrella is alarmed
don't have it spring on you
with its platinum mouths
and hat of blood-ridden fur
It sings to the vile eggs in the garden
which silently creep into your lake to melt away

And as sweat pours from your eyes
to change into salt
the gates fashioned from your children's bones
are swung open
to release the telephone of cement
to disclose the statues walking at midnight
inducing you to fly into the rubber castles of the sun

from EROTIC POEMS

1946

. . .

Upon the earth eyes opened in wonder,
As trees flowed within me
And dreams followed snow.

No longer did I see torture
Or hate, coiled like a snake:
Ready for the constant attack
—On man himself, imprisoned
And fearful of the sun's power,
Born in uncertain times
Of myth and death.

There was no feverish cry
From the depths, or from above,
And I knew this was the island
Of an exiled heart.

Yet this island is before us always,
From life to life,
From minute to minute,
In a state of change,
But eternal as the primal images.

The world never sees itself,
Never regards its love;
Believes itself protected
And forms a pattern of evil.

But, those who see everything at once:
A cosmos, designed and ordered
In the rhythm of a heartbeat,
Love the image, but not the myriad worlds
Wasting away under a symbol of death.

It is here: the whole, of which the parts
Are both mirror and picture.

From a window I see the world
As I would see love
As I would see you
As I would see myself.

This act of vision
Is an act of love;
I speak among you
As I would among the dead.

. . .

You flee into a corridor of stars.
You sleep in a bleeding tree,
And awaken upon the body of trance.

The night flies like a bird possessed by fire.
Pieces of night scatter in an alcove of ghosts
Where a comet is our symbol and space our illusion.

We are two loves, two feathers blown over water,
Our garments washed upon the sands,
Our bodies flung to the rocks.

I meet you in the solitude of violence;
Take you as a vapour and flow as blood
In your body of music and haunting flesh.

Scenario

Blood stains velvet
As a girl passes like smoke
Through the heavy air,
Passes like smoke
To the drunken sailors.

It's strictly contemporary here,
Nothing archaic except velvet
(And the blood spills over it).

Nothing but fast love
And fast death.

The man and the woman in the circle
Dancing a samba.

First the quiet doping and casual loving,
Next the brawl:
With the Don Juans
And the queens
Breathing for paradise to come.

The early morning brings
A taste of ash in the mouth;
Welts and wounds;
The analerotics yelling for air.

Mirrors broken; bottles of gin
Slung from one table to another;
An elegy written across the window.

The last to leave is the girl at the bar,
Passing in the dawn like smoke.

Dressed in velvet,
Happy and bitten,
She waits for the noise and crowds
Of the next night.

From Dark Illusion to Love's Reality

I take to a caryatid coming alive
(Whose marble falls from her hair),
Moving over the ruins of cities.

Her life is ephemeral.
In her shadow I walk as the most melancholy,
Blinding the sun with a sweep of my lashes.

Within her life ends as swiftly as a dream,
And the future seems worse than the past
And no better than the present.

From the depths of an uprooted earth
No longer light forms,
But frozen waste is scattered everywhere.

In this desperate night I submerge
Toward an incarnate body in the sea,
Revealed to me, without pangs, as Love.

(My caryatid returns to her frieze,
Tracing like snow in the air,
An image of decay.)

I take from the sea this magnetic heart
(As the sun moves slowly between us)
To follow the pulsebeats of Love.

■ ■ ■

I open for you an ancient book
Breathing through the soil,
With pages of leaves taken
From an ageless, forgotten garland.

It tells of a wonderous flower
Born within us, but blossoming only
As we are lost forever
In its loving, deathless power.

And the book falls into night
To appear endlessly
Until the last mind's eye
Records its precious wisdom.

And I shall not move through this night
Before I see the flower coming forth
And cling to your flesh
For the final enveloping.

By the sea of our eyes
This flower shall be made golden,
And none shall make us separate
In the flowering fire of our souls.

Nativity of Love

In the long hours, torn from night,
The earth gives birth to us again:
The greenness flowing in our blood,
Forever in oneness, passes like dew
Between our lips, sealed from the world.

Rising from our first dream,
I see only the face of your heart
Moving from the trees to an island,
Perched above us: ghost of a love-land
Where we lie entwined in our bodies,
Given to the grass.

Your mask disappears in the sky
Leaving the veined star open
For my kisses. Your star, above
Pain's phantom touch, slowly entering
The net of my arms to sleep again
In the rib's infinite eye.

Though we may pass on from this land,
Conceiving us in the womb of love,
Our sighs and songs shall haunt
Its black trees and dark grasses
As I haunt you in the mirror of memory.

I seek you in the deep daylight
Of bodies, covered by leaves
And glowing crystals of the sea.

We lie close to the soil,
Joined to ourselves forever:
Our flesh invaded by the sun,
In deep communion and final purpose.

Autumn Poems

1

Under autumn clouds, bird shaped,
Pursuing the winds carving
Our faces in the rocks,
I take you in rapt fury
And before Time's calm indifference.

2

Today I am seized by the rain.

The rain walks, runs about in your heart,
I feel it moving, flooding the veins,
Lying in wait for my entrance.

3

I feel the turning leaves
On your trembling thighs;
Know silence to be water
Flowing in the darkness
Of a season of sighs.

This love's knowing silence
Flows toward divinity;
Is a finger of light
Upon grains of sand:
Our golden stars of infinity.

Answer from a Place of Waiting

And what is this: the meditation
And the dream you paint with an ink of tears?

Who has known a lover ripening for marriage
Will be like a tree growing

Deeply and joyfully into the soil,
Leaving her loss and pain to wash away
On the face of winter.

Overgrown with protective leaf,
Culled from some esoteric forest of your world,
You lie upon thorns
And think their juice is sweet.

No, better to die and meet as spirits
Than write as if we were dead.

Now that our bodies still call
To each other across the distance,
Let us meet to exchange our kisses in the sun
And move into entangling leaves.

Let us cast our eyes
Toward the heaven of youthful gods,
Consumed so many centuries past,
Rising again from the fire
Of their inviolable loves.

■ ■ ■

I am forlorn.
The berry under the breast
Breaks its sea of sorrow over my head.
Resting on stone, I think of my unending quest
For the morning star gone.

How I curse my own undoing:
Of trying the profound feelings
And weights of love
On the twig of chance.

Sorrow

In anguish, I hear a voice
Singing of the wounded animal
Turning on winter's garland

Of dead flowers. For days he has lain
Remembering his autumn birth,
Watching fire give way to ice.

Unable to die, he suffers
For his beloved, knowing she has moved
Into a temporary death.

How much pain the dark tooth
Had cast his way
As it drove deep into his loin.

His sweet flesh is no longer embraced
By the sun's dark arms,
No longer healed by grass.

As I watch him, I wonder what alien wind
Drove the savage tooth, as a sea,
To his body's star:

Piercing and breaking the rib's bone
And opening his flesh to swift snow;
—To leave him quite alone, panting

In the silence. Waiting for the medicines
Of spring to heal his wound,
And accomplish the rebirth of his beloved.

Night Vision

> More gold than gold the love I sing,
> A hard inviolable thing . . .
> . . . my heart is incorruptible as gold,
> 'Tis my immortal part:
> Nor is there any god can lay
> On love the finger of decay.
> MICHAEL FIELD

Last night, far removed
From the thundering chaos
Of the soul's decomposure,
I walked sullenly in the dark,
Coming upon the grass and trees
Swaying to the rhythm
Of her body's apparition.

I took of those intangible potions
We let seep into the ground,
And they were no less intoxicating
Than in the moments they flowed
From our kisses.

The mist guided me,
Lightly as a river moving through summer,
On the illimitable plane of extension
To Time's final expression.

∎

I see your hands between burnt twigs
And your hair, speckled with fresh grass,
Dashing like a seawave against the air.

We walk arm in arm in the country,
With stars and grains of sand
Gathered for apt communion.
Feeling the pulsating fountain of virginity
As if for the first time,
We marvel at the blood-felt meteors,
Rapid through our veins.

The sword of extraneous laws,
Swinging to disentangle us,
Is drawn toward invisibility,
As the cabin door opens
To the distending light of our fingers.
Then, you are again very much my own,
Graceful and nude in the moment's oblations:
A grape shared between our lips,
And juice of an eaten persimmon,
With the body's flavors,
Flowing through autumn.

Your beauty diffuses within me
As your fragrant hair
Spreads softly over my breast.
These are the lustful moments,
Empty of all harmful mutations
That seek to rob the heart
Of Love's natural order.

Now, as lightning cleaves from my heart,
You begin to take me deeply within you:
Our lips trembling feverishly,
Our eyes pouring their light from the sun.
Do not speak.
Do not even echo a sigh.
Entwined, rising and falling in oneness,
We enter silence as a sea of becoming.

Then lying in a passive embrace,
We listen to the resounding rain
Penetrating within us and moving
In unison with our blood.
My hands rest below your breasts,
You murmur sweetly between a soft kiss
As the joy of peace ascends
In folds of sleep.

■

The vision dissolves in darkness,
And I return to this point in time:

Reminding me of what is a phantom
And what is a shadow never lost.

I return to walk again
Among so many creations
Lending themselves to the primal things;
Offering their leaves and naked cells
To the moon's competent magic
And the sun's expansive divinity.

I know what remains
Between the conjured experience
And the summoned thought:
It is she, almost as a breath
And felt in the wind,
Yet forever present
In the *green whirl,*
That imperative essence
And spirit of my blood.

. . .

Unable to move and hardly breathing,
I am before the stars' alchemy of light
And eternal marvel of blue of sky into darkness,
Becoming balm to my blood's long agony
Of we two wrested from each other
In these dreaded days
And unholy divisions of our love.

The hoary strength of the redwoods,
Flowing as a river to my veins,
Floods my eyes with yearning
To see her being identified
With the whirling silence
Of these myriad worlds becoming One.
Yearning to see her as she wished to be:
A woman from the center of the earth
With a rose of fire in her heart.

The breathing grass gives quiet ecstasy
To my remembering nerves
That once wove gently through the soil
As her light shone from every living fire.

The minutes pass as though sharp thorns
Against an intangible center,
Where a wounded animal wakes within me.
The Light, bearing enemies of pain
As well as bodies of bliss,
Coming forth by memory, returns
To my heavy heart in sorrow,
Now unable to work its blood into flames
Until her eyes again shine forth into mine.

Spring's Entry

How shall we know Spring
Pulls the tide of rebirth
Peacefully within us,
But by the body's own fire
Rekindled through our veins.

Behind us lies a worldly night
Of guarded anguish,
Before us flowers opening
To the touch of singing lovers
Bathing in the Heavenly light of their eyes.

Two Worlds—1946

to K. R.

The wingless bird, only half-a-bird,
But having the power of flight
Locked in its spirit,
Threads through the prison seeking daylight.

Unresponsive blood through the veins,
The blood coldly, moving like ice,
Through the walls, in which the almost dead

Sleepers have no hunger for flower and flame
That wait outside and within these walls,
Even below the angel submerged in their hearts.

The ruins of the living are here,
Obscuring all light.
Dying roses fall among the crucified
Who lie in absolute separateness:
Dumb, distorted worlds.

How shall this wingless bird,
Outside and within all bodies,
Send forth its fire to the hand
That shall break the mirror of these walls
(As it would plunge into water
Or open the Heavens).
How shall it regain its wings
To penetrate the day
Now releasing its light
As light is released from the heart?

A Simple Answer to the Enemy

> Either the State will be destroyed and a new life will begin . . . or else
> the State must crush the individual and local life, it must become the
> master of all the domains of human activity, must bring with it wars and
> internal struggles for the possession of power, surface-revolutions which
> only change one tyrant for another, and inevitably, at the end of this
> evolution—death!
> PETER KROPOTKIN in 1896

It is an eventful year.
We live in a nation flourishing
On the blood of millions murdered
And millions more being murdered
Everywhere else in the world.

I sit reading the incorruptible words
Of those who chose defiance
To the highest evil;
What they foretold is almost incomparable
To the nightmare lying before us.

The Revolution has not won,
But it exists everywhere.
The trigger-like mentalities
That lead the counter-attack
Bear down with unequaled force
On the rising tide of revolt.

The people walk as if in a movie-dream
And work in the terrifying order
Of a chaos their bodies reject,
But their fear compels them to accept.
The bureaucrats and idle rich
Continue their reign of permanent war
On the sweat and blood of the poor.

Across the seas a monstrous child
Erupts over all Europe:
The final expression of centuries
Of accumulated barbarism.

The politicians spill their lies
Over our heads; the lies of murderers,
Rogues and fools whose hearts have ceased
To seek the light of Love.
The measure of their strength
Is the docility of those they rule.

Whatever happens, one thing is certain:
The end of a world it has taken
Hundreds of years to create,
But mere seconds to destroy.

POEMS 1943–1955

Ages in the Wind

what have you seen in the long black years, man?
what have your eyes told the cold and ice?
what of love and life and handsome death?
what, man, have your eyes seen in the world?
—you ask of the dark cultures and ages
    and only the carrying wind can answer you.

—I have seen the men and life crawling to death.
    then the branching of drops on haunted lands.

    man and the chains, that is what I saw.
    blossoms in fields through the Nile.
    springing from earth came the flaming white,
    and she the many thought was perfection.
    the chains are there, and the pull of fingers
    on the growing mind with lifted thoughts.
    the drawing room and the genteel, that too,
    with the book of verse on the mantel I saw.
    out of the thundering maze came the chaos.
    blasts of hot horns heralded the swift age.
    steel skyward zooming forged in a mass of columns,
    and the new burst on electric wires.

    I have seen the years, and the year of this age.
    I go now, for I have seen nothing.

Symbols

i. The Gift

For this perfumed box, you sent,
I remind you of an intangible gift
To remember me by,
Evidence of an enduring love,
Whose shadowless flame may you feel,
For a long time and in the final time,
Like a vibrant tremor at your spine.

ii. Dharma-Kaya

Not unlike, I imagine, Adam
Before the Fall, a man in coition,
Rousing great power out of dust and clay,
With the first star of night
Brightly in his loin, is carried upward,
And knows the wordless speech
From a quick rush of water,
Transformed among pebbles and rocks,
And through the toneful wind
In a darkened forest of moving trees.

Another Autumn Coming

narrow is the way, which leadeth unto life
MATTHEW 7:13

No, we shall not weep, but this heart
Now become as aspen leaf,
Quivers in the late summer forest,
Awaiting a gift of the heavens: a meteor,
A pearl to shed its light from the center of the heart.

How long ago was that other autumn
In which we walked out of dust and clay,
Renewed in our selves; and with the fresh spray
Of an otherworldly water mounting
In our spirits like fire in a hearth?

The way remains the same, though our dream
Is a heap of ashes, fallen into the dark earth.
But somewhere in a sphere we no longer enter,
I am surely drinking from a cup
In which you poured the wine of our love.

I sit now in the quiet vision we fashion together,
And remember your slow graceful limbs,
Moving over the leaves fallen from poplar trees
And turned to gold under your feet.

I remember the day fused with the night
In the dawn of a moment's eternity,
And hearing your voice from beyond the starry wall,
I know what we knew together is the way,
Now and even when the seasons are no more.

Golden sands rise from under our feet
And settle far away between the sun and the moon.

The New Year

Into our lives falls, unsteadily,
A rush of the moon's light,
And only a few drink of it
With the veins of the body.
Who stand possessed in the night air
Or fired by cooling drops of rain,
Washing away the evil within them,
—Who, but those bearing love,
Entwined in another world,
In another time?

The air changes.
The scene escapes me.
Suddenly, I am reminded of you,
The ruling classes of a dying age,
Impotent parvenus
And arrogant fakers,
Sweating away in the whirlpool
Of unprincipled action
And wielding your passionless power.
I look angrily about me
—To the streets where people,
Become targets, will fall dead
And the wounds of war will again
Spill blood over your lives,
Crossed with guilt
And sealed in a lie.

Revelations of a New Order

I

The five swords, palpitating fasces,
mingle in the colors
in the sounds in the velvet.
What I see through the margin of desire
I see by the sign of their meeting.

Across the great divide,
I laugh at you, the euphoric demon
laughs at you, for you are not
where I am: where everything is glowing.

Now passes gold under my flesh
and opulent jewels to scatter the day,
the sons and daughters of day,
and the sores and wounds;
amulets to drive away
the people unhooked from limbo.

It is, then, gold with a thin film
of blood travelling the rocky surfaces;
bright beads and scarabs
to conjure up the winds of purity
and the word to end all words.

∎

Where the animal strains in the overflowing cup of
the mind, there I am: in the jungle of specialized tastes,
                    the black roses mating the man-
                    eating plants and the mandrake
                    root growing through the body of man.

All that is of value emerges from hyper-perception—
Distortion—and the vision of future catastrophes; from the
sudden invasion of a mind not my own in the world. This
I will record. For whom? For MYSELF, beyond denial and
beyond indifference.

Finally, arriving at my self
the wild bird escapes
scratching and scraping;
in its talons the flesh of the body
is caught up in shreds!

Being and non-being lacerate
the soul, until great wings
bat the void with a sound
of muted thunder:
the necklace of Kali
descending in spirals of color.

■

I sense the cataclysm.
      The underground overground
      the torrents and the deluge.
The Destructive Angel windwardly
     scattering every
            monolith
            tool and book.

... Where the golden blood sings
out of its open, golden, mouth
the song of the void.

I look to the flood gates
shattering, heaved-up
out of the pent-up fury
they would resist.
From the pyre, new fires
... from the fires, new pyres!

■

The five swords unmingle
in the void.
All entry is worth the passing!

II

"The horned god roams the dark forest . . .
. . . the man who is masked in the skins
of animals, takes on the horns
and, in godhood,
        the working of the horns.
The recognition of his fated form
(the desire and the possession)
is the beginning of his priesthood,
his kingship."

He, who is a journey of myself,
traces the number of his calling.
In his divining stare
turning ever inward,
he names himself
the giver of hemp
and the rites
and the word of hemp.
He draws the circle
enclosing in the emblem
of his godhood:
the green man,
of the horns and the cloven foot,
and pressed from the hand of the Queen,
he speaks an amulet of words,
shaking the trees. The Enemies
wait beyond him, but watchful.
His kingdom, as Bacchus with his vine,
from the cast of the plant
takes root in the cities
and the temples—the fires
started for the burning of flowers
and leaves. At the crossing of the winds,
under the morning star, the rose
plumed and the violet plumed, fly out
returning the treasures while the Spring Wheel
turns in the blossoming flowering.

From the inspired fumes:
                    the rites,
                    the dances
and slowly forming itself,
the inward mingling of the senses,
                    the Paradise,
its flow of blood, its permeating existence
closing the night threading the day.

                    ∎

At the whirl of the dancers
at the striking of the horns
earth and sky pour forth
each other; the vertiginous eye
of the god fires forth everywhere
light from the mirrors of Paradise.

Break of Day

The city whirls, pivots and sprawls like a cat.

Through the spiraling smoke of reefers
Each touch, each sight and sound
Would turn the real into the unreal
The dreamer into the dream.

After the knives have flashed
And the pool of blood has made
Its imprint of flowers on the street
The aimless wanderers, the busy and unbusy,
Break in air like splinters of ice.

Ashes, like stars, fall into the sewers.
A bird, hatched no longer than a second,
Falls from its nest
Fated for no other wings than death.

The disquietude of an evening
Settles into the dawn

Leaving behind it an alcoholic moon
Trailing the eye's quick sunlit glance
At the lions of day
Reaching with wet paws out of the sky.

This Room Is My Cosmos

There is a secret Knowledge out of the brains of the Navel, on the edge of the Being who summons me. Tie this fish of midair to the azure stream—inclosing the minute time cannot inclose — by a lake swelling with the waters of the Navel.

There is dirt: there is a secret Knowledge. What word, what hand to rend the hells of the hunchback globe? What knife to slash the wrists of those already dead? Put the *ones who do not see* under their own blinding lights; empty the immovable into immobile hells: the hand of my hand winging the fly whose buzz pockets the ear and coils in space, fallen into the fly's head.

There is no time to cleanse the waters. There is a secret Knowledge. On solitude, the heart is simmering with lead veins to print M-I-S-E-R-Y on the brow of him who comes to summon me, caught-up, speeding from lairs of the spatial animal who clutches the Tree of Life plunged top-side into the earth. The minute salutes, through the One Who Is Not I, all the names of the god—

(His ashes glued to space where he is exhumed)

Descent

Along those well-known, but rarely inhabited surrealist corridors winding into a labyrinth — SILENCE in guise of a Blue Woman, faster than light, spills through the cage I hold in my brain: maledictorious milk.

And I put out forever from the most favored view of lambs cut up by diamonds struck from the throat of an Eastern Queen, descend, not without a certain elegance, on a cluster of night-birds and violets, exchanging a manikin for a corpse.

With the aloneness of a thief escaping cinematically under the streets, I summon that wayward look scratched from bare walls where the shadow of a kicking horse is cast forever; scooping up petrified tears once the oil to set off machines of Desire. Pitting what is eternally lost against what can not be, I hear the voice of heroinic sleep ask: "What fever of regret propels Desire out of the mouth of the cave?"

Stones hurled in its face, Desire—humming like a sawmill—is Desire unmasked, sniffing bouquets left over from the Day of the Dead.

Inside the Journey

Quickly, I rocked between waves. Quickly, I got the god on the wing. Quickly, I picked the tarn from the twirling top. Quickly and quickly, and faster, faster: for the kill of the body's anger, for the win of the lost child, for the fall of wizards through revolving sheets of snow.

And so I walked all the streets become one street among the renegades who go unmolested, half-asleep, to the gardens of childhood—in the largess of a white love once a pink, pearl-shaped object on the horizon of their longing; a white love in a black space—no time in the land of nothing but time.

And this was my dream that lasted from some dawn to some midnight in the fallingdown room overlooking the oldest graveyard of Manhattan:

> the poisonous stars: *benign*
> the rootless tree: *nailed to the sky*
> the black pit: *enclosing ladders of white light*
> the icebergs of the mind: *floating to the tropics . . .*

For a long time I saw no other sky than the ceiling of this room where, from a chink of plaster, hung the image of paradise I embarked for like a ship to the Orient. I could hardly move my head. I could hardly say the word to ask for water. I could hardly conceive of *another* life. I threw the hex down, I swallowed the spells, I put the tumult down. If I spoke I would violate the wonder of that silence. If I moved, I would break across space like a knife cutting cheese. I knew all the constellations of infinite duration where my thoughts that flew away one day waited like brides for their bridegrooms of the infinite.

In another time, I was making blueprints for the Eternal, but the work was interrupted by some ogre who jumped out from behind a slab of magenta sky, and I was mesmerized on the spot between the poison I was wiping from my lips and the face behind the face I saw looking at me from the sky I was using as a mirror.

Anyway, I broke the spell. But another wave of invented emotions sank and another light fell on the crest of the wave: escape was a door I kept shutting all around me AND on those who were carving me, symbolically they said, for the first course at the restaurant for the initiates of the lake of love—which is to say, sperm ran high that year, breaking over the brains of those who know how to conduct themselves properly in *this* world: which is to say, life goes on gathering wool for the mothers of all the daughters whose tongues spit live lobsters and whose insatiable desire for some seasalt paradise makes thunder break in my skull: which is to say, very simply and without metaphor, that my brain was oppressing me.

—And that is not the most of it—for I took a look into the great vacuum of *this* world, in order that the journey in space of that life that puts poetry to shame, since it strained at the risk of all my senses becoming nil and hurtled me further into abysmal giddiness, would terminate at the junction where I might be able to move while in a state of suspended animation, since if I did not move in the vacuum the vacuum would move within me. And this movement of what is lusting to annihilate the sense of life (instigating panic in the mind, heart and liver) and taking its place, therefore, within life itself—would only lead to my ejection from *this* world.

It is this Vacuum that makes possible that daily hell kept going to decimate the scapegoat inhabitants of the earth, inspiring nothing but apathy and further pollution, revolving on the sexual hydra—at one pole—and fed through the swine mongering mobs at the other pole, in order to do away with the memory of what WAS or MIGHT BE—and as I opened to IT I saw its Body that is a vast machinery, in perpetual motion, for the sole consumption of a certain kind of etherealized excrement transmuted out of the bestial layers of the human condition become entirely the cretinized image of God with whom, be it added, this machine copulates perpetually . . .

Animal Snared in His Revery

He breathes through his wounds.
The herbs that would heal him decay in the labyrinth of his great paw.
The sun sends medicinal currents to the wobbling island under his sunken tooth.
With agates of rain, the sibylline garden (oracles speak from the flowers) conceives grimly poisonous minerals traveling the earth veins.
The animal, blackening the light with an orb of his blood, reads on the televised leaves:
—SLEEP TERRORS RAGING—
                    —EXIT FROM DREAMS—
. . . and the green mouth cracks open underground.

Elementals

Lethèd fonts sprayed the mottled grave.
A disintegrated spade awoke as Man
                    sacking clay,
And flung its burden on the plain.

Two black birds
With taloned eyes

Screeched on bones
In an open, desert cave.

Two black birds sat jaggedly
On promontories
Of Man's distempered monoliths
(Who felled the birds
And put his burden on)

Two black birds picked his sack of clay,
Beaked his bones into the sea
And turned on the cave:

Two black birds perched on a bough
Scatter the flung burden.
Man drops into the sea
Two bleaching black birds.

■ ■ ■

Beneath occidental peripheries
Oriental irradiation leaves ambivalence
Of the farflung time:
To parahypnotic menageries:
The falconfaced siminan Cat
Martializes for apocalyptic sonorities.

Morassed climates underhinge valleys
Deserted by a tare:
        Fling shadowlands
On the bright pandoms—
        You are the coat
Won thinly in a burntout room:
        Dragonfurnaced,
Who cracks a shell for prophesied volcano,
        Earthquakes
Round your dark om-tarantuled side,

Western scorpions
        undersex
                dreaming the eastern.

from TAU

1955

. . .

To see this evil from its core
He spent himself on margins
Crystal edges umbra-ed and broke,
Splintering by measured denials,
Waiting for the hour patience intersected:
The giver capsuled whole the spending parts.

O Mad Love where untempered
You remain, tunneling trains of art—
Deflecting horizonless
                    depthless

Light
      on this voice—these sounds—
A heart whose wails you dream
Into actuality swims halfway
To your always perilous obliqued and
Always
      vanished
           shore.

The Owl

I hear him, see him—interpenetrate
those shadows warping the garden pathways,
as the dark steps I climb are lit up
by his Eye magnetic to the moon,
his Eye magnetic to the moon.

I have not seen him when windows are mute
to whisper his name; on that moment
erroneous bats slip out through the sky.
His lair conceives my heart,
all hearts make the triangle he uses for a nose,
sniffing bloodways to the brain:
the bloodways are lit up by his Eye.

On a sudden appearance he tortures leaves,
flays branches and divides segments
the sun has drawn. I do not falter
—in the dark he fortifies.
His color is *green* green,
to distend him over the earth.
He does not fly.
You meet him while walking.

He is not easily enticed to manifestation,
But stony silence, petrified moments
—a transfiguration—will bring him out,
focused on the screen where all transfigured bodies are.
You must be humble to his fangs
that paw the moonball dissolving in the space
from the corner of your eye:
he will trick you otherwise
—into daylight, where you meet his double while running.

By night the deltas of the moon-spilled planet
are stoned under his wriggling light.

By day he chokes the sun.

Shot into the Sun

for Gogo

Empyrean beaks oscillate the wayward scene.
Chrysanthemums pulverize marble lions
The marigold space empties
Into solar hieroglyphs.
　　　The Bird is found,
　　　RA

In a desert pearl
Sound—soundless—violetized light
And rolled into a fever of seas
Felling rind on the mountain Cry:
　　　Vincent found The Bird.

Resuscitate the voice of RA,
Bring battled cries on the wind the Rose inhabits
  Antonin spied The Bird
  In pieces on a beak of crow.
  Do not seek The Bird.

To ascend the Cities of the Sun
The poet of overground fish
Impales subacquelent monoliths,

We have seen the screamed voice
In halls of checkered fear,

Volatile fingers guard the hood of time
Where a wall is time enough to spring:

Sound here, Found Bird, lies RA.

Going Forth by Day

To suck the sign from circumvolutions
He can cast diced divagations
To the four winds: Nothing and the sun
Will speak for him: He speaks from the sun.

On temporal levels, on this level Now,
The personaged past interpenetrates
On the weird, slung head
And screams   screams
On all sides of the snakes of Tau.

Cosmogonic amplifiers erase minumumed
Signatures of daimoniacal configuration
Whose greater space passed into future:
Fire unlocking by saturation
Eye of the sterilized Tau.

The blueskimmed, dancing vibratories
Stipple air with kra/cries,

A shaman calls from the Old Oak Bough
A garden grows into the sea

The Sun in the Jaguar City
Televisions the northern changes:
By tropic instigations
Scuttles the clockwork panoramics.

    Who breaks the tree of life
        drops the key to death,
    In the Vacuum's glare: dies unknown,
        earthcloven into cannons
    Of the wrongwayed men
        blasting space of cosmic cruelty
    Where the humbled are.

A city of escape hatches—

The Snake flies down The Bird
        Sounding sibyl scream:

    Infinite suns secrete the gong going day.

    ■ ■ ■

Ground grade guard the crucible
        Cook air
Toward the Air: into materia Immateria
        X
    the Stone
and transvecticize the Earth,

    Fire
Crackles beneath and above:
    Watergrown
stars overoute the wordtide.

    This Eye before (am
searched for) Interspored in darkness
    For the Shades kept,
R a d i a t e s
    A Light
O time pure flowing
        Sun
          Chariot!

Riding cantilevered spaces
        Is seen
                to see
                        Interemanations

Of the flowered spiritscapes.

∎ ∎ ∎

Out of crystal beginnings
He watched the sunbleached sky
Trail before moonscaled ceilings
Where light ript the darkness down,
        —his love loveless in a cloud.

Where wailing shadows run
And tripled bells resound:
Over monsters strangled in a tear
And seascapes that bend the town,
        —his love loveless in a cloud.

What is the name of the pitchforked head?
Who sleeps in a burning bed of hair?
Why call night to play with day?
Where is the hand making change stay?
        —his love loveless in a cloud.

∎ ∎ ∎

In a garden that isn't, but will be:
Glasscrowned in a laughing sphere,
She swam an eye to a cornice of the sky,
She veiled light with dark
And lit the bird: free.

On a smiling crevice of street,
He cuts, for death, the diamond of her eye:
Star plumed hands put it
Burning on his brow.

Winds bend and soar from fire
And ice ript from the Core,
The Bird, their emblem, is enigma
Circling a thousand pits of sleep.

They curve, craned in a surging stream,
Until spasmodic rungs flame to leap
Toward a deathbed star
Of the spherical deep: they rise,
Drop, love, bird/ript in a highted dream.

■ ■ ■

Flame gates open to water gongs:
Roll to the wayward depth
Before & After the caves of Sol
Gave emblem to desire and its death
In sunken seleniol floors
Loosed loudly in Amores:

The birds of Amores poise,
And poised plunge
Into high depth,
Stretch a gleam to wing in,
The birds of Amores triptik to a Musik:
Fall on planets bluedanced on no walls.

A tongue grew tongueless:
The breath, a wail of stars
And black sky: a flying milk—

O the snake strung blue sings
Vibrationed for Amores
Through a glass of golden fish
Rings dry earthgongs
While windwhips dance Amores' birds
Into a golden ball
Whose tides circle Circle
No rounder than their sound

Upon the seaswell air of fire

And the high
        earth
           water.

    ■ ■ ■

She sped to me a winter word
When wound in welts & wounds of dawn
Black lights flayed on growning ground:
The sun blecked on us & swooned a summer artichoke.
In winter's spleen
A rant of graves grew in a thorn
Of that her sleep, that spent a shrieking vein.

These words tied in a spool of snow
Now they trail at the serpent's tail:
Cut under a wind.   dark and silent
spaces between all the letters of the world
Up in the burning brains
Of the sun's new infancy.

She spoke and the wind roared spittle
She speaks and children freeze in a spin
She speaks my eyes ogred on the wailwind
She speaks my head halted
She speaks a word to sleep me down:
My time to burn the dark sun down.

To the Music

How their nerves tangled,
They tangled in a crowbeat head
And slowed, headlong, on wintry cobbles
Of the headless moon: Their fingers ript
A darkness of heady sprockets
And they shook a bloodlet Arm

Down to the pit of the leafhung moon,
Tangling alone in a birded tympany
Where green arteries broke
And their blood bleat.

How their music wailed!
They wailed in the shade
Eaten by solar lunar glass time seeded
And looped in a Dream
Of greenlit panic and jellied fiascoes.
The wind ate them dry on the holes in space
And bounced them back on grails of lymph
Where the mottleheaded dropped
In a stance of play,

And the madmonths whirled
To never-die-alone,
And alone they died in a lie
Of the wildbleet sound of starry truth.

O how the body died!
They died in a solarsluice of the jaundiced moon
And crowed the splice/lunged field:
The cottonweed and sabre grass tipped
On a giant derrick of their sound
That was an open wound:

Bloodless, they walked through the trees
Where the singing arteries unveiled,
And a thousand moments were clipt
On the flower that waved in their heads
To the timeless alone at their dreams.

Question

Not I, but it, should die
when it twists against sinuous walls
diminishing me in a jaw of stains death made:
not I, but it, to stammer in voids, shriek hells
and once it dead, I live!

make my brain swarm with sibyl
                              and it: staved in a hole.

To me, monumental, it cracks blackly
oozing gigantic pain—but must be whipped on a grave,
        and/or sacked by stone veins:
        I, then, pour sticks of white blood:
        sublimity glyphs me in a wired cave.

If this will not, rocks fall upward,
the hour turn into a straight line
and it: redescend the stair by invisible hourstream
(as it has said) or it and I change
a space between, and if it be there
where shall I arrive to its death?

        ▪ ▪ ▪

To the flat lands by the hills of Suum Nar
to MarMagAgog, onto sidereal semaphores,
to leech/hung prayer fields of Avadon
to Triptika on the sunbelted Nile
        where fish is god
to stars unravelling the numena/number
        snaked in iceflames of Baruda
        whirler of the wild,
to Smarachet: the wingedvoid, MAAT
        drives a gull cordons dual divulgating
        on the Queen of the Air—and her wailing sisters
        enter, going, to aethereal white light.

An autumn sky secretes chalkfrozen spermatons
where nomind plays and the secret body swings—
on a matestring of clouds sunsets
        loop and double
                in burning, benzoin, air—

O rocket me,
He who is mine is I

and wins the Sky:
A Sun & Moon ago, kissed to stars,
a momentary string of sands to go,
                    arriving on the silent   sea   roar.

   ■ ■ ■

18 beings and The Other
combine to make a residence for God
and the light of which there are no parts
disintegrates hell messengers
screaming bullshit in the face of the light.

In man there exists secretly The One
who shall raise the water
to cover everything
and raise a great Wind
to harness the water
and he, who is the one, is full of light going out of him

   ■ ■ ■

Broken language hisses
a tare of wind
flies down to drawbridge spiritual margins

There is eating of light
there is matafanga of intention
there is/will be the broken hood of spirit
A spiritual margin be splintered
and opened—attacking all corpses

The corpses shall fly down
straight as light
No brazen ones shall feed
Reborn their lives turn three times
ungutting the secret curse
Death will fix their circle

They will become a mirror
by the fire of darkest Cold
whose light traps salamanders
in a flash of golden ice

Nowhere shall the corpses live
without Keys I shall bestow
Unknown futures manifest
on visionary gales and waft
to the grinning grimace
of supernatured space

By my Return let the hours dissolve quickly
and the fonts be given over
The calendric wheel invisibly metalizes
on an unworded leaf of the Golden Head
that shall cover the chalkfaced
that shall open the time of the Dance

by the serpent to know it
by the serpent to coil it
by the serpent to speak it
by the serpent to bird it
     like straight light
     in the Word of it!

EKSTASIS

1959

These poems follow chronologically in reverse. The exterior interior and personal vision—erotic, mythic, magical and devotional—I have hoped to make clear by placing the distance between each in a continuous time sense and-or when the ekstatic breakthrough occurs as the metaphysical whole. These poems, then, of A KIND, have made a book though written between 1948 and 1958. My object is a revelation, in manifestation, of beauty—its world, natural or supernatural—and if it shows forth, if it lies ensnared by the hidden operations of art and inspiration (for so, here IT IS!) with music and rhythms discovered, worked and evoked, well, then I invite you to travel the depth of it.

LITTLE DO WE KNOW!

The Author

C h r i s t

Death,   sunrises
beatific the winter's
rise. Blanch light
on rivers seen unseen
Born CRYSTAL FLESH
FISH IN A CLOUD
L I G H T   LIFE

Glory crasht on time   .   Angel   tongues,   MAGI
and burden of the stars   .   In   the   F I R E
elliptical HEARTS convex   .   Impossible   beauty
CHILD,   MARIA   WOMBED   SAVIOR

Light   and   night
street   of   geyser
clarity's   theology
s p a r k s   on   the
pyramid's diaphonous
U N K N O W N
Understand: advent
of the Spirit, sudden
come of the Spirit—
bulb, face, plant, legs,
pipe,   souls.   Euch-
aristic   blood   on
a   w h i t e   banner
suspended   in   the
A   Z   O   T   H
three magi on the road
and star wheels to
B E T H L E H E M

Fragments from an Aeroplane

1

At first you took my fault away
then I did not care much
now you give me this fault, too much!
you give it to me, this fault
that it follows me around in pain
groaning alongside my soul
shaking the shaft

crushing me
as if it were a load on!

2

On afternoons and busses
the mind catches no satellite
and while the day is being cooled
—arcana beyond the bleeding head—
I see you, my soul   in a vision   SAVED

3

Bonjour he cries I'm not here but gone over the plateau
I'm not at the sacred hill at karnak
I'm not a true believer formed from the womb of God

He has lied!

Inferior ladders lulled him in his sleep
as the murderers of the dream passed
as the planets effaced in water communicate
as the saints inebriate the silence

4

Golden light   at Tehuantepec
men in shadows   golden light
              at Tehuantepec
against shadows and solitude lumed by green phospher
              yellow   stones
              at Tehuantepec
       golden light   against the shadows
solitudes in green phospher
              yellow walls
                    women
                          mellons
            the
                    jewels of the air
                              FIRE

5

The far country of beasts windows dust I sing
and the whorl of spaces I sing
immensities and flowers entangling in a steel fountain
minerals I sing hung on shadows
the far country! eros in damnation!
       lions in hail!
              houses of blood

crowds, legions, nations
crane
out of water graves and ladders to God
                    turning the unleveled EYE

6

I'm here alone
              Where is HE, God of the PSALMS?
Where's the way to the garden at work within the rose?
       —perfumes that made me drunk, light life—

7

Tonight walls fell away
     and this desert gave birth to you
tonight your fountain hands flowed and signed us
       in benedictions of intellective night

             outside, gates and towers
                inside,
the King miters gold to bridge the space
          and wind
          and rain
          and air
          speak your NAME

8

    This world is evil
        say the saints
            out of the Christus
not of this world
       as they go by
when I didn't even know they were there!

9

The gull flew by wires and stones on what mythos built

              CLOUDS
and bells sounded seven times
         (an underbelly wing of him!)
I have my window open
the lamp on the roof broke as a mirror

I think of you, Land of Weir
my house of water on the hill
my dreams in a naked crowd

Interior Suck of the Night

Narcotic air
simple as a cone
spun
interior suck of the night

blood shot eyes of my geni
As the first branch of clouds hang for the infinite
I go across streets with candles aimed for lost windows
your NOTHING engraved on a cherry button heart
your smile folding over the tables of the law

Opium
in a butterfly's dream
windows open on broken stem of pipe
chimes, cuneiforms
of the marvelous and you! my innocent
a shadow encrusted on a light beam
your eyes
the daughters of your eyes!
I see the salt spoon of the sibyl's you cooked
my hair my threads my nails with!

■ ■ ■

Iguana iguana
a giant slime lizard stuck to a wall

Cacti razored the night by candlelight
on ladders weeping to the moon

Antique music old music
fell from a rock jagged temple
into the throat of Indian prayer wound
around the Virgin beyond the black box
they carried in Cristero
with the beards of Don Quixote on!

Les Langueurs Allongées

I

I've lived in rooms, rooms, rooms,
Unlocking
I've lived in a house, house, house,
I've lived in the mantikoapocalyptic seer's chamber in Calais

    Q K you   c
              wandering
                  the river's green current
       this death move to rhetoric

I've killed them, stars and chains of lust
           before magi, magi, magi,
        Cavalcanti on the stairs
                      La beauté

2

           Method
          millimeters
       and crepe glass windows
       and black and black and black
     — tongues in a case, case in a slot, slot IN —
   This triggers the madness of street hushes crowds streets
Opens the wounds of bed glass desert crowned and shot in Mexico
    the erection of pyramidic shapes
       marmalias beneath crepuscular agates
         I drove tongues, grapes, kif, pearls,
          God everywhere — all, all, all!
           beckons to music, to the
           music

Sheri

I walked you
sank you in black glass
the trouble with the stars is
they're too far from my eyes to yours
First Wing and last pages of the albatross
I satellited you   cocktails on a petrified face
The   l i q u e f a c t i o n   of the walls of the city
For the Lord made all things   green
opal eye,   lice,   dung
for jazz, green is the essence
of the lightfooted CLOSE UP
like a mandolin sneaking up to you
naga naga nagai
first whip of the Lanch cornered room
Beatrixed and
marveled
on FORTUNA'S GATE

                    W
                    h
                    a
                    t
          g i f t to bring
                    n
                    o
                    w
                    o
                    u
                    t
          of my heart in
       chaos as I remember O
     Love the voice that came
    down from the tree and fell
    on   my   heart   like   a   veil. Pax!
    O Lord the peace you spell out
   silent between the rafters of your
   Heart built up in your House I come
   to   wanting   wanting   to love
   Y   O   U

Ball

Where earth dropped into sun
    giant sky without stones
        I'm going—Mexico City to Veracruz
the road a great green fire

        I am smoked to dryness

Stars of smoke who made this road throw up
                              your eyes
        which are closed in New York

O weir I can not sing you from that quiet street
O prairies have not seen you close your eyes

A tomb of clouds to receive you
        by the fog in your veins
    BASHO
      eaten
by the sun from the page   I wait
                   as long
                 as a   star

Mysterium Mysticus Ecclesia

The immensity coming back upon itself
A deep jawed lion
                skulls under the Cross
        curled serpent, emblems of dead empire

The immensity coming back upon itself
songs bled on a crooked neck
        jowls opened in etheria
streets go-on-up-to   moons   in the Dark
                the earth immanent
no statues among legends, ghosts, haunters

The immensity coming back upon itself
                art, life, death

Dead Smoke

Ambivalent miles, sorceries played, we drank from hatred's lake
Giant jades immanated spells, I played the windows of Hell
Perfumed birds out of emblematic halls
Cut fire in two—caves yawned walls, cries, tigers
A mile below Saturn
Presence of damnation
Shades in the meadow enlightened the cows
Who made the walk of seas go round
And legends, iron stalks in the forest, carved the geometries of Azoth

Winds have not flown longer than time we stopped
Whose sail hit the rooms where you looked into voids
—A beast on a star, Jaiba on the moon, the sunken tooth—
Stalks of madness tripled fire
And sent gardens under the sea
Mountains fell   dogs howled
You—O dark side of the moon—
Interlaced light—shadows went on the water—
Undeciphered glyphs, stones of the immortals,—trophies bled in gold!

■ ■ ■

D   If you will come you will come
E   I can not see you for your hands tremble
I   If this is the time I shall hold it
R   The stars have gone over the mountain
D   Meridians later your smile broke glass
R
E   If youth dies the immortals are born

o
r   v
g   e
a   h
t   e
n   i   l
I   w   I   e
B   O   C   c   t
o   V   E   t   h
d   o   r   g
o   m   i   i
w   i   c   n
n   n   y
g   b   b
i
r
d
s
I
put
my ner
ves   over
my eyes my
veins over my
skin and think
HA!   I   decipher
the talk of the gods!

Confirmation

"Climb down here"

                It's a voice and a hand

"Fall into arms cradling the sun"

"You shall walk straight and dazzled

        out of a wall, softly
and fall with a cross on your lips
              space of living sleep

You shall go up in a rose"

The hand of water
              the voice of fire

John Hoffman

road that announced him
road that did not see him
eyes that circled the sun

he was an aerolith ON
     there's a sign
the sun circles the air

a tau beneath the sun
these shall further
a road becomes an eye

if the heart circles the brain
     mountains of thunder
he shall bend under the tau

beyond the broken line Sol

. . .

Ah Blessed Virgin Mary
pray for me I live in you
to sleep in God
and die in God
to praise His Holy Name

O Blessed Virgin Mary
ask Jesus to embed in me
   a sword of sorrow
to kill my sin
   my sin that wounds His Wounds

Tell Him I have eyes only for Heaven
as I look to you
   Queen mirror
of the heavenly court

. . .

Man is in pain
   ten bright balls bat the air
   falling through the window
   on which his double leans a net the air made
   to catch the ten bright balls

Man is a room
   where the malefic hand turns a knob
   on the unseen unknown double's door

Man is in pain
   with his navel hook caught on a stone quarry
   where ten bright balls chose to land
   AND where the malefic hand carves
      on gelatinous air THE WINDOW
   to slam shut on his shadow's tail

   Ten bright balls bounce into the unseen
   unknown double's net

Man is a false window
    through which his double walks to the truth
    that falls as ten bright balls
    the malefic hand tossed into the air

Man is in pain
    ten bright spikes nailed to the door!

. . .

    As some light fell
on the inescaped facade
  stains of interior cancer
      intervined the stars

    bewitched by time, a long room
of rooms who opened on you
         I
         R
         I
         S
the street corner flew into Spring
    , precisely a lily or an iris—

The Poor Paradoxes

For it is all blest by God
    water, earth, stars, souls
which is to say, all is blessed IN God
and what is not, is not
for God is that WHICH IS

I, in God, bless you that you be in God
    God blessed in us as we are blessed in God
and all is in God in His Blessedness
and all that is not in God is NOT
and this NOT ends at the beginning of what IS

that you are in God who is blessedness in the nothing
of ALL THAT IS
and is nothing compared to GOD
Who is all blessedness in His being
COMPLETE, without need of anything

Scorpion Bite

mozart the light of day light beams are fingers
are antique clouds
are loadstones
light beams entangled, heaven and the god enter my breast
Christ IS the marvellous!

Our Lady of the Snow

There's a glow to the wind
and medallions fall from the air
There's a miracle!
thinking no more lovely miracle today
than the May Day Our Lady made snow fall
on Rome
in the Fourth Century Anno Domini

The New Evil

it came to the night
it rained dung, white and wails

we read its name ript on the sodden movie screen

Leda was not more prime

swans issued out of Hades

      by invented eyes and ether's fire
it came
it was enough
IT came   the walls leaked leaden lovers
it came to the nail in your shadow
it came to the imperial cabal strapt in mummy fat
it came, came to THE MONEY electrified by mother blood

IT CAME
the shot ran out the door into the bullet's head!

Boobus

Last night Mike told me he believed the stars are alive
Today we walk with the yellow haired child
Eyes of the auctioneer's furniture
               fell into mirror specks
the mirror specks reflect Mike's wife Joanna
the expanding universe of Foster's on the corner
                  of Polk and Sutter
A four or five headed portrait of Ginsberg Corso McClure
                    Lamantia and Kerouac
I hope La Vigne paints it
Haselwood is washing his teeth
The yellow haired child like the light in Foster's cafeteria
      Boobus McClure
       is making all kinds of metallic sounds in the kitchen
Publicity! Public spectacles!
      Artaud writing against the superstitions of the text
The morning is burnt with smells of cooking and cooked stars
It's nirvana!
It's the last goof!
It's pungent silk worm disease!
It's beautiful ship of state undulating its ribs!

■ ■ ■

PUT DOWN
        of the whore of Babylon

High voltage mires got into her jaw
as she devoutly lit up her spine in front of Mammon

On the slopes of the Sierra Madre de Chihuahua
they dance night fires
cross themselves by mirrors
blood shot emaciated men who - they themselves tell us
        FELL FROM HEAVEN!
dance - light fires - eat bitter earth fruit
in a sense like manna - O man! O man! -
    the spit of plant lice
    or black markets in a pearl at the unheard sound

For the wails of self pity
    for the hysterical salesmen of ideas
        for the goodwilled destroyers of words

THESE
must be PUT DOWN
                        for they 're inside us

and foment saccarine sweet whores
like this ONE
Dancing
to the tune of sly poisonous health remedies
    that make my head exude dung!
    that put saliva in my bones!
    that dish out infinite possibility of the
            imago-magpie of erotic ecstasies!

    NO!
        NO!
            NO!
not for this panic of idols coning our time
                    by false angelclocks
but for the descended dove we make it to live!

McClure's Favorite

The very thought of a poem kills it!
that's not right.
PUNKS! However How Ever BLINK OUT
Come lion   -   come tiger   -   come ocelot
come coon   -   come weed   -   come leopard
come saliva   -   come STARS

gongora! gongora! I think you're the end!
GONGORA, are you the greatest of your kind? I mean
are you poet's poet of the poet's greatest poet's poet poet

Man! he squints out Dido hollow ash lines
—chemical incendiary
swings the Mississippi ARABIC
ON a flamingo ghost
in Plato's socratic circles THE BIGGEST HIGHEST PEBBLE POET STILL

To the next poet who writes THE LAST POEM
give Gongora or
silences
OR
in the gardens of Granada grow beautiful deers
down movie houses of your limpid arms' pits
affectionate ladies

I knife a gape of a word to swim through

MADNESS! ABSOLUTE MADNESS!
will make you uncomfortable, swift hip reader
super cool cat whose rake splits my tendons
and blurs big bones of BEING RICH!

Observatory

Smoke
tilts in space
sylphonic
downward
into an appearance

a beast a myth
    an intelligence
where are edges and limits
      you are instigations
hallucinates or realizes
and fires peremptory images

      Love
snaked by
      thru multi
   multitudinous Void
equals Death

      What permanency, Air
invigorator from sylphs, mercurial
spirits, geologic geometers
      PLACE
of initiates initiating occult pacts
zohars whose one book sealed
      in mythological golds
UNTOUCHABLE
        SPRINGS OPEN

      It's zenith!
zodiacal beasts phospher
and stars devoured white!

      Cosmical games are wars
not deciphered
      shift spaces O essence of smoke
not less black
      a being
      a world
      a sign

YOU DO NOT CHART MY REGIONS!

Masks are not clouds
under the air speak
"I am rivers riven Zoltecs lightninged
what sleeps awakens geomancies of no metal!"

. . .

What made tarot cards and fleurs de lis
        chariots my heart to shackled towers
The priestess maps apocalypses
        Swords catch on medused hair
            Mandolins woman in a garden

They scaled the wall, they fell from a wall
Les fleurs de lis illuminated on an eyeball
            came out of the wall

            they fought in a flower.

Symbologies systematized from sweat suctionings
made theatrical cruelty extend souls on a pensive
cloud turn   turning incendiary incentives ON!

        They came to PEACE
and wailed in gavottes
    monsters cooled there mothers
in bubbling craters
                    angels
        dropt leprous booty
On a high flung season they blackened blood,
                            climbing the walls

A fleur de lis on a charging horse swam up
        into the moonclad Knight
his lady on a wall
                raped
                        moon struck by wands
clapt in a bell, his lady shook fleurs de lis on the wind

            Mandolins
        in a bile styled peace
                explode!
    Knights go scattering swords
The Tripled Queen on a resinous wall
                    apparitioned
as les fleurs de lis
            luminescent

under burnt out flesh
suddenly gailed
                    TAROTED
on medieval   stained   glass

Terror Conduction

The menacing machine turns on and off

Across the distance light unflickers active infinities

Under the jangling hand set going in the brain
                    THE WOMAN
menacing by white lacerations
            THE MAN
menacing
in a timeweighed fishbowl of the vertical act

and the woman and the man menacing together
                            out of mutual crucifixions
disgorge
            towers for the dead

            the woman menacing
the man menacing
the woman and the man menacing together
            BUT
THE CROWDS
        THE CROWDS MENACING
as eyes take off for NOTHINGNESS
in night rememorizing the primal menace

on a day in a night crossed with butchering
polite squeels humdrum
                    WHAT are all these

    waywardlooking   scorching   haggard
            grim
perilous   witchlike   criminal
            SUBLIME

drunken   wintered
                      GRAZING
          FACES
                FACES
                            going by
like icebergs
              like music
                        like boats
                                  like mechanical toys
LIKE
        RAINING
                SWORDS!

Intersection

                ■

No longer scouring mangoed islands
no longer doves flown from my fingers
no longer the first wave
                rainbowed
over the white stone
                flinging
light to the black reef

No longer the razor from a sheath of stars
        over the face of day
come back from night
                        no longer
nautical sleep to float me by the blood cry of doves
on miasma, the sight of crime envelopes day
under cover of love

              ■

An old look follows me thru the town
a look of daggers and autumn winds
a look that betrays where it came from in a pool
                at my feet
fish comb water and change it into fire

It's useless to ask who's behind these eyes
set like stars in snow
or name the creatures coming alive
            out of the exploding iris
A supper of iron and mercury
is spread out on a table of green water
and the knives, forks and spoons devour it!

I follow the lights of a swayed bridge
and that old look's thrown up from the bay
            at the sputter of dawn
Night does not come, held back
by pins and needles spilt from the sun
—an old look of ties undone,
of lambs martyred by the will of the innocent—

This look on the uncrossable bridge—
an eye closes on a rough surface—
if it had power I'd demand atonement
if it spoke I'd speak back
if it were a body I'd wrestle with it!

            ▪

I'm thinking then
a chain of words
breaking at the fistfall of words
I'm thinking green funnels of light
sifting white water
flown in blue
that cut a breast of honey to free the air

Here
take my breath
out of all the cities I haven't seen
from quick pleasures I haven't noticed
from a room without doors I wouldn't want to leave
Take my breath for your breath

In a secret room I dream
      the eye of the father closing
      the eye of the mother closing

the eye of the daughter
            opened

They look to the winter sun
that lifted a golden reef into the clouds

I'm thinking some impossible drug
flown by a hand not a hand
            but a tongue
not a tongue
            but a whip
not a whip but a cup!
I'm thinking
going down the street
too long to be seen
not wide enough to be missed

                MY HOUSE IN THE CRACKS OF THE PAVEMENT!

            ▪ ▪ ▪

It's summer's moment in autumn's hour.
I walk over a carpet of leaves
Fallen on a hill overlooking the city
Watching the clouded moon cut
Like a white diamond
                across the sky.
The godly animals, roused from sleep
—Flying serpents and the many eyed of the ancients—
Come out to mate on the lawns of heaven
All about me a fierce fireworks of desire.

In such a moment I would make a necklace
Of these leaves, rustling and golden,
In vision of her the whirling winds have taken
Breathing into their sleeping veins
All power of earth air and fire
                joyous in her love.
I would be no more sentient than this bird above me
Its breast against a receding wind
That is time broken by the beasts of heaven.

. . .

It was a time I didn't see the beast
I walked down to the flat country
in a room watched the gull
     FLY ON SILENCE he kryd
My coat covered the stars
       the bird gave me a cap of hair
Good, God, wind and bloom of air sat down, came down
         on an empty sardine can

"Come this way"
      the object shall not possess—

    I am the master of the unpronounced word
    I have come thru places where speech is fire
    I have named all things holy
    I have revealed ALL the mysteries

I slept, then, on a bed of the inexplicable
    the gull in its silence
      a shadow   lawn
       it is the beginning of time

      crystals
        on the window pane

Binoculars

GREGORY CORSO

mexico a dark mouth   terraces burn the morning

the clouds go under
      the waves,
        Cocaine

ALLEN GINSBERG

      a war on the new york waterfront

God is everywhere

CHRISTOPHER MACLAINE

toms toms stopt your poem

Mexico sings the Bird Lost choir

you are NOT mad

MICHAEL MCCLURE

goats, gangrene and The Stars
yr head turnd in a song   For death
on the mouth
on the lip
on the suck

JACK KEROUAC

the whore in the loin cloth
the light on the undersea bottle
BLUE

JOHN HOFFMAN

No one to match you
you went
to watch an albatross

jealous won't find you

FAREWELL FINAL ALBATROSS

Who is the star dancer the turn the glide speed the changes

GOGO NESBIT

mystère mystère mystère mystère mystère mystère

GARY SNYDER

The O valley Jangle

Stone particle shown

In old mud hut

Mugur Magur and Lud

so soon! ah meditation!

HOWARD HART

the spoon the unconscious
the tooth the growl
        a splitting rod in the bad morning
            yr black coat on a wicker basket chair

PHILIP WHALEN

Kali slipt on the kitchen sink
        on top of a berry nut, you're the wall
                through the g-string
also you've got the YMCA by the ball!

    ▪

COME

HOLY GHOST

for we can rise

out

of this jazz!

from NARCOTICA

1959

I Demand Extinction of Laws Prohibiting Narcotic Drugs!

—against you, psychiatrists would be conscience of the people! no more!—against you, doctors, druggists, sociologists, idiots, asses, the whole fuckingload of shit perpetuated out of STUPIDITY to elevate that most detestable NADA, that void attempting the determination of states of being—of BEING!—and which goes under the name of safety, fuck yr safety, WHO NEEDS IT?

Meanwhile yr much flaunted machine age drags with it incredible ANGUISH, INSANITY, STUPIDITY performed on a MASS SCALE. The plague is on and fear stalks yr hearts, you bastards, bastards precisely because you are rabblemen, public selfish security hounds, because you have no saints among you, because you are the pissants of all time—grey, black, dull, dud suited little men and women! *you* are not going to AND DO NOT HAVE THE RIGHT to tell me or anyone what to smoke or not smoke, eat or not eat—what's good and what's bad—you stinking prohibitors of the CURE for most of the world's anguish—you, turds, fuckedup middleclass liberals and notsoliberal intellectuals DROP DEAD WITH YR ASS HOLE MAMMON MOLOCH MONEY MOTIVATED LAWS ! ! ! It is I WHO AM THE LAW ! I DEFY YOU TO SAY IT IS NOT MY HUMAN RIGHT TO USE ANY GOD GIVEN HERB PLANT AND POWDER FOR MY PHYSICAL AND PSYCHIC WELL BEING, or in any way *rational* to obtain THE DIVINE DRUGS *at hand* without having to deal thru a clandestine, profiteering, criminal underworld—at prices made for millionaires!

Instead of sensational news mongering the leftovers of countless unfortunate junkies—why don't you learn the truth about the Heroic Drugs, why don't you move to lift the bans on narcotic medicines that never harm those who know them and need them—unless, of course, they are FRUSTRATED BY POLICE disorder via a self-destroying illicit TRADE, plus the creation of phonie addicts thru sensationalist literary and news accounts that, by distortion, create curiosity about narcotics during the twentieth century prohibitions, and among those members of society who—if it were not for excitement, danger and romantic come on of narcotic underground—would never have come, in first place, to knowledge or desire for the drugs. Leave the REAL ADDICTS ALONE!

Idiots ! become wise as the authors of the Holy Scriptures informs you, for you are not GOD in the name of the idol of SAFETY MIDDLE CLASS PROPRIETY NORMALITY AND THE OPINIONS OF DELUDED WRITERS—Coleridge, like !—topped by all the disorderly grumbling having its root in IGNORANCE AND STUPIDITY from all 19th and 20th century advocates of WAR in the name of a "peace" that doesn't exist ! or if it does, it's HELLISH and get rid of it !

I DECLARE WAR on your lack of intelligence, socalled lawgivers and arbiters of
every man's pain ! I say ABOLISH THE PROHIBITIONS ON THE SACRED
NARCOTICS—stop the sensationalism ! To the dark ages with yr crime producing
"law" not yet fifty years old, whereas the Temples dedicated to Opium and Hashish
in the Orient were built FOUR THOUSAND YEARS AGO !

License the true addicts
Give them pure heroin and controlled habits !
Hands off marijuana !
Keep peyote free !
STOP KILLING HUMAN BEINGS WITH YR DAMNED LAWS !

Bones

If bones weren't enuf for fuel, the new york Giants invented grindings of the Screen—
                    that we were killed by television
in the streets of new york, circa 1949, phonie, egotistic war by business delegates,
                    rice christian supported.

A CAP OF HEROIN COST ME TWENTY FIVE CENTS!
I saw Antonin Artaud in a dream of Sackcloth
He scored for me in Washington Square
We cooked IT in my kitchen room, Yugoslavian junk, the greatest!

       ∎

For yr hatred of contemplation
this gross caricature of sidhi
        sidhi means Bhang Smoker
We have GONE THRU!
and I say, Sanctuary! sanctuary!
whenever yr accusing finger farts, economic double talker
                go shake the tits of art!

In other words, partner, we sprung him and the others
FOR this must STOP
                        putting down sidhi, i.e., hip
                i.e., enlightenment via marijuana or any image of
        mystical states, extasis or no————!

Opium   Cocaine   Hemp

ten hours trying to score for drugstore cocaine or morphine A DRAG!
we watched doctors' lit offices—sour faced hispanic closing down with a smile—
and young fear struck where we beat him for blanks
—while waiting! hanging! dying!
man, it IS A DRAG, mexico city 1959—USA everywhere—
only I dig the climate
at least you can talk to the doctor
though he prefers, PREFERS! staying inside the limits of the stupid law against
my need for the sacred medicines—*the salts of the POET!*

■

What is the worse drag is WE DIDN'T SCORE!
rich users can make it, though—
but they don't always need it way the poet pained for end of
        pain and the sick ready for visions need it
I don't know too much about the rich, but the cool ones turned me on
        cocaine
exhibiting two foot long ivory and jade opium pipes
WHO WENT TO ORIENT, returned from before 1917 or during wars with no
        laws against opium or hashish—
in the middle ages they were Monk's remedies, as it, man, when the monk had balling
eyes and chose not to make it, he had recourse to 3-way concoction of belladonna
hashish opium, or opium alone—this last TEXTUAL, check it if you don't believe me!

■

Getting high is an art. I speak of the initiates to marijuana, hashish, peyote, heroin,
morphine, cocaine (O king of high heroic drugs, I can marvel of the VEGEWEIR-
WORLDS!) and pure pleasure, love god among the drugs, OPIUM, sweet black
translucent Opium, my first and only cure! For who doesn't know these and know
them well, each in its turn or in combination HAS NO RIGHT TO SPEAK OF
THEM NOR TO JUDGE THOSE WHO KNOW OF THEM!

For I am the LAW.
For I tell you the pain erased by Opium can be equaled by no other pain killer!
For I tell you that the circulation of FORMS in the certain sensitive far flung states
offered by SMOKING OPIUM are balm to the poet, the hermit, and for this reason
alone BLACK OPIUM CAN NOT BE RESTRICTED BY MERE STUPID
MAN MADE LAWS—for it is aid to the process leading to contemplation—this

much said enuf, stiff, pigeyed and fat tempered! woe to you who stop my march into the RAW MEAT CITY!

For I am the Law and I say Coca is GOOD
Coca is dying one in the Inca Cosmogony
Coca Leaf is on the flag of Peru!
Coca is PANACEA FOR MANY ILLS
Gabrielle D'Annunzio the poet sniffed cocaine!
Coca stimulates imagination brightens time stimulates intelligence
Coca is an aid to fastness of thought brings you to the snow heights of the Inca
     worlds makes you think of Great Inca Prince, son of the Sun, son of God, Inca
     Great Inca!

it is so cool up here!

Opium, Put Down of Laws against Opium!

The yellow idol was knocked out I expanded
Rooms of beauty raided me up to God
The infinite opened its eyes
Metaphysick, magick, and musick,
Opened wide the windows of my soul

Image of images
Aereal flight of eternity
CESSATION OF PAIN
The Order! the order!
Nothing but time and nothing itself bearing roses!
Whose?

The long look of sylphan eyes
The concept in the nutshell
Concrete Reality Billiard Balls
Expansion of internal ekstasis
Including the mono of Eternity
Tigers of Infinity—
Nuctemerons, I hail thee! for yr Voice
Maketh the image of the maker of no images!
In this FLOW
Angels, sapphires and sands
—Oriental pearl cut from Gromyko's lip

—This tribute from the lion of America
—This anguish be damned!
—This anguish be rid of!

Come on! give me the medicines I need!

Memoria

Jimmy of Morphia,
                   Mohammed of the Sacred Plant
        Al Hadj who spoke only berber tongues

        Come kif of Geni
        Come kif of Anghor Vat
        Come kif, Orient, Gold Coast
                sacred green eye
           around your burning flowers, they dance!
                AH GEE GA HU NAMANI !

           O Hashish!
Flying fingers flail flagons of fabulous flamingos floating flamboyant farewells
                on the fabled City's Gate
O Hashish around the fires! around the palms! O Gardens of the Goat!
           O Hashish!
                  —her knees on terraces
      For beauty twining her knees caught arc of her neck
And on the Portuguese in the Bay, she washed my eyes in white
Marijuana in black light

           Marijuana en las puertas del diablo
         All night long, the chant charted
             and fell

        All night long, aztec messengers arrived
             and fell stars!
        All night long, end of time
             jaguar in her eye
                  Typewriters hung in Ant Eater's Garden

        Macchu Picchu loomed—crust of Sky
            it fell
Marijuana seeress spoke sibyl sentences silver and cut the throats of time!

POEMS 1955–1962

SCENES

1. Füd at Foster's

Bowl of cold turkie fool
A roast chicken liver louie
My cigarillo's going out in a spanish bedroom
Jazz is for free
Coke is for free
Junk's unlimited and sold by Agents
      that I can make poems that I spin the day to
      Tim Buck Two that I lose tension and my head
      floats forever a far inscape of lemon trees AND
NO MORE REALITY SANDWICHES! ! !

Can I ever get up from this table?
Can I ever stop thunder?
Can I make it to windows of fur?
Can I soup up her eyes in a can of star milk and shoot it for light?

Can I read in the park?
Can I sit on the Moon? Can I?
Oh, stop it! Oh start! Oh, make music
Though your arm is too thin
    and the jails are too small, sweaty AND STINK!

2. Immediate Life

       "he who is without sin let him cast the first stone"

These are not poems I wanted to make
Ones I wanted to didn't come out
They're stuck in star thief land
My name is Philip Lamantia
And I go around with whoever
Which means all kinds of weir persons I like
      junkies, tricks, demi poets, mads, holdupmen, squares
      priests, monks, professional bums, beat jews, jew haters
      spade trumpet players, potheads, zen cats, anti-spades

super gigolos, coke heads, murderers, okie poets, smugglers
put down artists, hippies, flips AND
    BLACK SUPREMACY WHITE SUPREMACY AND
    RED INDIAN SUPREMACY WILD ONES! ! !

My myth is my people
They make grass grow on sky fire and
Who knows when the ghost of Edgar Allan Poet lumines my nights?

I am high most of the time
The sickest of San Francisco all around me
I AM THE SICKEST OF SAN FRANCISCO
I WANT OPIUM! ! !
Police confiscate opium
I want police to give me opium!
I want them to stop busting noncriminals
People who want to recover their sense of being, dig!
searching for God, smoking marijuana, eating peyote
And—because Chinese afraid of us deny us smoke of mandarins—shoot heroin!

For we're all niggers and mandarins now
I'll buy all the smoke of Chinatown
I'll buy all the junk of Oakland
I'll buy ALL!
For I'm rich with free gift of grace
And the point is that if you haven't any other way to taste
Heaven marijuana coca and opium make it for you
For me—when I'm in pain—they take the pain away
If you're square, o.k., but stop pointing IGNORANT STUPID SCANDAL FINGERS
    AT ME!
AND getting us all locked up!
If you're hip you know what I signify
If you're listening you'll see me thru the scales in my eyeballs
        and weigh my words WELL!

■ ■ ■

For Real

Black Tom
kills if you snitch on him, he sez
but never kills anyone
   the indestructible connection
who is never busted but killed by the police.

2 to 20 yrs
for stool pigeon who wouldn't turn Black Tom onto the fuzz
        when the fuzz set him up for the bust
            told the fuzz no man I can't snitch
                on Black Tom
Black Tom they killed . . .

Who three months before divorced
        Trixie who's fucking the man
and said when Tom broke off with her
      You black motherfucker, I'll see you dead

        Three months later the Man shoots Black Tom
              in the head.

Rest in Peace

Al Capone you were a tower in the midst of/
Al Capone you were a strike breaker! a blight on the radical movement
The Italian anarchists hated you, Al Capone!
However some remember with glee the good old days
of the Capone era, bootleggers, jazz buffs, boxers and junkies/
Al Capone——yr foot, yr stinking black foot! it's a black lyre
out of the pythagorean scale!
Al Capone—it's cool, ok, it's the end!
Al Capone you have no singer
You were not Giuliano, hero of the people!
I refuse to sing you, Al Capone
I go on, we all go on
Giuliano's a myth and your felt grey hat floats flat lands USA

to spume ridge of Trinacria where the Door to Hades IS
—racetrack around the pool of Persephone—
Sicily, yr dark mother, Al Capone!

REQUIESCAT IN PACE/

Inscription for the Vanishing Republic

THEY'RE LIARS!

I've put away my deep veined love
It's pain, pain, pain
There's no other way
they've made the drug too expensive!
Police of initiates
I suspect Moloch and Mammon make you act that way!
and stupidity, more stupidity!

I'll go on without drug of NO PAIN

and the pains, dues I've paid, are not thy fault, O

Plain of Ekstasie,—no—but theirs who keep me

from yr gasconades of gorgeous veins

where I work you to muses, gods, to Divine Itself—images—

and I repeat, HAIL THEE BLACK OPIUM AND THY WHITES!

Orphic Poem

the whole crazy scene! who can make it!?
they call to me, holy fires
holy fires to send me forth out of Loon
holy fires behind stars
numena cabalas of Fiery Disk
a cipher in the infinite
holy fires written in letters of air
tongues of holy fire air

the sylphan disk of night
all the goddesses stoned
fires of holy night guiding us
we cut ourselves on the Gospels
holy fires sea islands of eremetical sea
the lute on the wave
marginal islands on fire
the waves of sea water gods
time in its joyous splendors
Jesus! Joyous Jubilant Jailhouse Jesus!
beautiful Jesus True Golden Number
as the Father in heaven does He do
who makes all things NEW
fire of the holy fires!

The Call

I, weir, sit snaring
    while the city flys
      overhead
            city that drips
                  scopolamine

For it was arranged, circa 1952

to funnel deadly nightshade thru the faucets

It is now decreed no one stops the mage-edged self

upon the hill of song, sibylant grove, superior sun cairn

At the pool, druids stood over the graves of angelic warriors

Today we have called you up
               SACERDOTE DEL JAGUAR

on the mountains of Yahnah peyote and the seeds of the Virgin

Prince of Bogota! king of the whitefaced! blue gowned!

riding the fields of cocaine

triangulating return of the Tipi flue

      O, beautiful nature! O cities of the sun!

      angels entwined in yr cloths

      over midnight fires

             Bird Shaped Emperor

America waiting THE TEN THOUSAND FLUTES OF SONG!

Politics Poem

The mismanagement of government is a stare on an owl's face
automobiles have closed their bones against the decree
The State IS Machiavelli!
as we wove thru street's half light, a junky
leaned his arm on the stars of my sleeve
The Election electrified the Last Bank President
Limpid the streets! limpid the hot economic bubble!
limpid the bovine government! limpid coming out of Hades!
The Sovereign Gold King was stript in a ring of bones
The master suicidist complained with a mouthful of nails
Marvels of the tongues of poets!
marvels that stop the rise and fall of markets
that do away with markets altogether!
off the trade winds, gigantic odes fell for sale

Master of the pine needle toothless hovels of heroin
How you cover the world, dust, with yr mouthpieces
I have been sucked dry by political weather
Empty heads roll, mock elections decided by tyrannies of liberty
I am an auerhahn going before John Adams

You have despoiled the Empire - greed, quick profits, the gods of War
———Woton the bug-eyed flea merchant lice of the temple steps———
DUNG, you exhale yr matted hair and rumpled old cars decaying in front of owls

    —The sting of yr Purse! the sting of yr purses!
It's the rule of Women! Women the Strong! Women the Powerful!
Verboten their words twine like snakes, phony empires rise!
Junk. poetry. junk. poems. time. the Stone and the poison I love!

Lava

Sometimes when at Popocatepetl
who brought down his wisdom in igneous downpour
      upon which ten thousand years have made you god, Volcano
          man peons conquistadores hotshot mestizos
              I think fall out secretly in awe and fear
    to think of you raging again with forests of lava,
    timber of hot nature—this dream
to crush human stupidity!

              Come! Volcano! DREAM!
             come volcano ACT!
      come Volcano! fill the world with yr wisdom, Volcano!

From cool currents beauty erupts
    O convulsions of the earth, come!
              Sweep down on these brief pilgrims/ SHOW THEM POWER!

    ■ ■ ■

That I burned by the screech owl castle in Berkeley Hills day the bat
    tore ceilings I went thru mirrors several times

    .movement of blood over green vegetable planes of imagination.

          It was peyote! peyote!
Jaime's pad, anthropological apocalypses
          farout stone readings on glyphs
             theAirswelling!
It was peyote! peyote! the rush of cascades of colors
    transmigration of races tribes
        American Indian presences
            .one time 9 of us saw in a room A ROSE CLOUD
             .The Ache! Advances among us, Chiefs!
Olde Indian Wisdoms, I celebrate you Washo Group under the Tipi
    from nightfall to sunup
        we looked on glowing coals
          sitting on our haunches, earth close

Going Out
                    and In
                              Breathing the Great Spirit
mysterious communicating God of earliest time
                              Love and prayers of Love peyote button
        at dead   center   on an elevated clay holden
        poem, vision, old men with feathers, long chant of the woman
                              out of the tipi after dawn—

New York Blank Poem New York

new york the asphyxiated head of new york
new york a zipper thru the cranium
new york a gold thread on a suit of calcium
new york nothing new york grey beard, old grey beard

I eat you SMACK
        new york I eat you SMACK
                the roll of their granite heads

                new york smack IS new york smack!

hello. hello. nyack. smack. nyak. nyak.
                a column of plate glass dust
                a spindle of hair hoisted from reconstruction streets
        of no construction, over construction
                        —even the bleet of the Avenue
                together it is NOTHING, new york!

a further intake of winter
        a loon paradise
                a lone street
        Orizaba! new york Orizaba!
                the coasts of the main Crank—MU!

new york, pillars of pain, new york die, new york live,
new york WHERE'S YR NARCO TREE?

                              from Mexico City, 1959

Cool Apocalypse

Cool is seed of the wind cool is wind with breasts of sky cool is cool
forever your eyes looking for me when I was cool as the scene could be
cool is the Empire State may it get as cool as the old Chrysler
Cool is for the invisible police as they materialize into the gorgons of Ghent
Cool is for the atom bomb when it doesn't go off
cool is for my bombs going off cool, cool, cool
on every floor on yr lips of rain and shine, cool Stan Gould, cool!

Cool I'm made and cool I'll flow thru billows
hanging over cool streams of Incan snow where it drips with delight
high as a mountain cool as cocaine
cool as the greatest high
cool as the point the Arabs surround you with talk, cool talk
like thousands of leaves of grass
cool like Miles
cool like con men returning you to your money
cool like Pres dying for Ike
cool like the first Inca Prince of these states

Cool is the magician at work that he maketh The Stone
cool is the poet who hangs up all time to see
cool is he who digs The Holy See
and again cool Light Life greatest cool I know...................Jesus!
          Greek words come in
russian icons instead of the movies
                  cool new instruments to bring you on, cool Dadio
          Circulator of the light, coolest Dove! cool this poem
as it cometh to that coolness where I confesseth forth
     THE UNSPEAKABLE!

Apocalypses

Frightened ones of my country!
Deluded ones of my country!
Insensible, for the pain of AngSaxMoney Success Stupidity
Intelligent ones of my country!
Look to the holy madness and watch Christ Highest Aviator

Look here to the Indian Prince who's first Feather of peace
From the Dove who lights yr path, America!

The light hands of yr intelligence, my country, is come!

Let art be done here, let Mad Hermit rule
Let Prince be Prince Inca Poet of the Andes
Let shmohola be revered as a Sage
Let the junk heap cock itself
Let mom be fired from the Bank
Let Nut, son of JerryBuiltState, be cooled and put down!
Let lute singers abound, mantic moons pour!

Move the great wonder in each socket of your brain!

Look, the children of light reach for the Cross at the horizon of Rose
There we have made it, at last
                              joy to the sons of God
Joy to the daughters of wisdom
Joy to the far out bum whose wisdom you can not put down, for you all seek it!
Joy to the madman saint on his subway trip
Joy to the numberless lips of Shepherd women muttering their prayers on cheap rosaries
Joy to the poor, crazed by advertising advertising advertising sex no sex
                                        sex no sex SEX

Joy to the mother of God conducting us to the core of Her light
Radiating His light, Child with a universe crossed in His Hands!

I tell you, citizens, minds, business men, liars, learners, hip, square, alike —
The key is love! for love created us, love is our being! love or die!
Love before you Who is God/Come to his feast/eat This Bread/Drink This Wine/
Be lightened by Grace Walk from the flower of reason!
Be enlightened by the Divine Spirit! Do not hesitate! Fly evil! listen or you shall die!

Blank Poem for Poe

Poe, mesmerize me with a hymn to Mari

You are a HUNDRED AND FIFTY YEARS OLD!

I break my forehead with mysterious signs
There are ghouls in the forest

—you go on, music, beauty, aubers
.THE FIRST CONCRETE CABALA

.January IT IS THE YEAR OF WONDERS!

.an old man carrying a basket of bread
.this will not further
.sent from a hole
.a wimpwab
.a sky urchin
.pass the peace pipe, Sc maHula!

a wing a diadem a flute
a jaeger a jaguar a junk
a tuna a witcherie a FLY!

Poe, Poe, Poe
        Poe, Poe,
                one, two, three,
                        Poe,
                    Poe,
                Poe,
                    POE!!!

VISIONS

∎ ∎ ∎

The marvelous unveils its face in front of me. The crank of my bones beats the angel boxer from nowhere in the chipglass face.

Ardent Souls, we merge into the landscape.

I remember the time I was thrown down my soul severed from my body hanging as if by a string—one to the other and I was taken up above myself left sweating and weeping, old earth body nothing but shit and there in the High Paradise lost or not I don't know, I was met by a Messenger-bearded-who said YOU'RE HERE TO SEE TRUTH and I was in bliss further out than any earthly one, great bliss, that I wanted to stay in that place of radiant bliss lights and color I was looking down on my earth body and I repudiated it and all its joys for here I was in the essential joy of the spirit and my soul hanging there by a thread to this body DOWN THERE that I said I WANT

TO STAY HERE AND NEVER RETURN TO BODY AND BODY LIFE EARTHEN DEAD
NOTHING—for here was all truth beauty wisdom loveliness heavenly bliss paradise
I was born from and was TOLD I could return to after I had WORKED! and so I was
SHOT back to my body and earth and beautiful spirit vision is now told,

Samadhi!

■ ■ ■

Did I appear in angeltime or did the Angel appear in time,
          all time?
This question answered I walked straight into street of veins
             an intricate casbah a bewildered palace of destroyed works
I am a seer for whom the Revelation is intact
The Revelation! Of ain-soph God of the dreamers of the Ancient
          One
Beatific in Christ   Elevated in Christ   Maddened in Christ
          Illuminated in Christ!
Joyous in Christ   —   the first fruits born of negation, strife,
O ye thrones tremble! O ye blinded of eyes—woe! - for the
          feasts of famine - - golden rice thrown on swarm
          of hells blank as glass window on — Tracks of
          Paradise - -
              here's the number of the Lamb's light
here's superessential dove look of light life
            discerned above the genius of the race
          beatitudes in a sweep of arm, gesture, magnificence
    in miracles
          invisible visible white light manifestations
          of His Elucidations ·
        worked in darklings and lights off these voices who
        attended me That I
Speak the communion of saints IS ONE - in time, out time,
        blank time, still time, time of all times   — —
        Hail, thee, poem of the Holy Liturgy!
          emblem of silence waving!
    The Church in its lowering sea, the flag of Patmos seen!

■ ■ ■

Last Days of San Francisco

No understanding! that's how it—/ !
streets of water, masonic columns vaporize
chinabowls scream in steel bridges

       an old subaqueous tune, rambling
Goldengate spangles, Ferry Boat—Yerba Buena, isla del sol—a
hundred moons vibrate to MONEY, dissolved in yet/pot odors

Yadawack! speaks out of the Dream—how many hongos you eat?—
"the people" fornicate under Narcotic gods
moving
       Paris Panama New York India Rabat Macchu Picchu—moving
  —I.E., I'm moving
          noted:
General re/making of earth and ocean

      flag One:
  "God has
a monopoly on poets" wrote Paolo Lionni, nineteen sixtyone

I say: see the mountain of signs inside me!
Subscribe to this poem CHA WAHLA YAAGH!
Great Montgomery Street flairup! the charge of the Wap Handles
Direction Two: race, movie, suction cup of dreams—their heads
   honked   flattened out
In the Riots—General Disorder—I keep touching yr cocktail
   deposit boxes & elegant toilet seats—
               I stood on a Great Plain of California,
actually Gobi Desert—on top of white steps/plateaus of many heads
looked up to the silent giants breathing OUT STERN
                  KNOWLEDGE!
The peace pipe.
I hold it high. Gitchi Manito, his spirit liveth! his open gesture
   folded in the Law, lotusvoiced brother on the mountains of the
   Five Finger Lakes
this radioactive   HI YI HA/HA LAH!

Sounds of bleeding earth! water! the ten thousand gulls / Water /
   slabs of enormous sky full of eminent beggars drug addicts
                  lonestar detectives
John Hoffman's Albatross. I draw a Sacred Sign. You can be off

to yr bird's beginnings—I sight land—Saint Andres' FAULT
LINE TO BEAR WITNESS TO
A FINAL GONG!
GONG OF THE WORLD OF SENSE / GONG OF EQUILIBRAL
   STARS. their pyramids by—
Oh! Blank/space!
                   oh chabaroti! spansule/hound!
to be stoned by arabs—"to fall into place" at San Francisco
                         Chalk Wave
   according to the behaviors of Weather, first tonload up
      from 1927
So many luteplayers dead by heroinrayguns in   ¿is it Caryl
                             Chessman's heart?

Flag three: there are no accidents! There's CLARIDAD!

in a mirrordarkvision you can go under fast—in moan of
   Cracked Glass—
Bring the alchemic! float the transmutation!
Back from the mountains, Harry Smith saying over again: Dizzy &
                     Bird stopt atomic apocalypse

This much known: the Peace Pipe Sound! the rasp of THAT
   harmony! sunrays on the Ocean! picking seashells in Yosemite
         Forest—nightmen chanting above Lake Tahoe

the seer's voice, arms making the Cross
              the seer's voice
       rambling over siberian steppes
          the seer's voice/ Harry Smith
    in New York: your brain is a map of aurora borealis pin/ points
internexing the String Game—Polynesia, Alaska—my thoughts
in CHRYSTOS, light of all poems, I.E., maker of new
territories
EARTH/STAR
I see the Cosmic Intervention! I see water over San Francisco!
I see God putting you down, moneylovers!
PLAGUESVILLE!
The astrologer: BREAKUP BY SCHIZOBOMB I see oceans over
   Berkeley!
I see
   the Angel's
      FIRST WEDGE COME DOWN!

34 Words Six Lines

boons, bears, bagels, bundles, bindles,
banes, bunks, bags, bums, brains
motherfuckers, beasts, bridges, fields,
wars, whales, wigs, bangs, hash, swim, zonk,
great, stakes, balls, beat, cross, clap,
junkies, grimaces, holies, huka, soul, sun, mother!

Time Is as Eternity Is: On the White Road: The Muse

When first I saw you we built a bridge
linking our cities for a thousand years
Between us orbs of old races touched in nets
entangling our thoughts in a blue wine glass

You were given to me, a rare crystal
never seen before or since
Looking at you I watched an entire evolution
of unwritten history take form in a sea of comets
above your head   I scried a marriage of ice and fire
I made a lantern through your eyes
and searched one soundproof palace
where one luna moth sang in an abyss of flames
grown from the floor of your love

Together we watched for ten thousand years
—the first five an age of monsters
and I laid open to the plumage of the stars
magnetic wands and gourds fell upward in a dance
that shook the lice of the ages!

Dawn where sleepwalkers are tortured by the dragon
you led me away to the land of my birth
where fire is my home
handed down from a sky of water
The sleepwalkers drowned
the moth died
the ancient races danced only unseen
within the stone whose flint spark marked your pain

When last I saw you you wept over a jungle of glass
where El Mano de Leon set a boat of plague
into that people of dispossessed kings
whose dreams have gone mad above their heads

Witness

Because the dark suit is worn it is worn warm
    with a black tie
and a kiss at the head of the stairs

When you hear the dark suit rip
on the heart's curb the hurt is big
    rose flesh caught on the orange woman's buttons

As you talk metropole monotone
        antique intelligence
as you dress wounds by peyotl looming the boulevards
women hunt their children from you
who look out
        lit *still* inside of a dark suit

Advent

Jaguar in a Picasso eye—Stravinsky fires!
Picasso talks hamadryad fire hydrant minds
Who make death belch down death
Europe in rains of decapitated titans cut OFF—

NOW
Over our general motors neon sign I'm walking
With Jack Kerouac
The Juicy endless head of American Prose
We pray loudly in a lotus bowl—the Gentle present Jesus
In blue torrents of our rain
That washed us down mexican volcanos while we climbed
THOSE mountains of incense
Myrrh Frankincense Aloes

The Cherubic Wanderer Angelus Silesius
Out of the seventeenth century
    "TIME IS AS ETERNITY IS"

We come to the great mandala of New York
In church of Saint Francis off Herald Square
Where the blue slippered Virgin Mary guadalupizes the evil serpent
I saw drop down an elevator shaft At the Elevation
Of the Host I make a turnstile confession
Too ashamed NOT to ask forgiveness The green red yellow neons
Sound like Sister Mary Consolata's absolute up-to-date prayer
Blinking
    JESUS, MARY, I LOVE YOU, SAVE SOULS!
Jack's outside in tathagata vision—the real world
In front of you behind you over you under you

From the heart of this world
You and I haven't anything to be afraid of!
New York! New York! the streets alive with rain!
Automobiles swim in Bird time!

It's the night before the night before Christ Mass
Within us God is *not not* love!
Around us the people
                    . . . O, Holy Ghost
    America you ARE loved!

All Hail Pope John the Twenty Third!

Oh Pope John save us from the Light haters
Oh Pope John make new mistakes so we can correct the old ones
Oh Pope John make the altars vibrate the sounds of Our Lady's ointments
Oh Pope John I love you in the Divine Spirit / just keep blessing the peace makers

And bring back the East to us
Rejoin us to the International Christ

Oh Pope John, I don't know what to say, but make Church EXTERNALLY
    MYSTICAL AND HOLY
Send great messages to the people
Keep taking porno art out of the Vatican

Show the Mass to the People, Change the Mass!
Commission the Watusi to compose Masses for all Africa, for the whole world!

Oh Pope John, why have we had to wait so long for you
        all this time since the Fourteenth Century?
Are these the things I won't know until after The Last Judgement?
Why O Pope of Divine Madness and Holy Sanity
Why has the world gone evil, mammon crazy, middle class and more stupid than
    ever?

Now we DO NEED YOU to point out to us the Way of Holy Fools
For only thru you Who consecrate, guard and give us the rational milk
Who is only Source for the Sacraments of Divine Light
Do we have our being and live! Infallible Airman, Mystic Funny Man I love you

For you are a real lover of Jesus
        —alter Christus, maybe!—
I'm going to sing you yet, though I might have messed up again. . . . !

                Amici, I'm hip to the Catholic Scene!

May 1959

A Poem for John Wieners Written on His Paper

Who's the white Lady?
can you answer—I cant make it
who's the white lady?

We walked in yr room talking of the white lady
we walked round yr room with the white lady

It came, I fell back to the white lady
we made it—what turned on in our heads?
We go thru a Door of Heroin
and it is poetrie
—there must be some way OUT
—the answers are infinite
I await the sum total
of answers flung back to me
in the sea where I become something else—

White lady turning around in yr room
talking of us! A dream! I float the log
of chance, Fortuna—a bad shot—
it's alright, Mercy is ours
                              —we scored!

. . .

Shooting down to L.A. in an open car
all night remembering sad beat faces in New York
            if the stars were colors of her eyes
                    that I could hallucinate Atlantis
                        in the foam of sea
                            and imbedded in rock a sudden beauty

            that I had forced myself up from God's breasts
                to see the road twisting
                    in the American Dark
That she was balled in the night.

The Juggler in the Desert

A pickled hen descended upon the head of Orpheus
        on rams, goats, graters
                            the poem, a greek invention
        under forests, final and iron, the wild fawn said

                "Marvy, monde sans limite. . . ."

                Rose of the Eye I love thee
                Rose of Skull under carpet
                        of the sky
            Rose, Rose, I can never see!
                Rose visible as automobiles
        Rose cut from lyres
                    world limitless
                    in Rose banged
                for they come out of her, sprites

and sibyls,
                    Rose of the Sandman, I love thee!

Rosa Alchemica we seek thee!
    Rosa Alchemica to speak of thee I die!
    Alchemical Rose sea shells open for thee

                    in its sudden mandragor you'll lie
                            face down to heaven
Rosa Mystica!
                for you the snow people revolve

                    at city of the Air
                        herb of dew
                    Delicacy made of nails
            Waves from wombs, wombs
                    before Mary
        Rosa Mystica! Holy Woman lighted by afternoons
                in the temple
        Woman lit with the sun, crowned by stars
        Womb of universes turning over in her eyes

                    Child with alabastor jars
                playing a game of vines, Child
            of the Golden Ball, landed swimming to Spice Island
    They brought him the spoon of the sibyl, Three secrets
        Aromatics that bring the head down, raise invisible
                            fires at the destructions of
                        the world
                    I call thee back, in Skin of Glory, this world

Scat

■

Yah nah ruhk
  alou ya lepgleb lop amouri
        tes ogeen
  zin zin tuun uh mutsini!

■

  o yi may yoma
  o yi may yoma
  o yi may yoma
      o yah meh ha
      o may o olé
      eh hama lo
      o ho ma ha ma
      ma ha ma hey mo
      mo hey o ma hey mey ma HO!

■

  eee yah nacoma
            eka ztsa
            eka ztsa
  —eepz, clergeragob bulay aba bob
      amatzuleb betzagong
                        ari ah
              lemeto, insigi, chi chi chin
                      stomala, stomari ack

• • •

in every way i am dazzled by you

you cross the street by the hurry in my eyes

in all ways you return to me
though i do not always find you

we are useless to each other

i am fighting to get going to get you
a plume of cocaine
for your forehead
that has ceased to remember me

what i remember what you may remember
is rolled up in cotton clouds
and i see them about to beat on your conscience

what is the wisdom of writing you!
                you don't listen!
for you are everywhere at once but me
and I'm gone!
             where anywhere is you will not go

never to put to sleep the brain of my voice
that doesn't stop my cry your hurt
        your death these stars upset
           in the circumnavigations of the bed

Jet Powered Suicide

Just before landing—
      eerie sound like metallic gut string of
      atonal eeeeeh!

My first con on the system
my first big income justification of
      pariahic wandering
the poet paid off by oblivion
thanx to airline insurance!

the what's-the-matter-with-him ended
and some sad
young beast now conjures the fatal axle
change—more than orbitical tilt—
stares thru my magic as I stop
the flow of verbiage
coming from fission of flesh
become spirit and vice-versa
my phantoms ride to port
as this plane's wheels crash land
and recover
and what if I should smoke out?
Ah some happiness this could bring
by lucre's gloomy hook
grown beyond my frame's obliteration
Death I think I've felt enough
and seen a set of beings
black, snowed, god-like, demonic, uncertain,
and all my work, stunned, frozen
like this ghost plane thru window
while landing
the virgin girl next to me
doesn't want to crash—
and it's a grim joy
on brink of wide-eyed wish
thru oblivion's blinding core
for thee o twisting obscure futures,
        mine and theirs,

lost over Chicago

gods of antique blood memory
and angels form transcendent flights
even Moloch's maldororian visage—
sexual blue/stalactited tropic of
        mephitic duration
—and the whirling depth charges
and heights of love-light!
Ah the communion of spirits talking
vegetables, singing stars,
cruel gods gored my loves

I hemorrhaged for man thru
voiceless midcentury
Faults of sensibility
and those traps time set
for those mad by loneliness
and sane by horror's objective
        existence—
Nation of the Blind Beast
For it's best to go down to
death and live its frost
than pile up Woton's pride
better to love one night without
        strictures
release of Erato triumphant
than thousands of dull armies and
        prisons of psychiatry
Oh! foolish time, dryfucker's
        paradise
I would not see more
and my theme's Assassination
        stares out
to another world come
back from pre-dynastic real forests
devoid of gasses
where ghosts materialize
to haunt you Oh beautiful
        opium creatures!
Yes, fiends of sick religion
        and sicker mankind
under the metal Mocker—
my flesh bleeds cut from earth
though I'd return thru Jeanlu and drugs—
Oh oblivion's welcome from
steel compartment minds
having less than the moss of
        tombs
to show us—
Ha! I've come back from death
        screaming I
want to die!

Life that's not given to extasie
    /erotic wildness/
the outgoing ten thousand foot
depth and from it
    orgonotic light
Life that's less
        than
    frontiers of
        poet's madness—
eye of Unnameable Vision
        rolled on
        pages to
catch your spinning souls—
Life's not
blood/spurting soul knifing
    DELIBERATE
    CRIMINAL
    ACT
Is NOT.   And not—it's ended,
as star
        watcher
        skyred.

My Labyrinth

Under cover of black feathers mechanical men drift the Pleiades
My friend, you sing songs of burden
I'm singing of the silence of saliva, streets, stars
the invading of angels
at the moment of a singular embrace
        for all time given
to set us free among the beautiful limits

It's before my childhood
for all children ignited on a hill of visions
before this miniature of the Blue Lady
smiling down a wall soaked in tears
        it's here
in the net of memories

after the first fall tied on phantoms of anguish
come down from all the rusting pedestals of their moons
it's between plagues of saturated days wandering
both known to be lost and found in a mirror
                                        smoking my eyelids

it's everywhere
                in this passage of assaults
PRESENCE of a new star opened in my throat's wisdom
          Child! Hope! looking for the key in the roar of mazes

                                        FOUND
from my dreams to the door
the Great Door
opened by another world's FIRE

Listen I'm chanting always my way to you away from you
     what dies
                death
what lives
                on the road
                          of the white rider
          this side of
                     love.

■ ■ ■

Why write about "things"?
This map on the wall,
less exact than the one in my mind.

Take a shell of cotton
move a river south
exact a city with rain
paint a sign with stars.

Little do we know.

Chrism Song

Now you've gone and remained at once!
I'm in the remainder of you the subtle scent you left a bottle of oil a light in my
    Cross I am healed by your bone
it is a cool fire hour of origin circulation in calendar of twelve thousand hours
I went into your threshold in the twinkling of an eye
I'm lost to find your door, another door, I am whirling in your kiss of velvet flame

You are smiling your arrow eyes of unflinching light
your eyes the infinite door of doors
inside this first room of frog's loving krys I breathe fires out of your gaze

Oh! oils of health! oh liquid radiations thru Five Mirrors of your Head
my head washed by five rivers—PARADISE!—Oh! YOU Gaze Smile Face
frogs continue croaking your machines of no accident that perpetually play my eyes

It's the Organ of invisible fire cool fire opens its Palm to the Traveler
as You lock Chamber behind me I am eating you
translated into your northern light

I drowned like a sleeper daydreaming death

Your untitled translation of my being to Your Unknown Name.

    ■ ■ ■

make a poem your heart contained in mine
my heart enclosed in yours
it is this way the onyx burns
      interior fall of the city
this time i see the naked waterfall
    the perfect slow haze of motion
at the altar of your thighs
i push a canoe out on your hair
        almost landed
all the currents of the bath will attend you
for which we were created FIRST
for which we were intended to take possession
in a grotto of my fist on a net of your hand

        your face the eye of passage
between the azores and suns escaped from zodiacs
                        of my gaze
that you rise   roar of your black hair
that your fingers make a house of silence
between crosses of vine and hemp
in their courses my frigates laid atlantis   in a glass
for their coming to illuminate you
        that island sound, myrrhy beach
foot of venus triangulating mountains
under the mad monster moon
I own your body the boat of holy drugs!

        ■ ■ ■

it is because i cannot have you i have you
it is because i don't see you i see you
because you are not there under the bridge

on a rudder of your breast your eyes' ginger
the oriole in the heart
masquerades as a torch—it is because
it's too late that i send you to yourself

and the sea of sorrow shall not take you
and the sea of memory shall not hold you
and the sea of insane love pure love
        pulsates a fire at the edge
of all cities where my face appears to you
in a sea of Dreams —

                let this not be time
let this not be time at all
but the first look of the eyes
                poured on the air
        a pure death a pure love a pure
        sex your beginning my end

Poem for Indians

There are no more poems to write

    sudden transpirations

Why does everyone want to make them
I'd rather be an Indian standing
backed to a tree of visions
watching trout
eating bitter herbs smoking yannah seldom
prophesying the coming of whitemen

charged with an apocalypse of insane delivery

my legend Quara Mesh: "come back in
ten thousand years"

I will be sitting on the eyes of mountains
changing into a sun portal

I will forgive you the glitter of your slaves
I will teach you the path away from Moloch

    hi a yi! hi ya ha! ootzil-i-man!

Ceylonese Tea Candor (Pyramid Scene)

    for J. R., le Comte A. R. de Sales, and Helène

I'm the greatest poet this time because I was pushed off the Pyramid of the Sun
by Molock's Giant Black Crest Golden Lite
it was frightening alright —
I was fascinated I turned Aymon's head to watch it opening
slitted Door from the Second Ledge
taking 60 percent of our vision, optics, you could see it!!!
burning across the Black Sky, 7 PM, March ! O IDES!, 1961
It had a psychic effect reducing us to animal pulp
I was smashed my brain sent hurtling against the Edge Aymon
screaming come back to count the steps to the Top
A Mongoloid priest with a Cloak something started to hiss under

our feet on the One Hundredth Step thinking i find the
secret meaning of all those 200 stone L's! — elbows —
he began to run ahead of me at first I only thought it
was a cricket later knowing only Armadillos have
been sighted on the Pira Mi Di I didn't see the
mongolian figure but after getting lost unable
to find the steps down a million stars blacked
out by Mantle Night Aymon on the Third Ledge

perhaps 300 feet across
and twenty wide drifted away to the far edge
where hung skulls of victims,
BABIES INCLUDED 5 centuries before
JUST BELOW he was putting his foot
legs over the edge, about to go over
onto a hundred arrowsharp rock juttings
When I cried AYMON   COME BACK!   COME BACK!!!
from what I don't know I got the strength to dash forward
grabbed him by the hand away from the edge
hoping we'd find the stone stairway
and there were few stars to illuminate us down
and then, I looked back from the Third Ledge back
that is, to the Top of the pyramid, I saw THE SLIT
         OF THE GREAT DOOR OF MALEVOLENT
        LIGHT OPEN FIRE ON US   I SAID LOOK
      AYMON LOOK!!! He swung his head for a few
     seconds half way around and screamed again LETS GET
    OUT OF HERE!!!   I'VE HAD IT!!! we raced down
and the Black Shapes hundreds of them cut around us and
wailed a weird banshee sound of hell I couldn't quite believe it
but it WAS TRUE!!! we were being pushed off the
Pyramid of the Sun that IS the mountain of Hell itself
                and now I say unto you
     O fools of wisdom
           O poets of love and death
    believe my brothers in unbelief I AM SEER OF
MOLOCH'S HAVEN
     THESE SIX CENTURIES CONTINUES TO
       OPERATE 150 miles

north of
Mexico City
once called Ten
och tit lan built one
thousand AD by the Toltecs
after destruction of Teotihuacan
city of the gods . and conquered by
witch/driven Aztecs, bloody blackmagic
nazi/moloch worshipping sun devils of old
mexico who took the remains of Toltec High
Religion and turned it into degenerate center of Hell's
cult of bloody hearts torn open for the pleasure of all the
demons of the seven circles of the seven thousand webs of the
seven million fallen angels of God's solar paradise
And I say to you all take care on this continent that the
Hordes shall not descend who have been prepared by
Fiends who for 6 centuries officiate their rites of
rapine child sacrifices and blackmagic murders from
these heights of stone
BEWARE AND LISTEN TO MY MESS-
AGE OH POORE MANKINDE ON
THIS CONTINENT OF THE PEO-
PLE OF THE HOLY PERSON LIS-
TEN AND PREPARE AND
CHANGE!!! CHANGE!!!

make Holy Changes in yr lives
that we exercize
once for all Moloch and his human pawns from Asia's vast
colonnades of ice down
thru Alaska toward your shores, Manahata
all your Israel's dreams brought down in the
harsh swords of their Hordes of Hell for I know
from what I speak

Change into the sun
look into God's face which is everywhere
my war is holy my war is peace my war is Spirit over flesh
my war is the final way in the infinite stalking of your turnabout
rejection of your deepest truth

now listen if you do not learn now to see Christ in all others
if you do not take up your swords of the mind against the
mechanical materialist VOID
if you do not pray for DIVINE ENLIGHTENMENT
if you do not experience god OH POORE MANKINDE!!!
ON THIS PLANET YOUR TIME WILL BE UP!!!
AND there SHALL BE HELL TO PAY!!!

Rompi

— Rompi! Tangier! Rompi!

I fell into night the genii came
terrible genii nailing me into a coffin
This witness between you and the prophet of my dreams
I almost died in dream of death
the genii were cruel
kif/kif the genii were cool
        they let me live!

From cape of no highs
to somaliland of antique drums
—ganja in the veldt—
swimming fish fly far to far-flung regions
—Africa in my head!
leopards of light!
tigers of tons of terror!
devil masks coming out of every tree!
—watching warriors of the watusi way, I wail with thee!

O gingers of arabic gum!
O sweet kiss of the melon!

Where DO they hang from, the ouds of King David?
Songs of oriental america
ring from rafters of my heart
kif/kif—*swing!* rock and roll arab!

        all this way to Allah the merciful!

Crystals

Your eyes are alabaster sound
your hands electric bolts of rosewater
your wisdom fool's delight your wisdom sweet woman of blue gold
your voice is breaking bread
your voice the white cross light of the vision crux of the morning
your voice in a net of shrouds your voice over the cracked temple
your voice my garden of sound your voice my cradle of vision
your voice my game of words my puns of love
your voice crystal light in air your voice in the Golden Circulation
your voice out of crystal springs your voice lighthouse in darkness
your voice my refuge of light your voice Holy Place in my body

from where I breathe forth my love / all the Holy Ghost letters forming my tongue
    YOUR TONGUE to speak THRU!

        ■

            When I did not go pearls of wisdom I saw in Hell
great mountains of void, centuries of war / what I saw in Hell mounted
against the grey Bombs of the mystical death

My dreams nailed me to beds of unreason, foul hangovers of erotic
elephantiasis — OH EMPTY ROOM! — unable to speak BUT DRY TEARS!
Deserts! tears of grey void where God is believed not to be — God!
gone into God   gone from God   God is a long forgotten dream

                — muck of my face coming up in mirrors I smashed the
image of lust
with these bare fists the mirror rose as an Accusing Finger
I vomited among nail clippings
Suddenly appeared the being for whom poetry is made
in her lyre triumphs the distant dream of God
I understood Love's wounds I swam free of catatonia I went to misty isles
I went back thru the void

When I did not go I was going back and my eyes are FULL OF RAYS!

        ■

Your eyes of sun and I can't speak yr smile of joyous death
and my words form as the circle of yr voice

        ■

Forty days in a happy desert! 6 months in pax ocean!
too many cigarettes

I have seen Absolute Love I have seen the shadow on the Cross
Devil mirrors smash: in crystal apocalyptics I turn to the Orient

∎

"BLESSED ARE THEY WHO HUNGER AND THIRST AFTER JUSTICE"

Domine, sum dignus! Who is NOT worthy of me? I'm not worthy of Thee,
O King of Forgiveness, Lord of the Cosmic Ethic
only thru you, my friend, am I no longer guilty in front of tribunals of Anxiety
sin is nothing more than what you have forgiven!

I in you I am your Dignity humbled in human form and I am godlike in your Image
in you is my dignity that I am elevated to your Crystal Eye that I am moved in
    circulations of your Vision
what glimpses! *what* flames of somatic love! *what* peace in the midst of the
    Luciferian light — it IS darkness, cloud of confusion hate misery —
And you above it highest bird of all! and YOU suffering in it and YOU
curing us from it and YOU purifying us from satanic lights and YOU open
to us Thy Rays O Sun in my heads of Vision! and YOU GIVING THE PEACE!
and *that* hath no comprehension and I understand all things in Thee!
I, yr fool, at Wisdom's gate I so nothing and Thee ALL IN ALL!

∎

The body of the bitch whore or waves of mystic Babylon —
torn out of her skin! the stupidity of sodomy! I came down from her beds knowing
    it is NOTHING
I go into the Higher Mathematic
which is this, Babylon is sprung from Tingis thoughts of an antique Arab smoking
    from Le Café de L'Eau
. . . and the sea rose over Atlantis lost in water to remain the Sahara
looking out of the Bead of Pharos
to the other Babylon a spirit of evil Her Breasts THE HANGING GARDENS
you have come up out of fire
into Holy Fire
there is no Greece there is no Egypt
enlightened wise Atlanteans are my only Ancestors waiting the Turn of the Years
I'm in the Trinitarian Cycles
Going to birth in the Virgin's Womb I've existed from the beginning of time

I am completed in this moment
Tingis is no more America has the Second Revolution it's the no / rule Rule of seers
the State is infinite Compassion
the seers dance going in and out of Wisdom's Mouth
all the young men dream dreams
the plentitude of the Sun is Heaven's Gift to the earth
solar machines record the lettered sounds of poets
babylon New York is no more! the Sun City is born! Potomica meditates!

I AM AT THE ORIGIN OF THE SPIRIT!

■

THROW DOWN STILL ON MY COUCH
sweat and fire fire and sweat I was taken UP hanging by a string soul to body
Heaven is a rhythm of multicolored lights
it is the sound of color the color of sound in a motion of Silence
I was met by an outline of bearded prophet
I did not want to return to my body
I knew no greater bliss on earth

       fire of bliss ekstasis of infinite bliss indescript ekstasis

I said NO! I WON'T GO BACK TO THE BODY!
and then I saw the Smile on the face of the Vision and it spoke thru the Beard —
We have brought you here to show you the Truth of God's Heaven from whence
    you originated though made in time —
you must go back to time and find the beginning of Heaven on earth — the infinite
    you have seen —
he said, I must work to return — I came down thru stellar spaces
I saw planets I drew into me The Light I went down the shaft of interstellar space
    down to earth thru the ceiling into my body and the still body sweated and
    lachrymous pearls covered my face I got up and shouted I HAVE SEEN THE
    TRUTH!

for fifteen minutes outside in the night I saw THE LIGHT BEHIND THE STARS
LIGHT THE DARK
AND MY EYES WERE FULL OF IT!

indescript ekstasis
end of March 1961

Kosmos

I have lifted my soul again thru subconscious grey splotches of hell
I have nowhere to go but to God
Violent bodies twist in my nights
owl heads human jackals metallic horses gigantic ants
or cold grey void electrically operated by mantis-eyed humans
or burning pus of vaginal discharges hairs of sexual gorgons with faces of black
    sperm run from wire wombs
all this mummy cloth jacked up from tibetan time waves
at one stroke Light/Life dissolves these visions
atomic ray of charity destroys them

My crystal love shone from vapor, red, blue, green, magenta as I lay separated
I came down from green fogs
the King of Order rides out of blazing doors
come! battalions of spiritual war!
come! hallucinations of demonic legions!
I turn the pages of the sea I loot paradigms in a storm of whales I write apocalypses
    in Chicago
come to the door opening two ways in air
death by diamond eating gone to the door of bliss, Miss Death
golden death bliss of the savior's Head! o mystical megaphones!
it's the moment interruption of hallucinated stars
now fallen down in my room with poetry
falling with lights of shimmering brains, their forty centuries yakking Eternity!
a great circle of them, Menelik's bard making futuristic Heads
The Count of Free Verses, the ratheaded singer of egyptian death, his name gone
    like mummy wrappings in dust—other idiots of the muse!

Why do you come to craze me, Unanswerable QUESTION? and I am found by
    myself in this wheel—WHO I AM—
folded, again, in petals of vision
handed singing poison—am I made for light?
atomic garbage I see you atomic garbage way below this rocket room
I stab thee words at thee I stab steel heart of words!

In me Belshazar is doomed in doom's number spent
that I have come down from clouds
eating vanity drinking anger off tables of lust
scorpions my paradise meat, the Sun of Justice my spirit's fire
that death was put away, put down by Christ—o Rose of Light!

that you do not worship gold/spidery legs of usurer's scales/moneybombs of
    unconscious war liquefy
my weapons are trees of light, saith the Lord
my money aureoles of eucharistic light
my works of art incomprehensible to the masses
I am the womb of the transcendent Vision!
It's transcendent beauty of the Lord maketh love to speak

silent verticals of sound, crème parfait for hounds of spiritual milk pursuing the
    meats of God
never forgotten spoon globes, or forks of heads or blowtorch justice
gates of silence blown open by phallus of music
come to guard sweet melting mountain come to third-eyed castle come maruna
    comana alora tumari ceona
fire aureole wild celestial pinpoint to my heart balloon in God's eye
I'm talking this flower with seed out of an unknown planet
my eyes entangled in its bed of souls
into the sky of deified muck—soul most beautiful to be!
High I go into roots petals need—over me the clouds of holy grails!

Lap hap of words—lack word—word lacking—I uncover the beast in mind
I prefer glass rain to yr weathers
circles of dead dung O parks of Cincinnati
to odic feather steel tears of tits fried Boston eyes!
bloodlet from coast to coast, wearing Batman gloves, heroes of sinister subway
O we have come to invoke in thee—life!
O listen! my sounds are man's cabbages of light!
I've looked on horror's face and gone thru it!
my idiot legend face from magazine fountain screeching for the Absolute!
there are a million maggots milling in mad and asylums don't exist for them

Pepper trees of right anarchist power force, face to face with Dracula
that evil exists, that soul is to exfoliate
upon the watches of John Adams
money balanced by seers
that State is I!
my words destroyed in babbel burning air! one tongue of tongues!
I fell thee, politics! I fell thee, oligarchs! I fell thee, shade monsters
        of money cabals! I fell thee, Black gold button over New York! I fell thee,
        Army grinning ghoul masks I fell thee muck Aviators pulling switches of
        benzedrine bombs atomic war asshole I fell thee, submarine scurvies—
        America free of thee! the STATE IS I!

Initiation, be! initiation traveling the temple causeway
into fire of water, water united to fire, my body
left behind, into the Sun, from mesh of flesh and spirit
leaving the body thru the heart to go into the Great Sky
having passed from dung heaps of shrunken eyes

passed into and over the cloud of fear
having called on God having directed from my heart a prayer for my deification
to go thru fire to rise to tip of the pyramidic flame

To make of it, a record on the way to be burned
to taste water from this burning to be refreshed in eternal water to originate from
    the endless fountain
to be born at death to embrace Living Light
to watch a million diamonds open in man's mouth
crux of light on dark
crux action of my body on spirit
crux coming down of Spirit on my body
from wars at hilt of fires
daily fires from out of these fires of refreshing water
from this water into Sun O PRAYER TO BE BURNED IN THE SUN!

Year of Weir

Green coat my connection wears
big weir eyeballs
they sell the heads of saints in the marketplace
it is not the morning for exultation
we have yet to take power
by madness first
by love first
by wired windows first
by love—decretal signed by love first—
lots of fire!

Law? We are beyond the Law!

Claw, shield emblem of the Bone
irrational force in the mirror
where the Bone does not shine!

They come with a scratching star
with a mugwort of madmanes of the Head
that point all the faces of the Beast AT ONCE APPEAR!

Beast of mudajangi
the Lord of Youth
his head the spindle of stars
beast of prime Image held by talons of human flies
beast descended Gloomy typewriter in Amsterdam windows
cooked and eaten Beast
Art Herself, glorious Pig beast
marvel of gold ingots gouged into iron blood!

It is the poem ringing in my skull the poem
in shape of itself
pure spring of air pockets exploding a knot of necks

I'm jumping through Black Books of Beauty
lead of moon maidens faun of steel blood eyes of youth
I'm stealing crystal mountains

I'm wires of historical stance
Oh the God thing! say little children going upstairs

Origins of Weir

o my enchantment my broken fisted dove of eyes
talk their beams of nothing but you
take me wholed on the disc of morning
make my night flight, its light sun escaped,
Cross cut from Fine Mirror
        A jade in a jasmine tree, bearing three genii
I am Roderick of London, they screamed in tunnels and tore up
                        their hands—
jaegers, jaguars and Brother Juniper, Blessed Be Francis!

Jaw me, I watch for the Cross!
But plight me with new climates, I say LOOK INSIDE
Fly hedges, solitudes, sages, rams of women with forks for the sea
Fly O banners of Beacon Bays and sky over Paris On Days of Deadly Doom

Fly, or not fly, dovetail yr interiors
Scrub yr soulds
Become Aware, of Owl music, Popes, Pedestrians,
              I wait, cornucopia, Fly Cocaine!

                    Sea wave, Venus on top of the Moon,
          aquarians underground
                    unite!
          Here are the secrets of the sea!

DESTROYED WORKS *TYPESCRIPT*

1948–1960

EDITORS' NOTE: The Destroyed Works typescript is made up of poems and fragments that Lamantia initially discarded, then recovered and formed into an assemblage. In 1962, Auerhahn Press published a collection of new poems entitled *Destroyed Works*.

Destroyed Works

1

The magus knows he is not the magus
what eyelength ting follows the line on this page
and is broken
              X furthers A broken line
              is the circle the answer?

2

where sudden arrivals split the nadir extends
      the Great Man a magian interpenetration of zodiacal signs
        : the wind
          the clinging
          the first hexagram

3

black IS a clown is a color is a ting is a creative is white Black
   Tui commands
                    wind—time—clinging of the unbecoming
              but furthers south by sunshadow north
                 the Great Man lives here
                     spring unchanges summer winter changes spring KEN

4

learn the impossible
      it furthers to remain in halfflight
          the sage in the mountain's throat eats—east—
            to the silence
                  attain the unattainable.
     out of Ken
               silence the tables, invade the walls.
    out of Sun
               climb back dark, like, where white is pitched
               Is the great water crossed from below?
               sure it is.
                   above.

a dragon
                    feet of the dragon wave
                there is no dragon.
                        and the caldron's broken.
    dead dragons make big technicolor hearts weep and weep and weep

        5

    tedious afternoon by the lake painted face I circumvent
    I'm all asleep, not to see you, small obscenity
                        panoramically settling your buttocks
                        on the cowbelled sun. . . .

        6

    And then spirits danced out of all the basket woven angles
                and angels of a depressing room
                            I held up at the top branch of my head
    then the sun signaled with such unspeakable intensity
    that the black music was reignited
    a blood race from my birth
    end of the street, a platform :
                            held there SO
            all the elevators when DOWN.

        7

    So sharply he we all tasted of the void
    so indented in the memory of said frenzy
    for which six million bodies served as a sauce for ash
    so clear the time of the SAINTS arriving
                    the tremblings of Satan are written
                    in the inversions of the weather
                        on the attacks on the moon
                beneath the massacres of monsters
    I see, don't you? the angelmark inside the architechtonic geni
            spinning in the cloud

8

When the butcher hands you an ape
give him back the season of bells
when the man in the zoo complains
the keys start jangling in the sargasso sea
underneath the fashionable ladies wheezing among the giraffes
let's do it again with seriousness this time!
no time to put the streets in order for the ship of fools
floating up from the hick towns
the most intelligent statement, recently,
was a pie on fire on a spire of the Chrysler
in nothing flat I sat on a wart sent all the way from Paris, Ohio

9

Your eyes dimly aware of the crystal coast arriving
in when we sing from this air of full moon
tilted on love's hidden ledges
as I love you, early morning Mass of the almost mute

10

Some albatross wing moves in my mind
this moment the tropics exist
somewhere ante diluvian splendors rise
on top of white cocos and jungles coming down
over pacific sand
                    almost almost I hear
          the rain in the forest
              the moon on the cactus
                    the green eyes of maguey
and a thousand bird cries fallen diagonally from the stars

          return to batú bató the stars are calling
          twisted more than rivers hugged on red ants

11

On the mildewed hill when the visage waits for sleeping graces' rise
I have come down from mankind's broken tree
to see thee on my climb
for not on ledges of our being
shall cool water ripen into fire
—yet approaches of the tide—
I am washed to thee whose blood is sacred on the tree

12

It was the time of the frenetic be bop days and all the cats ran and went fast up and
down the fillmore all night long and in the day about four in the afternoon the
corners were wide eyed crowded with the beginning of the night that did not end
and everyone almost wore dizzy gillespie type caps, some with blue streaked shades
some english style caps or just black one—and I used to get up about three in the
afternoon Harry would be wailing on the pin ball machines near mc allister or geary
and fillmore he would have scored or i would have scored and we would rush back
to his basement pad which was enormous with one room about a hundred feet long
that once or still is used to store old brokendown plumbing machinery and had a
kind of cloister churchy doorfront and another room beyond the big one where he
slept THAT one stank of piss he didn't have a toilet so it just would lie there stale in
a gold plated spitoon. Harry was always wearing old sweaters white spotted jeans
big bulky half boot shoes he would have his beady wild eyes open in a crazed bennie
look he ate a hundred bennies a day and when he couldn't get them he drank the
nasal solution green dead green and a bottle of it equivalent to two hundred tablets.
By night he read old alchemical books, ezra pound essays and smoked pot, digging
the cats passing everywhere in the streets (hi, man !!!!!) on all the corners of san
francisco's harlem and then the grin would flop over on each side of his pimpled
face he conned his old man out of ten a week and then we would wail across from
the synagogues and the churches and even in the pads of the respectable poets who
put us down because he dug the scene and they later might or would dig it but
didn't when we were making it He waved his finger sometimes in a round funny
way sometimes pointed straight up or falling down from his arm levitating over
his two thousand books to the left and then to the right it was 1948 and nobody
cared nobody cared at all that he had come to the end of all things at the beginning
from the waste at the bottom of a pure desire to swing on bennies and gnostical
illuminations—Man, that chick and I were apprehensive he wasn't going to make
it, but he did, of course, raising and dropping his arms out of that eighteen year old
wisdom dug out of all the old men he put down.

13

How can I write long poems when the best ones
        the real muse things
            die with me half asleep in my Father's arms

14

Because the dark suit is *worn* it is worn warm with a black tie
and a kiss at the head of the stairs
                            When you hear the dark suit torn
on the heart's curb
                    the hurt is big
rose flesh caught on the orange woman's buttons

15

I shall write a song for you, mystical lady
I saw suspended in shades and lights
across from a full moon
                        who *is* you
who is simply *you*—still within the song

16

Image: players, green lit on the foam
in a hotel on the iron sea
: churning hands on veils
                        bow spent and anemic
but juggling—
            By exquisite cruelties
the most chic exigencies
            while my other self
lay interdicted by cannibals
            and said "I'm innocent!"

17

Where you were lost in the maze, mad love, there's a jewel vein
I found a bird alive on a thorn it sang CAW CAW CAW
there you waited helpless
old man flames in your eyes
had flown faster than Icarus
young god gone to weep at the sun
and said "wait for the wind's cry" John who died young

18

Congealed obscurantist mist curves under these pages
and robs you of poetry's bank a text in the shape of a comet
Beneath worn collisions of metal
in the sun's vast orange net haikus on coplas
a vast confusion in the revolutions of the elliptic
because no rule but one no to any
Let it be: Frenzy (the clarity of)
stand in and burn on and pass out to and drink from IT
nobody waiting for the sun at cross purposes
inside the earth by the arrows of your quivering breath, poet
penetrate the fins of the sand star out of the mist to the house of the sand star

19

Pain pools its city
    to the Giant
made of paper
    and electrical
pin points.
            The giant brain discovers hidden notations
(stones falling
                on tears)
A legendary interior
        premonition
seethes everywhere
monster mirth suddenly to explode
            into the dark canvas.
Like rivers of blood
        galvanic inclinations

go thru the still air.
          Late night,
resisting sleep,
          I wait for
possible lights
          to streak
from the living caskets.

Panic, in shadows,
          the city sense
running in and out
          of its arms :
the beautiful terrors
          turned under
by the climates
          and prophecy of climates.

          20

There is an immense hope flying my room
The blessed Virgin Mary is assumed into Heaven
The new world is explored again and new
Last night I walked on 9th Avenue and the moon was my guide .
The stars guided you Christopher Columbus
And I talked for hours about Spain
Spain is the origin of the people O love
And the streets of New York are again opened
          into THE HIGH RENAISSANCE
Arabic moors were running in its arms to you, Sun
                    igniting all the darkness

          21

Endure this desert, darkling
you are about to seek the rose
growing among these sometimes felt, hurting,
metropolitan, rock contortions.

22

Not the sublime among these baroque enscrollations
but a thousand angelfaces, star tilted eyes
out of sweating, sun baked bodies burning me
conducting me to silences
and mend my heart to God's—
O, rise sluggish soul, offer sighs
close to the wounds of nothingness
open into the Five Wounds
whose Body feeds a million mouths at once
thru Whom the voids are canceled
and death is hanged to die!

23
From a Book of My Travels

When I first saw the city I was sandwiched in a taxi attempting to get the effect grey
structures surmounting my vision my host brought me for tea and cakes to the Café
Nuit Blanche there sweating over the hot brew the place hushed with hundreds of
empty tables in some mid victorian (better left unexplained) I noticed that a suave
grey haired man had purposely tipt the chair of a famous ballerina in such a way that
as she was about to sit down she instead fell [off onto the velvet floor].

■

The tinkle of glasses met as I came out of the elevator into the gallery between the
waves of cultured heads I got a glimpse of one of the paintings but the effect was
more abstract than the painter intended since Rollo's face had been superimposed at
the angle of my stance on the hind part of the Great Beast surging across a rain forest
of petrified hair Rollo was foaming at the mouth he had just torn in half and in the
presence of its editor the double issue of MU one part he stampt under his feet the
other that contained Rollo's critique, in english, on the painter whose paintings we
had come to drink he stuft into his pocket in the midst of this the next thing I knew
there was the editor of MU swatting Rollo with the back of his hand like a glove turn
on his heel and rush to the elevator Rollo merely laughed out loud Everyone else
drowned in the frozen daiquiris.

24

The mountain spoke that I would enter my beginning
                    thru the sun portal
and arrive at my end no longer only of the earth
to recognize my Father
                    beyond the portal, my sonhood
It is He I travel to, traveled away from
and set out, this day, dead to the night that once overtook me
and which is scattered without power
for He has canceled the darkness
                                voided the night
The mountain called
earth called, the cactus bloomed
in a cry for my deliverance

25

Somewhere between exile and ecstasy a gathering point
A wanderer delves un-love gnawing at his heart
you are not arrived as expected
you are somewhere else
attempting to bridge the gap
up there or right in front of me
a Door (a vision I tell you
            is opening always
a very innocent onlooker in eternity
        holds the sun in her hands

26

This city any city opens its hands full of sea machines and sea saws and
this city any city closes its eyes against meridians of lust
this city any city calls us back to the love of the Father
this any city exalts us with the desire to be going elsewhere
this any and all cities frightens by the nudity of its streets
            the sensuality of its concrete mountains
and invokes real melancholia of the tower
where, ad nauseum, Adolph the last bearded poet peels off his flesh amid the bleats
    of the undersea audience

27

Poems! Poems! I keep seeing them all the time
falling drearily falling back into the black
where I look thru an owl's eyes
and somewhere everywhere I sense my Father smiling at my eyes
here I am sun stroked and all is quiet
and I say I am going to say nothing
watching things go past
while picking up water belly stones for the sling shot I forgot to take along—
These things keep floating all the time
                balloons and bats
                        hooded ladies and lazy leviathans
and a lot better besides
growing dark in a flower fallen down on everybody's heads
I see *you* ghost of the scorpion that God bless it bit me
Scorpion that drove me in a poisonous 24 hr circuit
to LA MUERTE
                death (o yes! yes! yes!)

28

What's all this howling about
Do you really want to break out
If you did where would you go
Do you want poetry

It's above you
Do you seek nirvana grace joy
It is under you
Do you want the certitude of a higher, less expensive existence
....
What IS ailing you different than Job
hot breath on a floating old head
        The mind is *not* in the brain.

29

        "this does not make it
        this does not say it"
when shall you end with silence

O, divine dissatisfaction!
I dance in pain!
Emptiness of empty rooms
invaded by memories, sea, clouds, hot sand,
where are all the great white steps
        gone
when night came and the palm branches sang?

In my dream, the gods walked over to us lovingly
handing out burnt leaves and the promise
that return they shall—
        within you, they forgot to say—
   "even *they* con us"
and you ran away from your spectacle face
made by artifice and the felt abstract Blade
   it was plainly too much! —
the devils dined, death flowered
     at the special hidden Core
      scream of blood, sperm, spit, shit
what you saw when we didn't see love at all

   30

In paradise net you threw me your head a pyramid carved on the
        back of the sun

     Beauty! Beauty! Beauty!
     COME TO ME
even in the shape of a crocodile

You grow on a withered fig
and, then, maddened on this emptiness
   void of life in one night bulbs, broken ashes, basins of flagellant night
all the atoms of war came in without knocking
like a breeze out of the caribbean
      or: making love to you IMPOSSIBLE
for it is not here, mankind, still walking from out of the ice
    cream festival of mama papa and dead kid between them
This time blood on the earth like a winding gut

   ▪

without knowing
                    fish of the forest
                         gas engine
          behind light
                              african apocalypse
the cities of this world jump out of their skins
anesthetized cones of concupiscent stones
I will NOT come to rest on the rocks of Gahenna
Oned with God who is in NOTIME the anchorites of the subways are mine!

Yeh yeh yeh
          in my tumors even   haters of purity
                                         bombers of the virginal eye
    down the chutes with your pragmatic madness evil
the lunatics make up the cabalas of goodness
the citizens wake up in their holier lunacies
won't know what bit them to the death of the mermaid's tire!

                    CRY KRY CRY CRY
     tired of your howling self consolations
          "we're not here, fuck it,
                    for this world, fuck it, WHICH IS ENDED!"
... And the new evil undresses in automatic nightshade
I gift you with it, it's for sale with weir worlds!
               IMMEDIATE POPOCATEPETL
which is how the ocean reads the dark and drunken basilisk
at the reincarnations of Belial down by the rivers of your towns and—Moscow!

     ▪

All the women I saw were stomached in art galleries
I was tearing down a skyscraper and got cut by rubbery glass
even then at three years to the helium records
I was anathema among them—they had their glassbacks to me
I ript out their teeth   they shoved their nutcrackers at me
I chewed their foreheads   they dribbled sweet warts and lime
my coat was too long   their hair trailed the ceiling
my bones went BUG inside the cloud I sailed to Xenia
she made circular motions with her adenoids
so her fur smelled like irrigated dimes
Luna on the telephone singing for the black markets!

I lit up the curve of her arm while Mico made a cyclone with his cock in the punch bowl
the only religion was Art
the only *art* took steps to defend itself in the war of movie rabbits
Moola!—that was the one I threw down into her mother's hair
which is worn by all of them now ghost by ghost shadow by shadow drowning by
   drowning

31

Against the tri light sky touched a band of rhythmic angels
Master you have loved us from the beginning
              long
                   across the bridge

32
Message

This way to the birds' descent
fly up by rekindled stones.
Frozen veins crystallize my brain
bones lashed by serpent's power
make a circle take horizon
from ten burning rungs I broke
and saw and heard An Orb
declaim the secret law

"Multiply to zero
dance incarnate words
the timeless shall be timed"

Interlocking triangles bridge the void
Ichor flows in ten thousand veins
whose frozen core the sun impales.

33

By waves fired on the carnivorous shore
lined by sea crab claws and breasted sands
I came throwing shells and beasts godfathered
                 for suns moons and zodiacal stars
My fleshcrested shore, eye gnarled in swung kelp tides,
my hands severed by sea and its knives

my time spangled meridians by the cauldron's light
when is night's ziggard lady
                    Drawing black wind
            from salacious waves
with a look plunged by phosphorescent water bugs
her head's foot spades my head
                        stringing stars, charts no entry
In a fish hooked heart, my time
                mermen scream
        and glazed gulls scrape my sleep

34
Loft Music (for Allen Eager)

The emptiness now
nails, water, slips, brassiers, blankets, gullets, grime
emptiness of it now
the long subways, the longer subways, the subways are long
are longer now
the subway trips are stopt up
on the red lights suspended in the darkest
            in the dark, dar, the throat of the dark

The toilets are not where you saw them last
you see   the white bowls with the crystal water
you see it isn't enuf but further to the loft
to the two thousand steps to the musical madness REAL
at the top of the loft the piano white alright
and the white trumpet RED
red drapes sixteen feet high
            open to the underglass nails
                            , mistakes,
you've gone out for hamburger, beer at eating place
across from the drapes
                    warmer inside
where the meats of moths and hung up heads
the tale even the road even the tail of spoons ice
there's a bald head on a chin
a chin in the stove
a stove singing for another who maybe walks in
empty

to the footfalls, to the footfalls in the long subway
above the electric sign post neons THE BLACK
                                neons THE WHITE

I think of my girl on a fork
taste back to the telephone
where the telephone over the wastebasket
in each room I walk into the aztec metal head goes round

You see the smoke of murderers
          —newsprint on hair ignites—
I'm thinking under the pillow's daze Image
                                        Drop Down
                                        Get Up
                                        Put clock
                                        To mirror
                                        Put film
                                        Sperm
                                        To the chair
          a mile to the hole
the hole back to the head
                        lie cool, open your eyes, see red
then CHANGE
          "no new thing"
                        emptier emptiness still
greater emptiness, further out HERE GOD IS not this, not that!
          nine times
                    nine times
as saint Dionysius the areopagite said

35

Down the chutes!
you can hear us
under the pressure clouds,
                        low.

This look box, Deirdre
    it didn't get sent
    it just stayed stuck   in Hades
    a star thief found it
    and sold it in Siam.

36
Cora

(note: the Cora Indians live in the sierra madre range of western
Mexico in the state of Nayarit. Pitayah, a delicious crimson red fruit, superficially
resembling the prickly pear, growing wild in many parts of Mexico. Yahnah is Cora
tobacco. The Washo tribe lives in the mountains near Lake Tahoe on the California
Nevada border, their original home.)

Through a village suspended like a star of blood
going into the rites of the old men
silence invaded me, eating the pitayah
Where they took me, the little Indians and where I ended up is a hidden explosion
    in history
not, certainly, an ecstasy in the void!
They chanted me out of the night up to their temple of the Two Iguanas
(a real iguana climbing the tower of my house)
First, the single line trek
with staves of fire
                up to their high places
music carried in their flesh eaten by the earth and its fruits
listening to the barefoot thud on a hollow slab of wood
            hewn from their forests of breathing stone
They made a circle out of me
grinning to each other inside the smoke of hot, putrid, narcotic yahnah
—plumes and earth colors—
that drunken grin a kind of altar for whitemen trying impossible,
            but effective, cures.
I was cured of them by their detached sympathy.

He carved my ritual pipe—slow effort
            baking the clay—
        and others lugged one hundred pounds from their heads
maybe the whole length of the Rio del Nayar

I began a feverish search for the caves of the old gods
—to bring back a cured feather, a stone
            a bag of medicines
came back with a few shoulder bags, peyotes woven black on white

Saw the high priest and chief
a shriveled up old man in the morning

sweeping out his thatch hut like an old woman
He grinned, too,
                    when I told him of the Washo Circle,
          peyote rite of the half moon
"No! no!—here little white boy we've got the FULL MOON
not just this half moon you've been raving about
but, sonny, you're not going to see it!
          NOT FOR A HUNDRED YEARS!"

37

          Saint Benedict Labre

Weary vagi, I'm a walking cactus
am now overlooking some works of the saints
one particular is for you, my time   the tramp.

38
Sphinx or Cat

     for Leonora

If this cat, a wrangle over cacti
whirls and prowls and purrs
                    cats moons decipher:
               a growl—
tigers emerge splenetic and concentrate
                              in caves:

          Maggoteyed poets
implant with cellular call
                         the wall
                    that falls
whose marching ants
          stop in a cove

Furs straighten on a string of lyres
     paws sprout wands: fangs
     humanity delivers dead

39

Many mexicos I dream while I wake up in the heat
the mountain sends me a sword of visions
I saw my mind overturn gold
and I came down with a leaf of it
                    and lost it
          in the aztec roar

40

Almost motionless, I move strongly and swiftly to devour new spaces
Have I no time, like a seer, to stay all trips for the voyage at rest?
for me, too, the arrival and the going AT ONCE
Less maps than the distance in the beginning or more maps later
a distant moon rivets the eye of black hunger
the sun suspended inside of my sleep
radiates by unquenchable rays—is this the desire of innocence
or, earlier, the innocence of desire?
A bottom of silence opens here when the motions grapple
I rush in for possession
I scream first later I'll sing

41

"I'm talking God"
          ARTAUD-SOLOMON

God I'm talking God
who flipped me out of my mind

42

No more than toys, then, these man/defying/made
THINGS
instead of ancient and natural
instead of rose gardens
—supermarkets, televisions, and all the rest of it
                    ensnare vision
while spooks of social spells
                              revolve the cars

I'm in a miasma of mental climates
and striking out alone
in a real desert of once imagined machinery: whirr
        of a new witchery
intended to drone out my   death SHOUTS

DESTROYED WORKS

1962

HYPODERMIC LIGHT

■ ■ ■

It's absurd I can't bring my soul to the eye of odoriferous fire

my soul whose teeth never leave their cadavers
my soul twisted on rocks of mental freeways
my soul that hates music
I would rather not see the Rose in my thoughts take on illusionary prerogatives
it is enough to have eaten bourgeois testicles
it is enough that the masses are all sodomites
Good Morning
the ships are in I've brought the gold to burn Moctezuma
I'm in a tipi joking with seers I'm smoking yahnah
I'm in a joint smoking marijuana with a cat who looks like Jesus Christ
heroin is a door always opened by white women
my first act of treason was to be born!
I'm at war with the Zodiac
my suffering comes on as a fire going out O beautiful world contemplation!

It's a fact my soul is smoking!

■ ■ ■

That the total hatred wants to annihilate me!
it's the sickness of american pus against which I'm hallucinated
I'm sick of language
I want this wall I see under my eyes break up and shatter you
I'm talking all the poems after God
I want the table of visions to send me oriole opium
A state of siege
It's possible to live directly from elementals! hell stamps out vegetable spirits,
    zombies attack heaven! the marvelous put down by martial law, America fucked
    by a stick of marijuana
paper money larded for frying corpses!

HERE comes the Gorgon! THERE's the outhouse!

    Come up from dead things, anus of the sun!

■ ■ ■

old after midnight spasm
juke box waits for junk
round about midnight music
combing bop hair
getting ready to cook
Jupiter wails!
heroins of visionary wakeup in light of Bird and The Going Forth By Day
the pipe's spiritual brain winters off the Nile old hypodermic needle under foot of
    Anubis
                            Mother Death
I'm at the boat of Ra Set
I'm Osiris hunting stars his black tail of the sun!
It's the end of melancholy   sad   bop   midnights.

■ ■ ■

They shot me full of holes at Kohlema's hut!
It's you who'll be butchered in my precise imagination
It'll be hard to withstand the reasoning of peyotl Rack

    many times my song went downstairs, people of entire hate and I
burned you in basements without tearing my face up
O people I hate the most! glass automobiles snake by to decay decay is living anthill
where yr automobiles lift their skirts and stiff
pricks of dead indians going in reverse
automobile graveyards where I eat fenders, bodies I crunch mustards of engines I
    devour whole gallons of molding chrome I whip cheese from cannibal hoods

O beautiful people of hate! your money fenders how creamy! your electric eyes
    stinking! your geometric reconstructions against my destructions!

U.S.S. San Francisco

No one completes a sentence I am in hell to complete it
above the cobalt bomb magic fog crawls in the hideous park of addicts
I buy ectoplasmic peanut butter
roaming streets empty of opium bridges open only to the south
Everyone has left
my compass points to the fifth direction in space your typewriter eyes
The beautiful Lul in a fog of peacocks
The beautiful Lul with swans in her face
The beautiful Lul turned into a statue floating the lake
The beautiful Lul who has taken my veins tied them to the bark
The beautiful Lul a vapor
her breasts vapor
her fingers vapor
her breasts vapor the beautiful Lul with lips
the beautiful lips of Lul phantom of the beautiful Lul
How ugly yr typewriter eyes not like the eyes of Lul gone a vapor
not like the last puff of opium gone a phantom vapor
O Lul I swim from albatross shark fins in game of light
O Lul your head gone to Egypt
O Lul your head city of Indian sand
O Lul
I stamp out roses of fire
O Lul
I drown in your eyes The anchor of heroin is thrown forever!

■ ■ ■

Immense blank void, melting structures, sperm steel, the last roasted cock,
    geometry of inert horizontal planes, phases of toxicomic monsters I open the
    door of the air!

My cock scratches the interior lint of fire, uncreated hair is the net thru which
    vaginal/anal spiders feel out corners of the universe—O cunt of bombs! true
    furniture for the Creator's habitforming drugs.

An old man in a temple
shucking corn.

The Antiquities come out thru the curtain of Fuck, they have reopened the holes of
   my arms
I keep chewing the leg of civilizations, at the origin of incest morphine is equivalent
   to the apotheosis of cannibal motherhood \

Christ is a rocket ship

Every time I smoke a cigarette the Creator has blinked all stars time pebbles of
   water in a trillion second of man's sodomite existence my words can not lie!

It isn't a question of love it's how you find yourself out and that,
   as the Master said, brings on anguish

"He who has known the world has found the body and he who has found the body
   has known a corpse"

I see white alone from this horizontal plane of glass obscurity the blackness I feed
   you is made to see white light

One day the quest for water was realized. I picked up arid cactus I sucked out God
   and dreamt civilization. The quest for water must go on!
                     My friend keeps talking in my head of magic herb Colombian
   Indians snort/shut their eyes seeing clouds and float around like clouds
I'm looking for the seeds of the Virgin.

   ▪ ▪ ▪

In camera of sempiternity you walk around figures molding dust

Amapola in white light Amapola before tribunes of furniture history
Amapola of Tepic in dreams of sand shore where spectral image of my friend John
Amapola of sempiternal Orient
black star of Amapola
white look of Amapola from a mountain of walls
Amapola commands night
seers shift in stars Amapola in clutches of white lice
escape of Amapola thru pyramids of lost light alone Amapola alone
flight of Corby night
Amapola in a forest of persian tapestries
Amapola the taste of spiritual sugar
                     Amapola in gardens of Araby
          Amapola born east   murdered in the west!

This World's Beauty

So much for poetic prosodic bullshit
images crawl under this slice of windowpane
monkeys are caught in yr eyes
Simultaneous reality falls downstairs in a wheelchair
simultaneous reality I step on yr blue poppy head
Jeanlu is off in the forest combing sheep of hair
T is for mouth W for mandrake Ten is not a number
I fix the Vision by a snap of my cat's tail
you see world you see it not/going into the distances of the spirit
it is Sky, ancient heaven, microcosmos, that this poem breaks to
I look at smoke like a pillar of God
I go searching spirits of wood
Morgenroth fumbles the locks of dream eyes open Morgenroth
Morgenroth urinated on fields of marijuana eyes Morgenroth
spilled on swords of history Morgenroth I carve yr face by starspilled mariahs
Morgenroth who has made world upside down/tilted the earth again
Morgenroth shadow in the phantom's tail/maker of smokeballs/volcano eater!
Morgenroth is the reason reason has no reason for being
Morgenroth is soup thrown over the garden wall
Morgenroth is bombed out rotting baby chair MY MARVELOUS KITE OF
    MORGENROTH!

RESURRECTIONS

. . .

It is I who create the world and put it to rest
you will never understand me
I have willed your destruction

It's the beginning of the flower
inside it's black ore I salute abyss after abyss

You are the exploding rose of my eyes I have nothing but third eyes!

This is the end of clockwork sempiternity is the rose of time

This flower talk will get you nowhere

I will not be involved with people I call true distance
I invite you only to the door of horror
Laughter
I keep stoning you with black stars

> Christ is superior to Apollo
> boddhisatvas are drunk with being God
> he who is living lives only the living live
> I will hate and love in the Way
> > in *this* is Being

I will return to the poem

   ■ ■ ■

> A theater of masked actors in a trance
> according to the virtues of sacred plants

There are those dying of hunger
mankind is sanctioned crime
men should not die of hunger

It is food, imperialist dogs! FOOD! not culture!

There will come Judgement swift and terrible
war

my actor will say in mask of sick dying poor man
> I cast you into hell! I die to live
who will bring *you* back to life?

Against this another whirls in a frenzied controlled dance
he dreams on orgies dark forces revolve
demons
incinerations of the spirit
the Bomb
in its mushroom flower actions round a dumb Black Angel cloud

■ ■ ■

I have never made a poem never emerged it's all a farce
    if I could unravel as this Raga into song
opulent view of Kashmir
thousands of images bearing light
light thru clouds the beauty of things
lit up slow unraveling of the morning

On a himalaya
this one in sight of heaven
outpouring
prayer of lungs sex eyes
eyes poured in abysms of light

the flight of horned heads
gods, cats, bulls, dogs, sphinxes
each head inside out a torso of fish

            Ranka u̇raniku
            bahaba hi olama
            sancu pantis droga
            harumi pahunaka

I never see enough
with those who fly tortoise shell in the infinite hangup
words slow unraveling song

the gods are vomiting
I am entering earth I am walled in light I am where the song is shot into my eyes
    O hypodermic light!

■ ■ ■

MANTIC NOTEBOOK

Apocamantica

Horror to tell red devils climbing out of ashtrays my inner humor collapsed like lava.

On this plateau boatskins overturn in my breath corpses float
luminous head
        sun
            shit
                rain
                      in a grave of crosses, lack of air.
strident electrical pigs. trance sessions under zapotec death. swelling bellies. livers
flung to space.

From where I sit money is talked up the revolutions come yaking money it is now
or never the Kingdom is before you inside you OUT! Magnetized to the shitgod—
you—THE SPIRIT HAD TO COME DOWN

shit spirit even perfect shit is a corpse
I'm not talking junk no hymns to madness the earth is a corpse Sempiternal life
or nothing Out of dung you came into dung you go The destruction of the world
is a meditation on money talk The revolution is come! All the worlds have been
destroyed! The Living One lives! A movement and a rest A movement and a rest—

It is coming, the aristocracy in league with iron hoods I pick its nose it picks
mine—aristocracy whose head was an invented slab of tombstone.

The heroes are coming! shape of indelible shadows—heroes in rapid
disappearance from shit spirit—heroes crowed—cooked— torn up by engines gone
thru the void!

Marvelous aristocracy rotting on communist dung! Tyranny of I in motion—
heroes who attack vampires who crush entire families underfoot!

It is you who are coming—Beautiful Destruction! I sing you, Destruction,
for your yelp live bodies of liver against this humanity of snake and dead dogs In
the highest putresence you glow like neon BEAUTIFUL DESTRUCTION OF THE
WORLD!

FIN DEL MUNDO

. . .

The poem says the bombs of America went off—mothers rotting that the chicks of
    war hatch and scream ANATHEMA!

The poem says you only think you're alive but about to be born your radioactive
    heliographs mock the moon's tongue.

Death is around the corner waving decrepit hands at the poem saying "what begins
    as a transparent globe turns into an abstract skull"

What wave mantic eye what wave cutting chairs of my soul what wave claws forth
    psychopathic night and vomits lungs and keys wave sucking silent wave thru
    demented cities.

The poem says JUNK IS KING/movieflashback to antique loveroom ossified sex
    organ room in the poem's mouth saying
at whorehouse in tropics Ananka high priestess of a secret cult
at Miramol thru jungles of copper bells—

I wake up in vapors antediluvian climates circle my room I'm twisted in a sea of
    motion I break out forms of antique script 20 leaves fall in leaden blights OH
    MUDDIED MIRES OF MY TIME!

Destroyed works walk out of walls into me into the poem saying it is an ogre's hand
    rocks my living tables it is a vast cloth
of cotton folds my body it is heart of sleep I live Visage
in atomic night of dark triumph where walls of the poem are
fixed in fire at the flying dragon's emanation thruout space.

Within me is the power to BE! TO LIVE! The dead are dead and the living—live!

. . .

               At the sleeper of inveterate cars
Behemoth at entrance to the labyrinth
               I take the image of the letter 10
Over infinite carpet rolled sideways
               I am hidden by funnels of feather

Who looks in stone changes mirrors into boats canals into weathers
and the masters of pestilence draw up
clock doom's head
wasted waters
opulent neck of the Indiana monster
shrieking with voices of terrorized women and children!

I make the gesture
A domed sky of flying tombs converges
Queen of sand King in the mountain's mouth
HEAR THE MONSTER BUGGER THE MONSTER CRAZE THE
MONSTER COME OUT!

I think a star in monster's mouth
Incisions of frosted flowers take up on its lake
its clouds turn into iron hooks
its oceanic tower turns in yr entrails

My breath is bridge into the Monster's
mechanics it is fear—Ocean—ocean of its roaring cry bring down
magic
horse rhythms in flight opening
gone into the Monster's sound!

■ ■ ■

THE APOCALYPTIC

■ ■ ■

The gods made a circle crying "Hellas! Hellas! beauty cometh out of ancient Greece Hellas! Hellas!" Their hair *is* silver and their voices *are* honeyed! Tormented, I turned into a ball of spirit sperm going full blast thru air which *is* decayed satan power! Holiness, mirror of demonic beauty, where is the image of holiness?

Love where I looked for you you were not, where I lost you you were found! You came out like blazing window When I saw your face jaws opened in dark ravine Love, what is your name in the jog of joy?

They came out, crazed orphics, vague, mythy, alone. Whistles of Hermes! horns of horror! their flayed horse ascends! angels mark courses of money mummies murder! The dead bleed on himalayas of satan dust I pick absolute horn a queen of owls stops short in traffic machines abandoned to the caprices of Caligula!

I sail into silence. The sky falls. The hands of Tlaloc open! They who jump from rooftops/lemons burst in street/who will digest them?

. . .

A gazelle fixated in clock work makes way for onrush of forest of no trees for anonymous figures of history caught in harp strings of Lady Death for the wailing foetus for hallucinations of other ghostly gazelles for Queen of gazelles retrieved from skyscrapers for robots bristling with pine needles and homosexual foxes for the haze of war
stored under dead apache skins
makes way
for revolutions of the Tobacco King stabbed to death in a dream of E A Poe who flees THIS MINUTE! the avenging compass of the whalekilling Memphis Lodge!

. . .

Lost in a crowd, the mark on his forehead untouched, his cat fell out of the clouds. For this police gyrated to him. I make it on the poem he said. The room he slept in turned into a star. Down he went against the magnetism of the Flush! They kept telling him they never told him they told it to themselves about him "expose you on mountain tops, see to it yr eyes lose luster, buy yr soul for sight of you going up in flames"

. . .

I've come to the time of brain crashed stars diadems of implacable women turn in sewers of Los Angeles. My corner of meat is a necklace of guts, Oh bug of eternal recurrence! I rip out yr time Sybarite emperors take over the thrones of burning angels. It's the antediluvian time of Nepenthe!

I've come to the time abstract paintings tear up the towns. Laredos of benzedrine! Denvers of heroin! Gabagava and the rest of doomed bones of starshit. The phantom is heir to the sphinx. Boxes of broken motorcycles jumble in slivers of blood. Professors of economic war dovetail into their books.

■ ■ ■

This is the night holding gum. I'm stuck to a wall of it I fly free of the wall I cry in throats of terror holy destruction everywhere! Walking into the chair's logic the tensions are jungles of 1964.

It is here my head dynamic sun reflects the hoods of helmeted gods. It is here dream of angels took shape. The vision mounts that I am lost in its fire. Power is mystery, watching the wall of the infinite lockup!

       stop

Mad hovel of form of light! it rides me, light 3 rings in shape of a circle a few minutes and I'm hushed in hell. Gorgons dance. I go clear to the incomprehensible. It is clear.

■ ■ ■

Sick of you, owl, talking nonsense in my head. I'm going to slug you with a foot of matted hair and a rusted firing pin from Medusa's conch. No more paleolithic new world postures! I want my madmen promulgated like atom bombs
hot coffee for the dead!

■ ■ ■

Empty visions blur my soul past Cyclop's, Nero's nights
Nausica from the lips of water
arrow shot oranges at Gibraltar
There is no muse in America signed THE GODS ARE DEAD.

■ ■ ■

Secret Weapons

I'm in agony looking or making up cannibal menus
eat the Nations!
fried pituitary gland of american general stuffed with pimentos
boiled mexican testicles *à la chinoise*
french bourgeois entrails, argentine style

balinese tits, pickled.
An endless list.

I dreme of sylphs what they look like
   never having seen one Mister Calderon stuck to conventional visions

     Take garbage
    take junk take garbage
  take english take american take garbage take junk
      take spirit of junk
    garbage school take garbage school
      take junk
     the imago mundi made from Dada

The lunch I spill on you is blank void either go thru it or die

it's the worship that counts

It comes down
     reni rakuna
The hand out of the cloud for Belshazzar
         mene tekel upharsin

It's time for bad pot it's no more junk time it's coffee poisoning time
  an endless list.

Table of Visions

The Mass is poetry in action a river thru which the Divine Blood flows
it's action veiled—slow—in sight like the river's transparent motions or there is no
  beauty in its turbulence
the beauty remains in vision of it.

The Church is the image of Divine Superhuman Body Font measured out by the
    Living One
vivifies the living of the same resurrects those dead after water
children take off their clothes in her presence

The act of looking on the Living One proceeds from is like looking on any image it
    is looking inside out the Living One is seen now!
optical vision is the image of looking on the Living One

The Kingdon of the Living One is outside and within you
Do not get drunk on the Spring He has measured out
constant sight of the Living One! you make love in sight of the Father!
Jesus, son of the Living One, measured the Spring as he spoke the doctrine.

Opus Magnum

To scream at you, beasts around the throat of Agamemnon!

    At halls of Oedipus blind
            at interior cairn at Carnac
                    at jaguar court of the Quiché flue
I came with Saint Germain
    washed the feet of lepers dried the tears of widows
        walked a long way to the desert meditated birds
            went the way of wandering anchorite
                chewed the bread of hawks
                    looped the dream of Constantine
                        was Bishop of Alchemia
                            made signs for the people that they knew the Christ
                                opened gates of Saint Bruno
                                    sat still in cave of Saint Druida
                                        spoke out against the rule of iron!

I came with banquet of lovers at ruins of Tenochtitlan
    swam the Hellespont of antique mystery
        landed on shores of Mu Atlantis Babylon
            made fast for pool of the underworld and
                ascended feet high into the sky—at rigalu of Tingis
                    ate from tables of undersea gardens

I came in company of the unknown saint
    prayed to Nôtre Dame in women's cabinets
        entered hermitages of Basil talked desert tongues
            was desperate in the medieval night
                designed crests for the Duc D'Ys
                    brought battle on the anglosaxon world.

                Soul in the night
                    Christ water
                make the wearer rise with Thee
            to drink with Thee the wines of paradise!
I came with Thee, annointed One, into mechano hells at desecrations of the Lily
    and said
No more this door/for Love turns in happy feet of fat light we watch with eagle eyes
in time and out of time—for Thee!

Deamin

What are you watching I am watching that we are watching
I watch the heads, they watch me
automobiles watch me I don't watch them
make underpasses overpasses—but pass me by!

Watching watching watching watching watching!
There *is* some way out of Guerrero Street! there must be!
when will he come with the big hypo?

It's what's watching me from the spoon
it's what's watching me turn on
it's what's going on inside the ampule

                Boats at Veracruz place to score a plane to Beirut

it's all over watching arabs cop for coffee and tea
        that must be the way!

                poets are outlawed the army has been digested by heroin the
white house evaporated the morphine president's shade is flapping the
asses of Dar beginning of which/maelstroms of Poe and apache ghost
            f l a m i n g   across!
what a mess! a scene out of time capsule last days of the world

You must imagine coming of Inca prince
my dim scopolamine feather universe from back of my head

This much is certain: the gathering of opium's a delicate art
the rocks of America are not beautiful
the dark oil geni has grown into a monster
        claw of the Mummy out of the wheatfield

There is no agrarian program it is all economic war!
I make war! I decide this tribe, cool! this nation, spared!
     this stupidity unlimited, put down! this slumbering beauty, waked up!
        this heap, fuckup, dead bitch—run down, put down, finished!

       I liquidate by magic!

From the Front

      Tenochtitlan!
      grey seven thousand feet high
      mist of dust—tin door open
      to slow motion immobilized traffic
      —girl at window—terrace—
      terrace a heartmobile—
      wind! dust of wind—wind!

      sail of dead ghost opium people
      fantast—the fields of Egluria

      these watches promote me
      venetian blinds, Chicagos of Zeno

      The mountain erupts
      landmasses grab the Pacific
      earthquakes
      the sky is peeling its skin off!

      Is this American mood? 1960 weather beasts,
         who tampers the moon tides?

      Reprieve. Sail of dust wind
      venetian mountain sequence
      zeroguns silence the street

mute traffics—desperate surrealism
backfire from motorcycles
waves over empty roof tops

Geneva of movies, who ate the dogbrick sandwich?
I've cut a loaf of it
and splattered eiou—chaos
slamming venetian blinds
click, the cat asleep
        aloha, tidal waves

Where am I? you answer
the question where am I?
who's here? who wants Veracruz?
what is New York? who is San Francisco?
Friend
where are you?
what to do   go where   how?

Motorcycles of atonal venetian blind dust of wind roof top!

STILL POEMS

Vacuous Suburbs

This silence doors shut against animals, spirits,
naked women over rooftops tearing down twenty pieces of ham
this will never be admitted to public record
policemen imbedded under phantom rails

      Can you find the dinosaur's track?
      Can you put yr hands on telephone wires?
      Can you find Socrates in some garden?

Red Indian spirits come thru veils of blood tears torment
These hours are still not put to rest
arrows mark the dawn!
gloom bell breaks
They shall not peer from windows
their souls shut up outside fungus tree
holding back spiritual floodgates
eyes don't catch ghost fires the spirits have deserted them
they who set up bad vibrations people more ghostly than dead Indians—
sleeping in bed knots of nothing.

    ■ ■ ■

This is the grey limit
suddenly a great voice booms no one hears it
a car goes by
typewriter keys have meaning my fingers have meaning my pains at back of head
    have meaning
there's a slight breeze I can tell because the curtains are moving as if
in a dream sequence

It's a drab world just a few sounds indifference
I'm happy now thinking on love way beyond contraries dullness zero hours

It's the way it is and I'm a god!

. . .

There's a mountain of houses upside down it's dawn nothing really matters much
you'll never be rich—I accept! this is love I'm going to love because I'm already there
This is my mind talking
NOT ideas machines—anyone else's opinion
what's important is not seen by eyes nor heard by ears
what goes on behind appearances
Pax! it's here! I know it at last!
Someone some one else some vortex of meeting final crystal open crystal beautiful
    crystal
nothing else matters
I'm falling from high places
It's so beautiful there are no images anymore
there IS a presence there IS a light there IS
        this incomprehensible transparent land
                sudden/complete.

. . .

The night is a space of white marble
This is Mexico
I'm sitting here, slanted light fixture, pot, altitudinous silence
your voice, Dionysius, telling of darkness, superessential light
In the silence of holy darkness I'm eating a tomato
I'm weak from the altitude
something made my clogged head move!
Rutman a week at beach at Acapulco
Carol Francesca waiting till Christmas heroin rain on them!
I see New York upside down
your head, Charlie Chaplin—in a sling
it's all in the courts of war
                        sign here—the slip of dung
technically we are all dead
this is my own thought! a hail of hell!
Saint Dionysius reminds us of flight to unknowable Knowledge
the doctrine of initiates completes the meditation!

■ ■ ■

There is this distance between me and what I see
everywhere immanence of the presence of God
no more ekstasis
a cool head
watch watch watch
I'm here
He's over there . . . It's an Ocean . . .
sometimes I can't think of it, I fail, fall
There IS this look of love
there IS the tower of David
there IS the throne of Wisdom
there IS this silent look of love
Constant flight in air of the Holy Ghost
I long for the luminous darkness of God
I long for the superessential light of this darkness
another darkness I long for the end of longing
I long for the
               it is Nameless what I long for
a spoken word caught in its own meat saying nothing
This nothing ravishes beyond ravishing
There IS this look of love Throne Silent look of love

■ ■ ■

I have given fair warning
Chicago New York Los Angeles have gone down
I have gone to Swan City where the ghost of Maldoror may still roam
The south is very civilized
I have eaten rhinoceros tail
It is the last night among crocodiles
Albion opens his fist in a palm grove
I shall watch speckled jewel grow on the back of warspilt horses
Exultation rides by
A poppy size of the sun in my skull
I have given fair warning
at the time of corpses and clouds I can make love here as anywhere.

SPANSULE

Jeanlu

By the window cut in half Jeanlu
Jeanlu in the opulent night her breast riding the sky
Jeanlu asleep like a nautilus smiling at Victor Hugo
Jeanlu bared on the branches coming from my third eye
Jeanlu if it is a candle of fire women blue in the night Jeanlu!
Where the borders break the caskets of lovers—MASK!—Jeanlu
In spite of icicles fed from flamingos Jeanlu
whenever wandering fauns drown and are reborn Jeanlu
going down in a dream of descending demolitions Jeanlu
waiting! waiting! as sponges of the sea in love Jeanlu
The earth is emptying Jeanlu
                    soon spansules of eternity
               explode you Jeanlu
          Jeanlu who is
               seer/sperm.

Morning Light Song

RED DAWN clouds coming up! the heavens proclaim you, Absolute God
I claim the glory, in you, of singing to you this morning
For I am coming out of myself and Go to you, Lord of the Morning Light
For what's a singer worth if he can't talk to you, My God of Light?
These lines should grow like trees to tie around yr Crown of the Sky
These words should be strong like those of the ancient makers,
                    O poet of poets
               Ancient deity of the poem—
Here's spindle tongue of morning riding the flushes of NIGHT
Here's gigantic ode of the sky about to turn on the fruits of my lyre
Here's Welcome Cry from heart of the womb of words,—Hail, Queen of Night!
Who giveth birth to the Morning Star, Here's the quiet cry of stars broken among
     crockery
Here's the spoon of sudden birds wheeling the rains of Zeus
Here's the worshipping Eye of my soul stinging the heavens
Here's Charmed Bird, zepher of High Crags—jugs of the divine poem

As it weaves terrestrial spaces, overturning tombs, breaking hymens
Here's the Thrice ONE GOD, imprinted on the firmament I'm watching
From where cometh this first cry
                       that my hands go into for the wresting of words
Here's my chant to you, Morning of Mornings, God of gods, light of light
Here's your singer let loose into the sky of Your Heaven
For we have come howling and screaming and wailing and I come SINGING
To You who giveth forth the song of songs that I am reborn from its opulence
That I hold converse with your fantasy That I am your beauty
NOT OF THIS WORLD and bring to nothing all that would stop me
From flying straight to your heart whose rays conduct me to the SONG!

High

O beato solitudo! where have I flown to?
stars overturn the wall of my music
as flight of birds, they go by, the spirits
opened below the lark of plenty
ovens of neant overflow the docks at Veracruz
This much is time
summer coils the soft suck of night
lone unseen eagles crash thru mud
I am worn like an old sack by the celestial bum
I'm dropping my eyes where all the trees turn on fire!
I'm mad to go to you, Solitude—who will carry me there?
I'm wedged in this collision of planets/Tough!
I'm ONGED!
I'm the trumpet of King David
the sinister elevator tore itself limb by limb

         You can not close
         you can not open
         you break yr head
         you make bloody bread!

Infernal Muses

GO! my calfheaded drone! O sheep faced Ana Stekel
turning into dove's dung, Ana Black Ana Noir
over niagara of bureau lips, rococo of bad taste
your brassier window of New York drenched in marijuana rain
Bianca dead on the chessboard field
Bianca of torn down elevators Bianca projected from mexican days of the dead
in true baroque dream
at the house in shape of a monstrance
only there on rotten colonial street autos de fe for you, Bianca
    jet song of blood/fires in yr toenails walls of yr great cunt emblazoned in bile!
I'm choking to see you Bianca
Bianca a vapor
at blackfender stockings burning witches hair
at obelisk of crayfish mornings mysterious Daughter Scorpiana
who nailed the corpse of wood on flesh
Scorpiana sculpted in white opium
head of Scorpiana circled by entrails
Scorpiana flown from wounds of women beaten to death by the Gestapo

Ana Black   Ana Noir   Ana Stekel   Bianca   Scorpiana
    Scorpiana   Bianca   Ana Noir   Ana Black   Ana Stekel

Crab

NO! you can't touch bleeding pyromantic LOVE! BREAKUP SADISTIC PYRES GLOW
NO! I/yes/we make love like manylegged poems
I give you the mirror to crumble by

Walking down street in San Francisco I broke the electric bulb's anal eye
NO! I forbid you Diana Invertrex! I chew yr corsets O Diana Invertrex I screw yr eyes

        Diana Invertrex dead jumble of bleeding machines
Diana Invertrex marauding suction cups of other muses' eyes
Diana Invertrex scatologic wonder babies
Diana Invertrex your wombs of wax paper clips german lugers

Diana Invertrex your hair containing porcupines your hair running New York your
hair paralysed by bat gleamings your hair spooned in the Glock Headed Universe

NO! you can't bury the crab eggs!
YES! you can smash all shopwindows of the future
NO! either I make my house in your navel droppings or YES! DIANA INVERTREX
YOU'LL BE FRIED IN COLORED GLASS!

The Bride Front and Back

for Bruce Conner's "The BRIDE"

Here's what you can put yr thrust into yr thrust in thrust into
thrust
into her
yuhu yoho yuhami
yugi yagi yug yug
uuugi agahama
gowhan in! put yr trust there! in yah go! yeba ya hiba ya hiba iba!

Mindless—puterin an letergo! my heap of hopskin hunk of hibi hollow hanging
hung up hair of hails an horrible honies of higher learnings
lean on X polarial pains of pleasure SHOT BY WAX CANONS

NO MORE DIRECTIONS

TO YOU NAMELESS HIMALAYA salutations from the font of wisdom! may yr
commanding Foot stink for Immortal noses—rhine deer!
TO YOU NAMELESS HIMALAYA I cringe in funicular aberrations of yr feline fenders
YOU NAMELESS HIMALAYA the name in smoke ice light fog I'VE WAITED A
MILLION YEARS FOR!
you sink named nameless unnamable forever nameless NAMED HIMALAYA
you sink I walk under yr sex fountain THRU THE HIMALAYAN VEIL

Coming up to get going to cut thru to make it out to further future
penetrations
to swim out towards infinity

these are just words

BUT SHE IS SOLID AIR FOR SHE IS MOVED BY SALAMANDER MAKING
    MACHINES BUT SHE IS SPOTLESS
SHE IS ROCK OF SICK AGES
FOR I AM SICK TO HAVE HER FURLINED OR BEACHED
    IN FOAM A SOLID SEA HALLUCINATION—
WHAT SECRET DRUGS in her womb?
what watches out of her toenails tied to atomic submarine breasts?
Who's torn her open in dark turkish skyscraper ATLANTEAN PRIESTS
    SUNK HER IN BELL AT BELLY OF THE SEA
    The Christians have slaughtered themselves!

Till the End of Time

    for Robert Kelly

You, there, face, strange sage
slant oriental eyes photo
graphing the american orient
bringing on oriental america vision
at the bottom of sylphan gargoyles
in flight thru a million labyrinths
I write with my nose to black wax
behind castlekeep of faces out
of a silent whirling dream WHITE KINGDOM! GREEN! GREEN! seeds
branches twigs flowers clusters vegetable veins!
cooked and eaten dieing love
    twisted into all the faces from the imaged grove.

There's an infinite plasterboard room of Glass Black
thru this infinite room my face falls into bits my veins
run as coagulations of dust thru this room the secret sprite
of Opium revealed   nude   basking in black light to
the golden sun in Amataba's brow
    I came
back
playing with third eyes   What does it matter
who knows who doesn't at the beginning / end / SILENCE
there's the dogma of the undogmatic height same as
depth of vision there's
this six spoked cross O Antique World Kingdom! Danger and fear

fear and danger pre eucharist connection to the Cosmos
in four directions of space   Original World Concept
it is again a question of GOLD / SACRED GOLD MASK /
of an oriental expression / minted with no help from Geo Washington

white   gone into gold   green   gone into gold
black   gone into gold   green gone into gold

Peroxide Subway

for Tom Burns

Prison of flesh exhibits her towers with tossed salad head—SOLD OUT—
on the Local, across from me, out of forty/second and Broadway
transparent stockings/an insane crotch of blond hair
hypnotic head tilted at 33 degrees   up
coming on BLANK /mammoth bubs bursting her whiteflowerprint dress
eyes pinned on dream ceiling of the mind's advertising art

Some other life I might have breathed on her or smashed my eyes up
      on her crotch
                        but now after turning on the Unpronounceable Name
weighing onehundredfifteen pounds   meditating Charles Mills and
      his wife   reading them Crystals   listening to The Centaur
and the Phoenix—his galloping Dithyrambs—
                        holding my breath for two minutes
      deep obeisance—praying almost all the time in this halfmoon
                  no/season night
      going to get Higher
                        looking at ancient TV movies
            digging this sensitive youth 66 days in Huntsville Prison
"hell on earth"   "git that cotton,
                        boy!"
      where you can be shot dead by trusty guards
      taking ten yrs off their life sentences
for every con *they* "git"
                  in now total recall of jails pools
                  Indian ceremonials   looking at long lost light of
      Antique Greece
                  smelling out coptic sounds—

gebye ol teaser whore who'd probably jump hysterical if
anyone even as much as touched her wriggling cottons!—

    still:
        that crotch was once a vision of love—forsaken?—
OH GOD!
       WHY ARE THEY SO IGNORANT BODY/HUNG
         SOUL KILLING MOTHERS?!!!?

SUBCONSCIOUS MEXICO CITY
NEW YORK

■ ■ ■

How depressing here I am after my nerves tonged hell!
cut in two by flames
not caring who you are my friend my enemy one inside the other
I am always walking in pain
Somnambulists in green shoes are hung on ladders over street's mirage
they disappear in artificial fogs transformed into lupins
I am out in the day dieing in it
I am thrown as a cluster of old sounds into the park
Blacksuited men having no faces stare into statues I WANT THEM TO WALK!
from frozen eyes the ray shall dart to finish off the population!
BLACK BLOOD RUNS FROM GREY STATUES
the unbreakable record turns in my skull
I have put a lemon tree in my window over the sphinx in my window I have put a
    veil
it is possible that no one exists
I am turned out of sadistic breasts turned into statuary it's the lemon tree burning
    in my window
all this time I am sick
my nerve/ends fart
I dreme of shit
maledictions press my hand in public places
I have thrown away a foot/long hypodermic needle into Central Park

■ ■ ■

Parades melt eternally where the park turned itself inside out
cups of ballerina mint tea float the vaginal shopwindows
that I am tortured in museums of frozen fifth avenue crowd
the sun is eclipsed by junk eyes
all that liquid money! in yr mouth, Maggie!
cocktails, rackety rack, cocktails—blonde jazz hair
I'm whirling back by furious subway
                    lion on the platform / coffee sand and cubalibres
winter's blue tooth ravaging lonely Flamingo on the Hudson

I'm the solar dictator blown away fragments down floating woman's water

down the streets by snowbird

■ ■ ■

I cut out, I mean there was no proper head to the time
inside it by gilted raindrop of telephone
to no room—just floor—
I cut out
that is, flight into ancient gods, birds and men shaped as tunnels of solar stone
going back over old road plastered down by sky

CACTUS
inhalations of Tloloc expansive drives of rain
now, head of five flowing fingers
the bush of fire behind old cobblestone canon
Quetzalcoatl's passage from the moon to the sun
at heart of the process, spiritual war to pyramidic contemplation
they, i.e., the Toltecs set up 500 B.C., even to Moctezuma's time

        burning water ran thru Chapultepec

            cut out to old Tollan.

■ ■ ■

A Note on DESTROYED WORKS and *later*

For me it is the Vision in its density and the truth of what I see
the breath is in the Vision and I come to the rhythms it is above
all a question of MY VISION thru which the images are focused,
the beat in the activation of this energy field, hence the density,
that the Being of poetry erupts out of nerves emotions skeleton
muscles tongues eyes spirits beasts birds rockets typewriters
into my head and I *see*, the weir pivot, at that point all is
Evidence Clarity Incomprehension Flame of Perfect Form and Chaos.

October 20 1960

POEMS 1963–1964

Song for the Intellect

Mere poets are playing in gardens of The Sky Arch
meats! herbs! Oh Tree of Living Bread! Oh Bread of the Spirit!
I die down in aromatics, resins, weaving bushes
                              fruits out of the desert
into seascapes of sky, suns of no name, your Heart of heaven
carved in memory left open to the darts of gnosis

In crucifixions my mad mouth whirls pleasures of the south
driving to Your north
in my west these smokes of cool summer rise in the east
My finger points three to the infinite
one is a womb
what goes out of me as smoke weaves these words
I'm pointing to you always Lord of living light
I'm drifting, cut to the quick of borning places
I'm firm in your absolute asymmetric sempiternal order

for others, I wish they MAKE IT—sadness covers the earth
You are poured forth like Sap of lightning
balms of Grace, superior resins, I AM IN AND OUT, YOUR KINGDOM COMES!

Babbel

is a language extending the sonic level of the poem—in pure song flight—to
maximum points and turned OUT to further dimensions connotative, denotative
languages cannot reach! Babbel furthers greater sonic energy output within
connotative, denotative writing by work done in heights and depths of LETTERED
SOUNDS.

Any poet worth his salt can make Babbel poems.

It is important to get ONTO SOUND LEVEL AND SOUND FLOW, resisting
connotative language surging from open, absolute sound of letters. My experience in
Babbel maps a world of SONIC TRANCE—AN ACT OF ABANDON TO THIS TRANCE
MUST BE MADE in order to *quickly* transcribe the sound of it into letters proceeding
directly from it. SPONTANEOUS IMMEDIATE TRANSCRIPTION.

Sande Rutman and I originated and named Babbel in December, 1960 in Mexico City. These first examples of Babbel poetry were made in December, 1960 and January, 1961, closely related to fragmental, similar outbursts in my earlier *Destroyed Works* (Auerhahn Press, spring, 1961) and to Antonin Artaud's "lost" book, *Letura d'Ephrahi Talli Tetr Fendi Photia O Forte Indi*— also, by descending scale of relation, to lettrist, gongorist, dadaist sound poems—certain poems in a spanish/latin meld by Sor Juana Ines de la Cruz—James Joyce when he wrote in pure sounds—Hugo Ball—jazz "scat talk"—further research will reveal Babbel's intrinsic tie-in to legendary "one language," the Tower of Babbel.

Babbel poetry is immediately communicable!

Poets of all tongues! BABBEL!

Babbel

Ali ben buri de asalium
      peres cadiscum shantan tibulil
dagamuri segur tiuti
     stanto raganimu
anta pastorico hibil tuhama orona carana
zet zen defea upanthal u turi
aganta la hara shamanture pulutiago napol tanat shapara duhuf tam anta tibila jibi
   tititu
      iri coco pastar bashili upu singel dama tuti pasalatho
        shu guwa datkut ubu bit tishpan nana har

ashun tag aley leti tus mada tus midi di di di tus eguut!

alora cum vora tomara se bulay falatora skuda eymara jenika falthosha perora
   dehumara
ostian gederbera cuculhoman hansar púdey hamakatumal O siberal!
   ah skanti cuculdiama! chetzen duria!
      EYE SHEY GALAMA HURAMI!

       sheytadi spuram kikitotam

egalahana ruda cum puti beobecharum soleana
freynaga porselten macha tivi dedotepelcopsm
      insta machanti fulgetubiri opaldara uraraturara
          sentacutzmari otoria reganduri ceycolm
panti! panti! isha pantavari
         impotrex laluga mehanda puspera!

New Babbel

chat chewlelathu chutz su matz mag muhuli!
        zutzi mewetch jedicumiflegem set
                metz coporal
     debubihalu debu debi di chan ugupta
                    netnitnitnetz capachulah!

     sadchat madchat sedchat metachat chetagon!
fleychat chetachat chetachat humeyhiahama
      chetachat
    metaphlotis mentacumachatchet putharagol
             chedchat
           chedchat
      nunigini
   ninigunu o COMOPALTHOS SEDZEN ZEBER ZEBER ZEN O BASHILI!

    triogoro midzi minimidzi zichi chichi chichi metzipufuka
        fucumidizi titzinococha
ybetmetil oskatmutmutmutackzin ackzin ackzeen ackzeen!

J. Weir

face of time which is no longer
three faces for the garden of allah
or
circular, orchestral, houses,
three figures for time, now, not now,
the felt of summer, sap
down windows

3 faces, figures, O face of
time which is no longer
time,
forgotten friezes on the window
always looking out of the In-Sound-Cafe
by wharves—

migrating bird at high noon,
albatross skyred by visionary
glass, stained by owl dust, perhaps?

flight of the Wing-At-Third-Eye-Level
i.e., Flaming Vortex become Red dot,
bubbling black, the faces loom, 3 smiling effigies

at the end of the Piscian Age...

MUMBLES

Bloody Neons

          10 milligrams de beta fenil sop ropilamin
10 sulfate beta finil sopprop lamini
·   am sick again sick again oh feb 22 65
in begining bird talk
          in bird's beginningszzzzzzzzz
                                        zz
                         zzz

          zzzz
shrupp lurp i'm falling in a sea of nesCIENCE
yes now Jack Smith's I am Jack Smith's
          America business
          is middle class is America's middle class
business
contact
Wings over HG Wells!
Dracula——draculahhh...
                         drack...
Batman?

is a whore's wing!
mineral essences purloin
momentous Clean Shaven
Women of Our Time—
lazily flailing the
men
disappearing Finally
LIQUIDATED FROM
OUR TIME
A Calendar of
        CocaCola Ovens
Zing Zagu! Zut Zabu!
Conga Lu! Congaluah! fresh from the Wars
and the Coca Cola Ovens

—Ching Chlung
            ching Lung
breakfast at Uncle Harrys
    Chinatown Ovens
Coke Suey—
Hung Su Fish of Cocaine Lil
&
death to all Seventeen
            bullion billion
            years of
        'modifying' 'praying' contemplating etc.
            THE «IT»
LIVING FIRE GOING
    BEYOND ITSELF
    «pre-cock»

who is
my Heroine, my
        Heroin

yes friends, Weave
    all Flaming Seas
        of No Knowledge
        Jack Smith   GOD
            PRODUCTIONS...........!!!

to think i spent 2 years trying to unravel the mystery
and here they plainly are ATOMIZED

SHANGHAI

GREENSLEEVES

Oslo Fumbalah
KLM KLIMOVAM
        Vac

Shumballah
the Place Fu
Manchu
chose
to meet the Fleet!
VinConglese
Crimes limited to
      3 CANCER
STRAIGHT FROM FART TO THEE
SEA OF NESCIENCE
   whipping across
      the Trance
Legs of No to Science
Marilyn Monroe
 ho hum — Cant get
    it, it up, this
      moving, IT, being
  End / Digest / newpoms /

duba duba duba du
duba dud du
shuba luba
lu bam
get on back to
   Old Pal Stein
take a Yugo boat
   falling falling
     into Der FUROR'S HEIL NECROPHILIPICA
     NUREMBURGERS
for Peace Pie's Piles
    of Boneless STIFFS!
sue Crazy crazy

crazier crazy
    they're crazy crazy crazy
    footnote:

The Acropolis exploded into
                a million pieces
New York opened like a
                jap fan belt
    & ties you to
    old time's atlantean
                    Obscurantismus

escalations:
I wanna Manna
        Pia Pu Pah!

i.e., who going to
        build up G—
            ge—God—up Again
        now we've
            straightjacketed him for good

Gad, man,
too much shit in the way
            I mean who's
            Clunk——Crank
                        ling,
            down my Nose Drain
                        Pipe

Take their ergs
        out & tie em up on
    Some SkyScraper
        Like NEW FLAGS
            FOR YEAR 2,065
        like Gee, whiz,
                God's a Nazi
            tastes like a Nazu
        himself Frying
                up communist jew nigger cunts
                Heil Hitler the Light of the World!
heil it, Fire

Fire Fire Fire
Rosa Luxemburg
Tits for Sale
they say the
Dalai Lama Tombs Taste
like Jayne Mansfield's Etcetera
1,000 years
rotting THERE?
put in
tongue right there
between His
test——
right—icles—there
son,
dont, quick,—
NAIL HIM
IN QUICK
'S LAST NAIL RADIO
ACTIVE
WATCH OUT
PANDORA CHRIST CUNT
SESAME SEEDS
voidWoid , , , , ,
mummblesmmmmbllllssss,
cumin up
Rite on time
errruuumbruuuummmm—eh

From My Athens Terrace Ruin

THE ROINS are
a thousand yrs old
or two
the mountains are older they say
TWO LITTLE GIRLS I WANT TO
TURN ON TO
YOU KNOW
THEY BROUGHT THEIR MUDDER FROM
SAIGON

8 years on some Roin Island Doing Time
watch yrself, son!
rauckas laughs lollitas of 8 & 9
whistling wolverines,
i means theyve brought back
hundreds of old
coins found in
garbage pails of Saigon........!
Athens! New York! San Francisco! this is
nowhere
.......pipi bandit poetry.......
ogu agu lugu.....yug yug.....
white panties slip
down acropolis roof tops,
a professional note Flap GROIN GROWL GRUGH!
sure I do you collect Stamps or Coins? huh?
and Roins.

Title: Ruinous Afternoon of 6,000 yr old little goils.

. . .

Going west east directionless pack to Indis
lower east side pad beach at Barcelona
all these possible trips,
stay here few more weeks
it's pre Spring out of the doldrums
Just shot up a mildey maxiton...
another two teeth pulled out,
one by the roots
nice lost maxiton effects, no doubt,
Nemi writes «heard you were on meth before
you left....are you mad? sure you are, we
all are or how else
could we stand even a second of it....this....»
uh,
uh,
what is it? zen lune, what is it, now
how he hee heeeeee di di di da dum

i'd even like to shoot up girls if they could get me high
& giggle like them all day & nite
balance off by extremities
this is very serious meditation type poem dont get me wrong, Sages!
        and sages I'd like to rub on like black musk! smells
                good & makes hash taste better.
                you try it sometime.
                Ding Dong Bells of FreeDoom, ringing
frantically into Presidential Ears

        read it anyway you like its still to be
                further mumbles in my broken down
                        Cosmos Room
                                yeh um no more
                        uh . . . sad sounds . . .

        ▪ ▪ ▪

At Random

One is the walk of elementals
Two is not the violet hand overturning the ocean
Treasure the cold hanging one
I say 69 and the figure 8 bulges forgotten on the bridge of crapulous cream

Pigsty the five emblematic faucets on the crest of lips
Belie the thunderous savagery of the septule kingdom an obvious mistake
There are 28 sections of the pool oblivion
As if 86 subjects for the experimental science of ocular dessication
Flew by at twilight
On glass rods stypticizing the colors of the segovian spectrum
I name my 12 arms cloven hoofs
As I am commingled with Satan milking his mother 190 days of the year

The hanged man pierced by fagots in the shape of tridents
Always the division of an apple repeats parallel bodies one ape one antelope
    gamboling on the turfs of lightning
The armies of trinity urinate a library of extraordinary ideas the cloacal figures
    masked with nine women in the throes of orgasm

Circled by decapitated phoenixes
I shall draw up my last will and testament
Disinheriting the universe
Requesting my ashes be thrown into ten thousand caves.

She's Appeared and Disappeared at Once

The way her body's cut by diamonds and the tallow stalks of evening
Blanketed with arrows
The sentence is tropical
Justice vindictive
She has eluded me with playthings beyond Greenland
Even when I strive not to find her
What eclipse shall narrow her escape

from SELECTED POEMS

1967

The Third Eye

Contra Satanas—
thy light is higher than light, angels
brighter than angels
Moons whisper their lights
it's the end of the world
Fasting and reborn, the Crystal forms out of moonlight & sunlight
Day and night, Green Crystal Red White Black Blue CRYSTAL!
Yellow Crystal!
Brown Crystal!

I am Hymnon riding hamwings of Aquarius,
beards of Samothrace, jonquils
from deserts of the sea

In my nights of white photography mountains fell
my heads rolled dice in heaven, my eyes poured out poison
In my day of love I saw   one rock
one strata   one pinnacle   one tree
one vine   one sprig of green
one flower   one woman I loved
I am Pythagoras agitator smiling from infinite blue coins
I am paid by light

light
is
house
of
MINT!

Garden   Light
of   of the   my finger is God!
his monies   garden

Waves
Waves   Waves
Waves   Waves

—it's indescript! I've gone into inaudia!
Maldororian waves! Angel I've seen
angel I haven't seen

            light of darkness
                        visitation of noname about to smash
            into *smiles*
        Here is face of old water man buried
                    in quickgreen lime fountains of
    Zut Gut
            accent over 'u'

        the waves
                    photojournal   seascape
                                        fin.

Blue Grace

                crashes thru air
where Lady LSD hangs up all the floors of life for the last time
Blue Grace leans on white slime
Blue Grace weaves in & out of Lüneburg and 'My Burial Vault' undulates
from first hour peyote turnon
Diderot hand in hand with the Marquis de Sade
wraps himself up in a mexican serapé
at Constitution Hall, Philadelphia, 1930

Blue Grace turns into the Count of Saint-Germain
    who lives forever
        cutting up George Washington
dream of pyramid liquefactions from thighs of Versailles

Blue Grace intimidates Nevil Chamberlain
feels up Filippo Marinetti
and other hysterics of the phallic rose

Blue Grace dressed up as automobile sperm
    My Claw of the future
    and the almond rose Rich the Vampire wears
                over the US Army
—FLAGS!
        AMERICAN FLAGS!

flying like bats
        out of 'My Burial Vault'!
flood museums
                where Robespierre's murder is plotted
                        —floated from Texcoco,
the Prince of Bogota caught redhanded
sniffing forty cans of Berlin ether!

                Hydrek ice blue teeth
        impersonates, psycho-kinetically,
the resurrection of Blue Grace as prophetess of the anti-planet system

Blue Grace under dark glasses
getting out of one hundred white cars at once!
Cars of ectoplasmic tin-types
go to the juncture where Blue Grace Glass is raped
        at the Court of Miracles, Mexico City, 1959

Blue Grace undressed
reveals tattoo marks of Hamburg, sea & storm of
                        Neptune-Pluto conjunction
Rumors of war
strafe the automation monster
walking to universal assassination
K & K and the russian poets
suck Blue Grace's opulent morsels, back & front
The nicotine heaven of Bosch's painting
emanates the thousand beauties of
        Christopher Maclaine's tool box
of mechanical brass jewels
                Man,
                the marvel
                of masturbation arts,
        intersects Blue Grace
    at World's Finale Orgasm Electro-Physic Apocalypse!

I sing the beauty of bodily touch
with my muse, Blue Grace

                                Spring 1963

The Sun Is Bleeding over the Sky!

The sun is bleeding over the sky!
Beauty be my prophecy and
youth my analog of wisdom,
to strike notes of wild wondrous song
where the rays of childwood eyes
extend far beyond the enemies of all natural ecstasy!

Youth's dream that zaps the zepher
of galactic sex! Youth's flood
of rapture's delight
that intercepts the candle of the sky
and rolls up its fire into balls of tropic night
lightning down the grey monsters of rational crime

Oh! Go out to the end of the world, Hands
of my surrealist youth! When all the trees
bent to thy rites
of savage runes and flights the sunbird made
on midnight's exploded jewel!

Diamond eye of rocket heads of youth!
Flame brain that banished the horizon
with a fourteen year old Scowl
of the Sibyl's spear
crashing down to living death
those who'd stop my march
to the rawmeat city of Flame-Sea-Sun-Ecstasy!

Ah, that I never forget thee, wonderwood
of phosphor youth! When forests of ink
flamed to golden goblets that sang my heart's
pure leap into the blood war rings of Thor!

Over the hill of windy rages
from the whorl of eucalyptic green
the voice of Ariel Morgenroth
did come down and bade me sing
the kingdom of Elsewhere off the shores of Never More;
it was and IS the moment you can not compass
—from materia prima to the specular stone—

where I kindle this paper
over pyres of prophecy:

Youth's dream
to burn down the dreads of dope
and dour old men's sickly sex
and sicker greeds!

The Ancients Have Returned among Us

in a way humming thru crystals of light—most unexpected—
the ancients sizzle and dazzle
not as we imagined nor can put our machines to nor
make comprehensible by words or songs or metaphors
The ancients have truly returned to us
and have unfurled flags of sudden Cloud Rings
from rivers crossing the most ordinary streets
on the way back from mediterranean flowers whose lips
sip the leaf-elevators of the natural man buried in the
dreams whose chrysalis snaps from the Dragon
of fortuitous events whispered at the Age of Cham
& sent hurtling from the steeples of Og
I can hear the ancients from the mouth of
fog &   dazzling wind sonatas beloved of hunchback adepts
& dismembered mummies whose Living Light
crackles from the diapason of This Constant Present Moment
they use as a bridge to remind me to be silent
& seal my words by carbon honeys & not to spare
the endless rolls of cellophane reaching Saturn
by the cross-fibred necropolis of the Hanged Man:
they caution me to Flamboyant Order
that repeats the dooms ordained by the transfiguration
of the banners of wayward heralds whose brains
fall blandly & sedately & fall again
through the overdrenched factories of neon blindness
& who cares? since it is all known to have been
fixed in the calendars of the Twins & read
throughout prehistory from the Secret Stones

cast on the Shadow: The ancients have returned
      & unfurl repeatedly into your Ear the scroll
      of living legends, the talk of multiplying flowers
foamed over books without words in libraries
          built by fire to the laboratory that dissolves
       constantly into an ocean of anti-matter
  Truly the wisdom of the ancients is written everywhere you can
      not see it and
secreted nowhere other than through the tachygraph
         under the cascade of capillary mountains
   forever registered before this instant gave birth to
its opposite which is snaking beyond the distance
         between you and I moonman & opal of the sun
  This arrangement by special decree of what
      turns night into day or brings the longest night
before the Lion that rips open the throat of the New Year
     when the ancients were the youngest gods burst
     from the bubbles of sperm spit   Listen!
their music played from buzz & bleats
   you can not hear except through periscopes
     set down among vascular whales
mating from the crisis of rock & shale under
    the disappearing atlantis of corn cultures &
reappearing before the wheat altars on
       the plains of the western wind & western winter from
      which the words & letters were handed down
    the elevators of Tomorrow over the Deluge
   the great night giant sends us today by blood-lined
cups swollen with ichor & flames throbbed from
        lyres lost to
      Sothis & returning from under that Sea
whose waves break from the Iris of the Ibis:
     These cups that flow like banners of molten lead
    Cups put together by Tartesian Giants
   hallucinated by the saints of Ys
  unveiled in allegories of the Tower floating the
  hearts of children
cups whose brims overcrowd now the rustling autumn
     Door to the invisible temple built unseen

in the cities of the satanic machine
   Cups the legends reveal & the ancients
     are beginning to pass around as if they were ordinary
milk bottles for the children newly born from
        top branches of the Tree with its roots
           going back
                  to the starfields of Every Night.

She Speaks the Morning's Filigree

Beneath him, earth's breath
risen from inward wars of blood:
        the youth's vision
is a vibrant string plucked by the gods
      over the field of stars

Through the night on fire with my blood
whose incense sputters your sleep and washes you
on the threshold caught from the Tinging Stone
I'm tired of cooking the ultimate specter of future poems
weak from demands of the mooneating children of the 25th Century
it's really so late to proclaim my youth of a hundred years!

But you, Io,
walking on sandals of almond & wrapped by hair of eglantine,
open the seashell that sings us back through storms of smoke
to the burnt altars of childhood that float
in milk I drew from dragons slain with the help of the sylph:
Clocks rant their dirges of woe to no avail!

Your sleep is my awakening
All the shadows lie canceled by celestial foam
Moon-poisons are cooked to the perfection of Tea
The sun stirs the cauldron Sothis fixes from your tears
that dance as diamonds on opalescent hands breaking the Seven Seals!
Over & over the dusk of the Chant from the plain of Segovia
rings up the veil through which the deities move prisms of desire:
the cup that swallows the sword, the wands that shake the stars!

Aurora the cat of the morning
has sent a message of aerial fire
to the twelve-faced Aerolith whose name is not permitted for reading
whose number is water & abyss of the bone
whose age is always about to become and
has always been no less than time

We can play host to the marvelous
and have it burn us to the salt of memory
where an invisible stone contracts all thought
to draw out the words
that shall crackle your sleep
to wake us up beyond the Pleiades

No longer tired now I've supt from the tombs of kings
and raced past the Giant Chairs of Tartesos
to mark the spectrum's path to where you and I
shall be buried in the seed of the Sun
I'm at the gate of the house built by no one
but the One who pulled it down
before it was founded from the sperm of the walking sleeper!
From this place my poems can begin
to take on the shape of candles
        and incense sticks

        as you ride midnight mares
        to undo the astral curse
                turn pages of burning books
                                or float
                freely
        on the morning's filigree!

Gork!

Or, My Personal Minute Reading On the Calendar of Emblems Proclaimed From the
Principality of Weir Which is *Constantly SomeWhereElse,* Therefor Unreachable by
Machines & Beyond Any Psycho-Physical Analysis, and Conjuncts Only *Relatively*
With the Phantomatic Distortions & Material Encumbrances Socially Projected by

Over Proliferating Mobocracies, Murderous & Degenerate Sciences, Retrograde Religions
& Politics At This Time Increasingly Oppressive & Horent Perpetuating Their Arbitrary
Prerogatives Out of Certain *Atavisms of Thought & Operation*—Steeped in Integral
Errors—*Known* to Corrupt and Destroy Our Humanity.

∎

It's one of those days when the moon jumps
out of its skin and the walls of the sky
crash down with a thud
of Saturn's rings: from the wind
that drops its eggs to the gull
who hatches them from its gullet

It's one of those days govern
ments war on the earth's dinner tables
& heads of state are venus fly traps
eating the scum of their slaves
from cisterns of all the phony capitols
of King Mob

It's one of those days I'd as soon the electrons
fell out of their atoms
or never move across my room except
to play endlessly *The Art
of the Fugue* since it's on a day like this
the planetary aspects are so bad if
anyone at all is not a Taoist—Be Still
& Act Not—an age of karma is set going so that
all future cranes & paradise birds
over bleed on the crests of all the seas
of our world, to the degree that on
Another One of These Days the air itself
shall strike down the citizens like a plague!

For it was on one of these days
the Perfect One degenerated into a
crocodile and the Sylphs of old
mated with the baboons who oozed up from
the Crash of the Eighth Moon!

Sagittarius Decan I 10th Day 1965

Voice of Earth Mediums

We are truly fed up
with mental machines of peace & war
nuclear monoxide brains, cancerous computers
motors sucking our hearts of blood
that once sang the choruses of natural birds!
We've had enough dynamos & derricks
thud-thud-thudding valves & pulleys
of the Devil Mankin's invention
           And soon
if they aren't *silenced*
and we survive the sacrificial altars
of the automobile god and the vulvas of steel
spitting molecular madness
through layers of satanic dust

if the complete crowd-manacled Machine
isn't *dissolved, back into the Earth*
from where its elements were stolen
           we shall call on
the Great Ocean Wave
Neter of waters
and the King of Atlantis & his snake-spirits
otherwise known as
           Orcus
           Dagon & Drack!
to send up calamitous tidal waves
—a thousand feet high, if need be—
to bury all the monster metal cities
and their billion, bullioned wheels of chemical death!
Oh, William Blake!
thou can overseer, if it please thee,
this lesson of Aquarius Clean Sweep
that Earth's beautiful spirit of purifying Ocean
shall stop these weights on and plunder of
her metal blood and very thin skin
to teach us Terra's song of taoist harmonies!

What Is Not Strange?

Sea towers of Sicily
    change place with the tongues
        of elephants borne on the back
           of the Ibis
              What is *not* strange
                among eddies of the
                  hermaphrodite
                    caught on the spiked hair
                  of foam—your lips, Diotima
                  result from the broken statues
              of Hermes & open
            with the click
            of all the fans of Murasaki
          What is not strange is
    that
  the shorelines of zipzap cities
explode giant coke bottles
  lighting the savage factories
    supercharging
      morning blur to
        Venus—Ping!
          Visionary hotrodders
            tear off their clothes before you, Geronimo:
           Epiphany
              in a starspangled leather jacket
                flapping on the hammocks
              of the bivouac girls
                back from their raids on the moon.
            What is *not* strange
           opening up sassafras seeds,
         golden whistles and millenniums
        of Pest at a single glance from Superman
        —he who is not coming back ever—
      as the Holy Biscuits
    spill endlessly dollar bills the future
  shall print their poems on!
What is not strange?

now that I've swallowed the Pacific Ocean
   and sabotaged the Roman Empire
      and you have returned
         from all your past lives
            to sip the snakes of my fingertips:

         Go Away & Be Born No More!

            DO A KUNDALINI SOMERSAULT!

Gothic Games

   1

When they do come bearing midnight suppers
wrought from Merlin's gobble machine
let it be hands *not bleeding at the wrists*
but slightly invisible
say clothed in a miniature seafoam cloudette

hands that slip elegantly
      out of the air
and let the dishes be chafing, but
bearing hamburgers with relish
and frankfurters from WunderbarLand!

   2

Take a trip into the grail legend
eschew those dull 'responsible' profiteers
who'd nourish you on video plastics
Here
at the castle
it's sunbeams for breakfast
and opal meat for lunch
dinner is unspeakable
and *secret*
but this much I can tell you:

the nutrition so ethereal
spiration alone accomplishes digestion
and the bloodstream transmuted
into a cascade of celestial fluids

Naturally
all is served from invisible hands
with a complete spectrum of sound
interlaced with each bite

From the walls, lips—
shaped like moon changes—
sing harmonies arranged from the
chaos of that *other* world
beyond the submerged forest where,
it is said, those who were once men
now become slaves of their inventions
conspire sinister dragons rocketing
out of elsewhere to nowhere.

Towers of the Rose Dawn

Having lived
for a long time on each side of
the bridge within sight of three towers
it was only after the bridge fell
thunderously into the water
that a great wave rose

to carry me safely
before the four doors of the castle
and spill into my hands, a giant key
inscribed with the weir-image of the head & eyes
of a green and beautiful beast.

Capricorn Is a Wounded Knee

No wonder the night is smeared with ectoplasm
eagle's blood flows over the planets
and we cast a spell for seven hawks to fly out of the moon
that silence may prevail
to so startle the noisy villagers
for us to hear the songs that break
from the lips of the air

Astro-mancy

The stars have gone crazy
and the moon is very angry
The old civilization
that rolled the dice of Hitler
is surely bumbling
into a heap of catatonic hysteria
Another civilization
secret for six thousand years
is creeping on the crest of
future, I can almost see the
tip of its triangular star
I'm writing this from lost Atlantis
I wonder when I'll get back
to the alchemical castle
where I can rebegin my work
left off in the Middle Ages
when the Black Beast roared down
on my weedy parchments and spilled me
into an astral waiting room
whose angels, naturally in flaming white robes,
evicted me for this present irony:
idleness, mancy & The Dream
instead of getting down to
the super-real work of
transmuting the Earth *with love of it*
by the Fire prepared from the time of Onn!

No matter, I'm recovering
from a decade of poisons
I renounce all narcotic
& pharmacopoeic disciplines
as too heavy 9-to-5-type sorrows
Instead I see America
as one vast palinode
that reverses itself completely until
Gitchi Manito actually returns
as prophet of a new Iroquois Brotherhood—
this needs further development—
I foresee a couple of
essential changes:
a Break Out Generation
of poet-kings setting up
The Realm Apart
of sweet natural play
and light metal work
matter lovingly heightened
by meditation, and spirit
transmuted into matter,
the whole commune conducted by
direct rapid transcription
from a no-past reference
anti-rational, fantastically poetic
violently passive and
romantically unprejudiced
Each one his own poet
and poetry the central fact
food & excrement of culture
I see you smiling tolerantly
O liberal lip (another utopian
bites the dust) but no! you just
can't see what I'm reading while
in the act of transcribing it
I know at least three other
supernatural souls who envision
much the same under different names,
but the nomenclature's not more than

the lucid panorama I telescope
as, on this summer night's
torpor, it passes from under my eyelid and

grabs you, earth returned,
into the middle of Aquarius, one millennium forward.

After the Virus

Am I happy? Were I happy!
Zoos of happiness converge
on horrors which is a wide paw
of who calls first from
the lip's underscore
Happiness not a constant state
The field of man's gore
makes bones shine further
to the suicide machine
We make the sacrifice tree grow
for its necessary leavens
burnished with an ecstatic smile
of pain—the oscillations escalate—
not a moment of happiness but
contradicted by the black undertow
What, then, is coming to be
from undergrounds too fast
in their bright plumages
flailing our brains
with the gash of birth?
Something storing mercurial islets
and fungi of being . . .
and sold for altars
pitched to the stars!

Coat of Arms

Pure as gale and mist washing my skull
pure as silk dances on the ocean's knee
    thong thighs of the walking coast
pure as Mendocino witch havens
    through the transparent plumes of extinct birds
looking down from the sky-people boat
exploding over candy castles
    the salt wisdom pervades
safe as the mummy's purity *is* from the congresses of fear

The night goes up
into the ventricles of King Novalis
and horned men descend the saline stairway
whose bones are lit up from astral lamps
of the great genii, Ignis phana, pure claw
that brushes death's meat
awakened without a body on the edge of the clubfooted wave

Going around blind corners, the sylph
breaks her teeth on the borders of three continents
I pass without passports—
rapid vision overtakes the storm
of this glittering void I love
and reveals everything in a speeding cloud!

This is the moral for inventing ecstasies
Freed from the clutch of memory
I eat the eagle's windy branches
    my eye the lion's cave
silver fluids fix my voice
that sings *The World and I Are One!*
What's newly hatched is born from dying seed!

To let loose a room's inner skeleton
I come from far places
dressed in the explosions of green lamps
It's the moment before arson
Taught not to look back
my fires drink a porous stone

The geyser speaks
at the house of the onyx mirror
My name is augur
these lips besmirch the dawn
My sword's a vaporous cloud
The tooth marks of ecstasy
wear the look of totems
and the dragon's vermouth tongue
Every arm is bathed in silver blood
    I read the spells of Egypt patiently

Even if I could not reach you, *supreme opal,*
the carnivorous sea is avenged
even if you erased the cornerstone of the temple
against the door melting with pride
I would marry all the stars sitting on the face of the sea
like a traditional wolf of the absolute
sucking down the dish served up by the flood!

O ponder the gaze of the forest!
Raise mist from the shore!
There's this gull punished by clouds
on the inevitable hour of genetic infantries
and a war on oracles
After history has washed her head
the grail heroes move over gigantic chess sets

Am I passive enough yet
to breathe the fire of the opal?
And walk over my graves
that withstood the cleavages of insect wars?
To wake up from death, *satisfied*

    the forest before me
replaced
            by a cartilage of stars?

Difficult First Steps

1

It comes over me like a gigantic faun web
of intricate dance and rouses black fire
Not yet prepared, but for
the clutter of baneful voices
I run the risk of being cut down
by the charging beasts of good sense
I have been nervous before
Human beans made me sick
and vampires insinuated themselves
too long into the crevices of my inner lodes
I shall take care not to listen to them again!

2

There is only this black ice forest
to whet my appetite as it leans
its invisible breasts for the
gelatinous lurch of my mind
I am not the first nor the last
to start off for this splendorous x-ray road
for which the universe was made
The swords of entire enchantment
cut the weeds overgrowing its hair
At each step I'm fortified
—when miraculous fingers
rend the mist we inherit from spirit-mongers
to keep us from the hungry foods—
by those whom we have yet to meet
and were not, as we, born from mineral minions.

3

There are mines of mysterious moments
that open their tentacular veins
dropping flowers with which the worker
threads his probes to uncover calyx

come from outer space—
x-ray visioned, their stamens
entwine us with other worlds
though we can not see them
as they shed the black light of dreams
Or now they come looking
into angel-swung litanies the sea irradiates
at the hilt of any night
in a jungle of black waves
that pour you, spines and vocal suns,
a caustic air
that spins me to the rock of enigmatic love,
affinities of the mineral diving board
that is my body contracting to the rhythm
of its murex hand churning the waters below
and only the starlight consoles.

POEMS 1965–1970

Without Props

for Nancy on her birthday 1965

High/renaissance clouds are terraces of dying light
mediterranean roses become nightfires of the air—that we melt on the sky/scale
by invisible flame the black clouds of the Boogie—that we climb the slow feather
    arc of light
to where nothing is what we thought it was and the One Look from the solar king
    is become
the spiral escalator to the secret treasure/room Each Moment
empties from the earth churning its metal blood out of water holding the polished
    jewel the air lifts
for the Ship gone forever from its Hangar where I'm making ready to mold your
    birthday candle of the third eye

There, here, having been & to be again NEVER BEFORE!
. . . these the vigils of all mantik art:

    THE FAERY CASTLE ONLY IS ULTIMATE REALITY
    TRUTH IS THE X-UNION OF ONE & ONE

Two & More is the Boogie's name

prayer is constant Magick, the single beam
coming from the Sky Crown: the sure stairway
that writes the stars as the Scales measure
what you see, how you stroke cats or when the time IS
to cross bridges between earth & air . . . Here's the burning mantle to put on, the
    falcon stick & suit
of lightning lined with secret scents: gifts of the
Black Sun
        to the Silver Morning: the minute before
the first day began! AND THE NIGHT IS PREGNANT WITH TEARS.

    . . .

There is no death, only sempiternal change
ashes eaten by the moon's mouth of dust and
the sun's sparks of germ fire lighting
stages of plants from ingested salt that

snakes multitemporal mind
to man whose crown of this same source is
prelude to another unknown king

    No death but
stages of becoming Being—the invisible
man whose hidden ecstacy makes planets wheel
essence of Light—who thinks all contraries into
complements & watches changes interpenetrate ocular
waves of seagreen, magenta clouds & winds of
royal purple
              ... to the sleep of Ra inside
mineral wombs and what sprinkles gold dew
                on eyes of dawn ...

    No time but hermetic dance of number
constant irradia and spiration—countless flown
            birds & one still phoenix

Thorn of the Air

On the   ... Madrid, last capitol of the silence ...

invisible   thru corridors of 9,000 lungs, wand/legged ladies
                protected from slow muffle machines

telegraph   which mysteriously commingle the clouds
                with you, city of the Uumm/wheel, city

—by moonlit   of suave chrome, above all: of breathless Lorca
                moons & Gongora shadows still roving, I see,

bark & twigs— the filly trees—straight as spanish truth!

a constant   ... El Paseo Castellana, 3 in the morning
heartbeat   —behold, this bluejeaned worker
transmits   apparitions sweeping the arboled pavement for
                cafe/heads to drink purely from these breathing

    Spain   ladies within & beyond you, that cross Two
                Capitols of the Silence: O pivot

connecting us   of evocation ... O mediation

to the schisms   of the marvelous! 1965, you are again:
of star & seed   first city of the western Serene!

    signed: the   open mouth of silence
american seer   that cups tomorrow from the thorn of the air!

The Flying Fix

As I write   The getting & losing of it
into   beer, my right hand
the secret   branches radiate from
      the sun . . . getting & losing it
some lion/   . . . going out from sun to seed to
tamer moves &   branch to fruit AND
makes light   BACK AGAIN
      . . . it's by losing *it*
stretch   *it* comes back!
beyond
Circle Pant   never question
      feel of sun & taste of
      light thru weathers & sudden
   while   heart/beats, fears sleep as
a winged   silence pervades . . . clear words
   Eye   O brothers!
flies free
from *snake/*   the brain melts away
into/bird

      SleepWaking by Heart/Din
. . . and east   heart of wheat, eye of beer
bound it   . . . the passing crowd asleep thinks
goes to   it's awake, but HA! no *questions* &
measure   LO! THE IMMEDIATE ANSWER!—enuf! or
      I'll lose it to say more—
the wind!

      they're selling socks, rattling
      tables, squeeks against the constant
      roar of the lion inside!

                 Paris, Taurus, 1965

Poem for John Hoffman the Poet

I take up my youth as
  if it were never
   worn out
and confront you, my friend
   across the attics
   where we watched
carbon monoxide clouds
   drench an afternoon
   America could not
       deny us
   though we had become
    strange beings
with *Maldoror* in
   our hip pockets
and the zohar
   obsessing me
to the middle of
   Saint Germaine
and no one can deny
   the great seal's
   enchantment
from which the dream
   of our native
    magics
  lured me
to the edge of
   heroin & roses
   of black stockings
those lustful girls
beyond our attic
    eyes
those sylphan witches
that strangled the
   serpent in our
   brains
turned into Arabs
  on hashish
   automobiles
when we walked

through the
sultry neons
soul mornings
tobacco tinted
from the cafeteria's
solemn
eyes
condemned
on a horse
shuffle
bridge
to the interstellar
spaces
between tarots
& I Chings
O lost angel
our eyes went
every which way
and learned the pig
from the doe
bedeviled the samitic
halting on the
thresholds of
cautionary
fire

Interjections

It is you, Maldoror, on deserted mexican hiway
a sick air of oil rise!
I'm mad—screams—I'm mad—SCREAMS!
the great white colored boy is raped at dawn

The green eye on my coat
loots the sun's paradise of green eyes
star caught in throat is a green eye
green eye is motley of greeneyed merchants
thru saharas of green eyes in melons, Green Eye
on Iman's inner racket ring, capital of world Green Eye!

I put you to sleep greeneyed living statue trailing corpses of
    crystal jizzm past sugar tropics rain and
black pearl
your one rival—greases—in a temple buggered by wolfbane!

        It is you, Christian Rosencreutz
in the surrealist star that cries with sphinx's bluefeet
triple dogmatism of apocalyptic night
the Rosicrucian horseman is butchered by Knowing Skulls of Mount Atlas

The world is very sad   a corpse

        It is you, Hermes Trismegistus, mixed up with the tutuguri
great cocks of knowledge are ript open by underwear
I have long since declared war on the adepts
the destruction of the world is an accomplished fact
I write from my head twisted in sirenGlass   invention   lies
        tortured   A Blade in the mouth of Invention TURNS

    Poetry does not exist
    the poet listens, looks
    is a receiving machine
    making what he sees

    poetry is that sword
    cutting the street from its asshole
    if I lie it is because poetry's truth is
        a mysterious lie

    poetry is made thru makers
            tuning in
    poetry is a quest of dead makers
    poet is living Ice!

    fires out of corpses!

    poetry doesn't mean anything because
    it is superior to life!

let the tree shaped minion pinion the wonder of drugged dogs
  fly the chasing lions ogre to ogre my forest reclines
bemused among tall ladies if the swamp
    the sierras alive with flagons from the wailing wind
     I wound up with the worn's desire
     and slip on the precipice where planets reel
      I am cryptogram of fantasy
none but Analogy rules disparate harmonies
     Heraclitus returns bleeding the dream
        Opiates recap my promise
      unveil the synagogues of chance
       spur window where the child smiles the mountains to death
The first day is creations's spell over ether
     American Blood be hailed!
     Poe goes through walls with dangling beauty's pall
     Have thee understood subliminal mind sur-limned
      Vanishing women appear with white wolves
       Our friends on the wave of corpses
        I am the light of the world secret as any day
       the mystery of all the days the night is a squeezed lemon

THE BLOOD OF THE AIR

1970

for Nancy
      at the secrets
   of the marvelous

■ ■ ■

TO THE READER
          I am not the I who writes,
but the eye is ours that parts the fire
in things unseen and then, seen.

I Touch You

I touch you with my eyes when you lie under spiders of silk
I touch you with my one hundred headed giraffes too secret to be seen
the rods & cones the morning covets awaken you
with my touch of tobacco eyes
and you rise from the snail's bed of tubular hair
I touch you with the breath of jet planes
and they are gone elsewhere to touch you too
I won't have you touched by sordid saints
I touch you with the hour that drips scent
snared from the chain of immaculate lice
who avenge themselves forever on the holy of holies
I touch you with the wind heaving the breasts of the morning
I touch you in the overcrowds
and they vanish
replaced by all the women who resemble you
and I touch them with the eyes of the sun

Annihilation of priests
I touch you on the threshold of the totem
carbon salt on the breath of the world
I touch you with my intricate rose superior to the fog
I touch you with heart strings of the veiled mountain
whose magnetic moment is the sight of us making love
I rend your skirt by the wind stolen from ancient castles
your legs secrete the essence of wheat
and your ankles brush the wing of crow
Your lips touch alchemic gold torn from the femur bone of poetry
whispering through archives of your smile
that beguiles the oracle who has a headache to change his legends
I touch your earlobe with the fatal elegance of the peacock lip
your convulsions gallop my heart of the rose hermetic and flushed by goats
    sighting prey
I touch your nipples
that touch heaven that is all of you touching me
the temple of your hips

the morning glory of your sex
the miracle of bedsheets and the sacrament of sweat

Rhythms of your thighs are the music of the spheres

You are more beautiful than the black buttocks of dawn
and all light has been given to veil you from the murderers of love

I touch your presence undressing the furniture
whose cries fill the distance between us
and you shall hear
when I touch you with telepathic tendrils
for then I'll come into you the light of the waking dream

■ ■ ■

You wait you wail
Across the silences
That are a struggle in the world
Obstacles said to be conjunctions of Saturn and the Moon
Objects—telephones—are taboo
Taboo the sky curled into leaden pillars
Taboo the river of racing horses

The sun spits on my fingers
Your little finger completes a sentence
Solitude is a flame of sleep
Jungles fold me in passionate bird omens

Where are you

The page is turning against me like a wave of horses
I'm unsteady on this continent
That throws its chains around all of us
As if we weren't here
Orbiting like apples through galaxies of desire
Your countenance in the clock I map
And your hands brushing the hair invisible
Step by step we come closer
To the Thunderbird's retreat
And beauty cries from a lacerated heart

Altesia or the Lava Flow of Mount Rainier

You are come to me like fondling depths I'm at the Pont-Neuf
Say I shackle and unshackle the meat drippings of art
A threshold of owl eyes spanning Mount Olympus
Turning coat tails and hood menageries of certain Parisian streets
The grave look sizzling pages of Nicholas Flamel's lost book

I would free the prison snarling from your feet

Your smile is my hurricane
And the ache of traversing San Francisco with guillotines of history
At every intersection North Beach to Mission Dolores

A gilt-edged XIXth-century edition of Edward Young's *Night Thoughts* opens in
    your hair
           What if it were
My turn at blindman's bluff and you were "it"
Running over a gigantic mirror
           On a cow field in Normandy

Blue Locus

It's here the glove attacks the hand
Everything is splendidly distant
your torso carved out of daylight
on the screaming horizon I've ceased to hear
because you secrete a whisper and the clouds tremble

The squirrel you feed is the familiar of halos
trailing your thoughts from the spirit lake
blue locus
promising the unknown on a hike to the woods

There must be a playroom of totems
under the lake you raise with the key by which you read my lips
On the fur road you travel
I'm to steal the squirrel's eye
... which is how the sun looks when asleep ...

and nail it over the photoglyph
in the space where you've cropped your head off

I want to play fanatically over your daylight
see the thunder-bridge return to the font
and bring you to where the dream emanates
through the paper-shackling reality
full optics
drenched with the juice of chance

O my lady of combustible cameo
your mouth of the northern lights
doubt's ease
and our blistering profanations
no more answers
you are writing the poem
who burn me with your shadow
that your body veils wet arrows
the birds that circle you
         breastplates
  for the army of love

The Talisman

Only for those who love is dawn visible throughout the day
and kicks over the halo at the pit of ocean
the diamond whirls
all that's fixed is volatile
and the crushed remnants of sparrows travel without moving

I find myself smoking the dust of myself
hurled to the twilight
where we were born from the womb of invisible children
so that even the liver of cities
can be turned into my amulet of laughing bile

Melted by shadows of love
I constellate love with teeth of fire
until any arrangement the world presents

to the eyes at the tip of my tongue
becomes the perfect food of constant hunger

Today the moon was visible at dawn
to reflect o woman the other half of me you are
conic your breasts gems of the air
triangle your thighs delicate leopards in the wood where you wait

FLAMING TEETH

. . .

Open your head of cisterns
Let fly the soft iron imbibing your mummy
This is the golden age
Walking overnight across the united states a state of mind like any other
Open your head of windmills
Let fly the queen of spades and the masked man of the sabbat
Be friendly to Cotton Mather take ether fly past the moon
Open your head of sallow dreams
Let fly the first mare the one come from the Azores
The second mare shall wear her breakfast as a turban
The third one the third one shall conquer Asia with icecream
Make up your mind whether to turn black or red
I kick over a high-rise apartment in my room
And what do you do steel eagle
Is the waterfall in your eyes burning
But a moment now and the hands of empire shall wither
Having dug the graves of the future the poor shall be walking in mailsuits
I have a window eating fog there's a riot on Alcatraz Island
The streets of chinatown are still adventurous I met an opera singer in my raw fish salad
She was on her way to sing Puccini to the Vietnamese
Open your head and find Narcissus there and strangle him it's perfectly legitimate
Let fly the churches of memory they're only prisons anyway

. . .

San Francisco melts as I come together
There's no need for music
I calm the waves of galactic eyes
We are everywhere at once
Like the fond palm leaves of my childhood
That broke from my breast of stars
O night of incandescent water bugs
Tulips dahlias and lupines hunt the bread of rain
"The Three Graces" in my father's garden magnets of my brain

Their faces light up the pool of nirvanic stratagems
Dissolve into the blood of the air

Fireflies and tiger lilies crash on white horses
Through the cruel landscapes Mrs Radcliffe's Pyrenees have their throats of bandit
    geography
Slit open by the fetid atmospheres of demonic chemistry
The vengeance of the Adepts may be at hand for those who blew up petunias
Palingenesis be my watermark
Whatever you mean Overthrow the world
The slap of Urania across reality's face
These gems of violent youth trickle down the nude breast of the woman I love
Are the thunder pins of water
Stephen Schwartz says I resemble an iguana
We chance encounter ourselves in slanting parks of San Francisco
The Ibis bird our talisman
As waves of little fiery lips lap up our ancestors
Under the eye of Horus Tremendous Convulsions
        We shall go out
                Transparent as the Devil

                ▪ ▪ ▪

The maginot line of poetry has not been invented
Working on railroads of Hymettus honey the traps are set
This wavering pinnacle to transparent fire bleeds on alembic water
Giantess o giantess
Your husk of sleep
Stretches my burning skin
No one is free
This area of freedom opens the basilisk's belly full of rotting books
Priests of literature float under the Ganges
Mahatmas descend from their hotbeds with the rattling skull
With zabaglione soaked in meatball sauce
Chinese mustard leaks from their temples that's all
Are we going through the door where the dead smile smiles of dolls
Manikins come alive
Their livers suckable as plums and raging stars
A garment flows on Grant Avenue

Forever to trap the visiting collars
That broke teeth on holy breads
Lucky money changes a monocle for a rose of salt
Genius pins us with the tieclip of despair
Joy beckons revolutionary ladies for the grand éclair
Two steps back or forward it makes no difference

. . .

With the opening of light in my soul
What more and how I swim free except the whole cemetery rise with me
There are no heights in the sparkling islands
My flesh rolls into the first refuge
Across the dawn's belly
Also opening along with the cranking metals of the city
Its soul of splintered being
   Its knobs of celestial systems
      And its look of wizard pigs

Hope rules out the equipoise of kings
I run into my friends coming out of drugstores which always know the time
      according to comic gorgons
That slip as powders into the air of imaginary bombs

The toilets are sleeping
And the fist of charms runs down streets deserted by its martyrs
Where one day
The cruel Whip shall find its anvil to wed the Dawn

Ephemeris

The room has lips to speak antediluvian wishes
         cloud wing of forest
                  carbonic eye from the sea
The child has lost his way and found
His human breakfast table fast by the coral shore
Morning scales the mountain
With the palpitating flower I found in my mailbox

unknown hydra service
aerolith express

The conjurations at noon on the streets of the most industrious cities
For the advent of purple arachnids
For a rain of butterflies
The simultaneous apparition of flame-lined ladies from the cedar beds of the future

X Magician
at once to seed the air
with musk giants
Clouds grow so softly under your skirts
I can watch the children climbing the diamond temples at every corner
And there's a taste of bituminous wine
For the solar incubation so rarely conjured
But for your hair shedding the stars
O little girls of the forest of cities

Out of My Hat of Shoals

Out of my hat of shoals
Mixed ladies in a park of seals
Transvestite fire and wink of water
Green flame rapes the garden tulips
Trees of nonsense bend their songs
Lips of clouds and kites of pain
I'm at a shower of windows
All the houses are made of rain
No more speed   we float
I'm happy with hermetic games
The toys of sleeping mathematicians
Triangles and compass of water
Theorems beyond reason
Hypnotic ladies read the future with the sweat of roses
I comb the stars
And they undress the moon with their nipples
The hunt is on
No one will ever sleep again
Sweet music of epicene bodies
All is pregnant with mystery

And the idols have been eaten up
Marigolds fume in the night
The day is locked in a box at sea
The sun has finally married the moon

Smile Berries

My lines of light fungusstone of hatemill and showers of love
Beyond these categories
Finally no name
Avalanche of scent
Pungent cinnamon spray
Pumice foam flower

Fear not children to skate
Through your happy dart of a wish
Even if it kills your parents
Better to hurt the dead than salt the young

We're off into ourselves
Every moment is light
I eat the sun I scale the moon

There are diamonds through the lattice of perfumes I steal from your hair
Wild apples war on the pickers
Their hands scorched by flames of white juice

The cherries will never fall except through baskets
And all the markets empty with human products

The better to drink them with I say
                              Smile berries for sale

Fantast

From a jet plane window I landed into an eighteenth-century drawing room
Where the Marquis de Sade and I were of one mind tasting pineapples
Cameo brooches burst and showered us with pomegranate fumes
From the wrists of Doctor Mesmer little commercial empires sprouted sent on slow
    boats to Boston Harbour

Where I'm smoking Copley Square by the laughing wheels of the trains of totemic
    beasts
Spirit-lined
I proclaim the empire of molten man one with all his precious stones
The trees of America light up the specters of Cotton Mather
Happily we shall live my hair burning the snow
My eyes burning forever over the Rockies Hello Chief Seattle

The Faery Chambers

The stereophonic angelic beauty à la Landini
O to be back in the frost-bitten middle ages
And away under the smoldering carbons
Spitting with Grünewald's demon
In the rose-soaked nights of the patient alchemist
Guido Guerci another sicilian subtly flooding the north with the *theoria* of colors at
    Isenheim
My eyes at the vision of diatonic numbers Blue the wind
Crimson the flight
Green the whorl of recalcitrant ladies
The dip harmonies
Harp honey
Oh for the slow tambourines I hear in the belfries of Adepts
The high seriousness of Basil Valentine's *Triumphal Chariot of Antimony*
Never again in chemistry until Fulcanelli
All writ by The Master "A"
                    across the façades of cathedrals
On the parvis am I again
The daily news cracked open from ecstatic faces at Santiago de Compostela
This is very dark my pitiful rams
And there are heavy ferous boots ferous horses ferous wars were preached
Everything went down the draining nose of Pope Innocent the Third
And Alexander the Bull gave the coup de grâce where gnomons
                    lurked in Fra Pacioli's double-column book-
                            keeping machine
The Emperor Frederick Secondo revived the ancient questions out on that parvis
Turning on the stereo record
                        beat of my heart to their harps

Seattle

I'm passing through this city with a smile of smoke
There's no one around but giant plastic tubes
Eat the mountain and slay the dragons
It's all the same slipping over venomous skirts on fire
The tubes whisper El Dorado with neon haematoids for teeth
Little homunculi and spaghetti dining cars
Dissolving dollars
I'm passing out in this city where the streets are jangling metaphysics the epidemic
    future propelled from Antares
I'm ordering sauerkraut with legs
Because I'm absent minded about the celestial weather
Very chilly between the ladies' chinchilla and her eyebrows are full of dragon books
The leaves of which I won't say spill but leak petunias
Better to take an apartment in the mountain at a high rent from the absent landlord
Stop Gorgeous Volatile
No one'll get out of here if I can help it without committing guilt without relish
The rites of guilt I say
The rites of guilt come with cans of soup and crisp gardens
Slain under the snowdrift pain Vetch the gorilla his name

    ■ ■ ■

Little hole of black hallucination on the wall
Tell me your secret bone of wisdom
Stuck as I know you are
               Little black hole in the wall
Within the salt essence of reality
And if you don't
The craters of all the women I've loved shall throw their veiled lights on you
And into oblivion you go

        Sibyl
Who opened her breast of infinity
The great gaping thunder flared its edible diamond
The sirens of her eyes surpass those of our ears
The place of love and the place of transmutation have met in the igneous air
Buildings have toppled into cups of grenadine or wine clouds
I have brushed feather sparks of blonde hair and discovered America

．．．

The mosque of your eye has exploded
Cathedrals with holes where shine the popes in their abortion of winged doubles
Your feet spread like vibrant chords over rustling plastic dolls
Bleeding american flags planted into your eyes knit with nazi stars
Leather brassieres wave through the universal televisions
Erupting Mount Rainier Popocatepetl and your eyes
Until the world's secret magicians yell
          "Please mend the buttons of my eyes"

Fall down with yogic tantrums my viper
Stare into Fifth Avenue through the flesh of Vietnam tingling with communist hair
     smuggled on airplanes from Java
Go back into the future
Watch the wind suck up the Kremlin
Get to work under the crotch of His Holiness Baboon Baby
Get high at the suntan hideaway of the Presidential Arm
Trigger your blood with toothpaste and vanishing paint
Commune daily with the columns of Graeco-Roman America

Into your slit-level underwear of the paranoiac cowboy
Dance lightfooted into your eyes
Look back into windows circling your heart of Indian beads
This is the end of silence you say
Sitting on all sides of the Atlantic facing the Pacific

Behemoth on the waters goes by
Advertising the lost books of Messiah Jesus von Heigelhauffer
Who is very interested in LSD rosebuds
NO EXPLANATION printed on suction cups of the mountains of the earth
Announces
               "Heaven is last night's orgasm
               Save yourself by finking on the Earth to the Moon"
                    AND
"Be sure to get yourself plenty of pocketsize torture machines made by humanoid
     toads
Who've computed themselves into a multiple population bible
Awash
With the bottle tops of your eyes"

Horse Angel

This word or this image
Whether the immense void to be filled from the ancients to now
Or the nightmare mane staring with crazy hypnotic starving eyes
Out of the oftseen painting of Blake's friend Fuseli
Don't know
But am tied to a thousand grecian pillars their horse nostrils migrating
And the stillness does not inflict any ice on their great hairs

      An upside-down Golden Fleece

The horse pervades
Horses superior to machines
Horses lighted with blue oil flame from the factories
It falls on them
Like an atom bomb on any andalusian field
It explodes not
Just the blue oil flame that's its metaphor

Horses watch me from my travels and metamorphose into mules
Transmigrating continents
      The donkey at Tangier
      And his burro on the road to Tamazunchale
      The road mendicant who was a giant of solar light Blind Indian
      And the moorish woman with the campesino straw hat sitting on a bag of
         esparto grass
All horse cultures
And the horse in dreams!
If I could speak of their manes hanging like metals
Hoofs tapping the rocks
And that wild look straight ahead in a fertile valley
                        the sun

The Comics

Cussing
the men are going home to work
on sleeping horses
and automobiles come alive
and return to the factories

wearing lingerie and makeup
Steering wheels chrome fenders and gears
leer at the computers
in the outer offices
and the engines—ah those seductive engines—
get into black boots and thrash the clouds
rushing through gargantuan windows the pistons are eating
with anthropoid teeth

Tonight Burned with Solar Slime

Tonight burned with solar slime tonight flung from the space station tonight purveyed by lugar vendors tonight the umbilical cord of this torrent of words.

You are no more the sinister angel but the white killer dressed in carnation milk. Your 12-year-old lips refuse the black dinner and the nun you raped is severely punished by the mallet of madness. I swim free. Nevertheless. Exiles. The tough nut of the night bolts the window on my dream more personal than what you think you may become or ever were. Pea brain is the star's octopus sucker or is not to be disturbed; to sleep, a poet Awakened on the shed of super-malachites and the luminous lodge *gained* is an entry to the beard's fame.

The hook of the telephones of the bed tear out your song "Cruelty annulled" O pincer of the invisible become the concrete layer of immortal conundrums.

I dedicate the rant blocks of New Jersey to the phony canals of California and viceversa; the solemn melancholic towers of San Francisco join their armless tomatoes to the floating cisterns of Seattle which I imagine carve the totems of Columbus Ohio through a visible network of telepathic geometry *That landscape on fire*. The mouth of black men forever sealed with heraldic signs and the snobbery of lost kingdoms found themselves New Life at the moment of supreme sacrilege when the blue iron teeth of false messiahs return to reign over the Potomac, long exploding its impure timber through the universal face owned by 100,000 poets I am or can be if only you, serpent from the inner mines, unload your main highway through the same state with no stop signs tattooed on the absence of public statuary. Though the state is perfect if gone to by the road that can not end ever into you, eternal sleeper, who awaken in the automatic trance: this trajectory to everywhere I oracle, mania outfield pitched to the cyclone's rebirth.

Flaming Teeth

The earthquake slivers
The broken nails of the nazis
Mister Fly and his obsidian mask
My father on his razor
Basalt nightmares
Megalithic godplanes click the xylophones
My wracking spit spits
Words are magic beans
Children of the flat-faced musicians
Cross the street into subtropical ice
Manuring down your hand split a hundred ways
By the onyx of baptism
Stop
I'm climbing
To genocide the look of you
A thousand shacks
Human faces
Synthetic clouds
O for the slaughter America pinned on its bottom
I'd give up the rasp of Europe
Beatific visions sprawled on coat hangers
And weigh the silence with real screws
The fists of dawn
I'm still too intelligent
Become waste of years
Cruel whistling from under the snow inside the floorboards
And asleep drugged poet
You're safe striking the buttocks of the dream machine

Endless
Filth
Phanes

With the 24 electromagnetic

With rich tongue doorway briar and the lost look of Astatara
With bleeding pens
Dracula coins are the final exchange
"M" on all the rooftops signs the invisible with your blood imperial

And no more tempests in the tombs
Put them to sleep with the war angels
Which are all the angels

■

I'm a monster in my work plates
Over glades of dark statues that churn your retina priests of the Drag
And the dust I clean my sugar with
Knock down smoke over the everglades I'm american as rusting rain poltergeist
    salami
And a hundred tongues at once
Bumble Bee Heaven's my name
Cycling in graves
Little Joy Rider stuck her prehensile gibberish
Into the orbitic Tilt Mechanism freely bestowed by the papal party
That secretly seduced the swollen ash
From which six billion shadows stood up
Every dictator I've invented
And dried up the oceans

Drifting in my green dope cellar dream
Mother of black immaculates and sneezing scapulars
With the senatorial poets elect
With sting ray for breakfast
Juggling the clouds and weeping O the mystery of so many centuries

Art with its capitols
Imitating animal sounds
Went by
For this disquietudinous feather languishing infinity on a pedestal of shoes
All the images of Jesus were slapped together like Israel
And all was cool in the opium fields
Panama was still born from eagles of Hydra
There were so many birds bursting the hinges of Our Lady
She was hallucinated on the clever spot the Son chose
The Electric Decretal Caesar-christus

In and out of the valley of death
The valley of death
Little invisible bibles saying "How do you do, are the rare climates moldy today?"

Just then the surgeon general master initiate
Slunk from his vatlined shroud of history
Imhotep—Voltaire—his name—
Would you believe it?
I'm going to go to sleep

■

I shall say these things that curl beyond reach
A fatal balloon
Resolving riddles
It's pure abyss-crackling vortex

And silence opens her lips very much like arson

■

Tomb rise
And it sees a vision of beauteous sexual bags
And the caravan of flutes drops its melons over the sands I am not
Into the fog I am
The infinite I become
With mad hands scraping the jewel of my hideaway
To rise to the black pinnacle Roman empires of thought
Fly down fast and around Amitabha
A succession of literary images cabalas insecticides
Nail your heart here

Stone windows grate their teeth
And the processions are inside secret rooms
The death ravens chatter

I won't let the precision instruments bite me
I'm obsessed by death fantasies

There's this silken road
Down here I can invent the moth to kill memory
Flay it alive
With gasoline wings
There's another road out of these rooms
Into the streets of elegant gawkers
Cafes have electric chairs now
And this is no road to travel

And this is the road to oblivion happiness
Cutup on the unknown and another acre of poems

Musick?
Here come the flagons of Isidore Ducasse
The speed which is happening
                              And the grave compassion

                    ■

The riot was mainly in my mind
Soon I won't be here stretched out on pillows of imaginary iron
And the evil jinn leering into my dreams
I'm vanishing like vanishing letters
I can't bridge you reader you'll have to find yourself
Going on slow as the blood I see drop over us

          ■

                Deflowering of technology
                Beauty the suicide
                Ice fevers
                Wrapped around your head
                Hers on fire

          ■

Even if supersonic sounds feed me with ithyphallic diseases and the roars of Aboreas
Was plain chant less tedious?
Answer me
Don't just stand there like the Tetragrammaton
This is truth
I'm obsessed by death fantasies
Husks
And the *Night Thoughts* of Edward Young

Death is a pineapple in the cake of death
Which wing?
I deny death I don't know why
Ask the swans who are rocking me under the chair forest

The dragon I saw
Small as my Jupiter finger

Looking back with miniature flames
The whole middle ages
And vanish quickly
Beauteous apparition I was thinking of war A poem
Beauty must be reckoned with

Penetrant Tumors

This is the U.S. penetrant tumors chopped with metal livers
The load of fairy fingers gesticulating war and the clothes wearing the people
Riding around the moon
They dream they dream
Their throats parched with dollar madness
This is the U.S. machine state
And a picnic in the fog is worth two in the vulva

Take a blood bath for breakfast
Drop the sirloin tip from the clouds
I've found the nut & bolt scratching the tide of suburban effluvia
Anesthetically wet
Let this never rest wild cock
This is America the enormous cemetery never to be discovered
But the slabs are singing cybernetic energy hydraulic energy

Don't eat the nylons off the women
Be firm and take over the corporations with dog pudding
India is looking away and Latin America is sleeping again
The Roman Empire keeps crunching into us in spite of the void
In spite of the alcoholic negotiations
In spite of melting candles on the Potomac
I'm patriotic as banzai
I identify continually with the hair style of George Washington
The filthy lucre games are almost ending
The invisibles are starving their unborn children at satellite stations at Rome
Religion is just a big dumb con
Laugh your fill under the Papa's belly who has designs on Brazil
O well the idiots still dance to the technological arts
Heraclitus condemned most of them to the smoke chamber
What do pygmies chant on the silent hour telepathy TV?

Back to the essential cope
The U.S. is a work state on wheels
And I can't stop smoking imaginary French gardens put on with masonic ceremonies
I'm wondering about the Great Seal and the *novus ordo seclorum*
The beautiful white mice in John Adams' elevator
Forever Our Fathers decree the classic sibyls
And the vengeance of Jacques de Molay
This is America a thousand islands of Gitchi Manito
Little progress since Iroquois cabals
The profits are yogic pins thru puritan cheeks
And the slobbering alcoholics
                              flagging

New Year 1969

The Analog

And the sea moved over the terrace into my marble stomach
that I saw the cleft on the rock disclose the Mason's Word
upon which were built the crumbling remains of Onn
treasure shored up from my inner eyes
the victuals medieval cathedrals secrete secretly
for the likes of the adepts
who smile through the velvet fissures of the centuries
that are Waves & Blankets of Stars
under which we are given, if we burrow long enough
for the hidden script, the Key to the King's Shut Chamber
that vanishes into the night hot with luminations
re-seered at the ice trance permitted to the high flyers
who with the correct gesture
at the right time know the precise moment
the Zodiac favors the conflagration of water and
the stillness of things about to become
when fire reabsorbs its opposite
the snarling snake before the plumage of the perfectly secured Peacock
Perchance the wave falls prematurely and spoils the little work
the Operator must beforehand arm himself with traditional shields
so that translated into the occult veins of his visible anatomy

the fox & falcon hoods spill volumes and sweat beacons
to throw him into the path which has no way up or down
and is never either way to the Ravaging Ferocious Mountain
... Ah what am I saying that my lips might be burned by angels and sirens?

World without End

Now I will take hold of the wind as the tons of weeds tumble from the mouths of fountains, and I can not imagine any bodies but angels yes. Always the wind bears the breasts of the bottom stairway, my heart shall be in the roar of attention, attention to the open flood gate, only no other voice shall mewl. For the person shall be submerged & surpassed by the Head the talking Flower of Pure Vision. Let us enter the wind's mummy as if it were not less than Genius, as it is I affirm the trembling lyres of Lycophron are greater than Homer's. Let this pass through the pharaonic knot prepared in the communal future where the winds shall unlatch all the leaves.

I spurt the heavy odors of the sphincter's hair. Together the prairies of America are cornholed into the mouth of China which is greater & less crowded than Portugal for the scene of the eventual leap of frog-poets into the waters of the wind. They spill their craps & leagues of white mystics this second into your laps, my country pens & fowls from under the Echo I ring!

The dragon is real and more beautiful than the photos ever and invisible medieval cards which did not depict its flash of jeweled vision. The pearl of the dragon is the splendor of the night, night from the beginning the foremost declaration of the sun's freedom. To burn thee black, my pretty flame, all women are undressed before his loon laughter. He spits the bible that's read too fast to be seen and is the invisible tapestry of the coming race. Already the burning neons foam under the beds of the cowardly vampires whose holy grace spins the office of lies inverted from ashtrays of the mendicant orders. Don't be fooled again by the leech window from the swinging dead bodies lapped up by members of the mystical trust; their banks smolder under the backward resurrection which is sweet as ether. I continue to lure the wind's eye I am one with the wind. There are no other friends. The avalanche begins!

Fog from under torpor's side and its veins above my hand raid the chrysallis dawn drenches with the tears of the machine I wash by the orifice of the caldron where magicians lie cut by glass and ply the trade of trailing buddhas, where the orient maneuvers the moon's leg twisted on rails of honey. Bring the sarcophagus of the immortal wail. I unwrap the box of fears and nail the corridor of nude wonders below the street that smiles. Black fire slakes the fist of water below the winter loneliness into the spectral slum you made, my chicken lair of beauty's corpse.

Horn of the summer. Soon the immaculate harvest. Two precious stones too bright for any eye. Hear the silence I vanquish. Note the lugubrious hymen devoid of its rasp and bleeding the milk of the Sphinx.

I have come again to the gate where the pearl water kisses the mine of light inscaped with the flower of entrails I dreamed last night. The waterway vanishes when the pure font ceases in the crepuscular vine dinner of the day we abandon to enter the true temple that is some secret inner night never more revealed than by the flower of water breaking over brains, the hands I print with the pain erased with enigma & smile of the pure land shake.

Let it be said on the hysterical sublime of this moment: open all the doors to tomorrow's liberty. On the flight of my eyes from the depth chamber's heart attack stroke of the light forever below, the stomach I dreamt is to be purged of extraneous influences who came in my youth and undid my clear sight of the dragon rite.

Peace is knocked over with a slumber foot, the match hair, pumice of bleeding liver and core of orange light. Fingers of soul dash the flames from pure saliva's soap, my life at the sacrament of black underground river POETRY THE PUREST LIFE. The world is irrevocable, transmuted today, and never shall day claw me to sleep but night wake the salamander's pickaxe. I cleave open the paper wall. The blood-stained fingers are pushed to the vanishing full pardon of the river and I am salved with the unflickering beacon roaring from the magenta whorl floating through the veil of Hermes Trismegistus, the original voice come from under the wink of 40 centuries. You curl the lip of ziggurats, you warp the palaces of resurrection: the glorification murder is resplendent with the purifying death whose nose moves my hand through the chinks from the underworld. Hail, Prince of Panic, I tumble you under the war bit.

Newspapers disappear, current vices appear as smoke tissues salute the bodies of the enlightened before the past began to draw the curtain of dust on the total eclipse my contemporaries imagine. I am beginning to eat light, straight *and of the corner stone* sprung up, grail-of-the-betel-lady, swinger of the nymph conch veined with the pest, thunderwing who comes clothed with high noon. I vanish to start the sun to roll its eyes from the subterranean chant that is and knows no name, Mystery of the clock that prunes the transmutative glance Look out of weir window and glyph god from under the vomit's shield.

O delicate white fang O child of roe O caught in your beautiful knot of blood I set you free for the thunder's kiss and the white tree, madrone of your first year of the kill. Suck the bark to your star's ease that illumines One, the cavern above the storm Two, the desire which is desired, and Three phases from virginal to torture. This is my valentine too warm for the mails of the spirit and so I send it on a lunatic screen made of shimmering paste over invisible bridges.

The secret doe takes up the skin of forests and converts them to the willowy convulsions of Irawaka *and before* when all the machines were made of floating cream black ice and the husk of our fruitless tears. Certainly in the future I care nothing for it. I am writing this now for you, then. You keep creeping out of the rose lip, tobacco horrors and the lust for drugs. At the terminal cage I free you I repeat out of the sad sadism of left and right. No more self-inflicted ants, you're close to the coiled element, the supreme root of fire.

All the mancies shall be mine who grew the trunk from the vibrated seed sent from the sun, though it traveled around the hospitals of hatred before it touched the magnetic stone basin and toppled into place under your belly's surgical history O poor astral anatomy so long bludgeoned by occult blows. I'm on to the whole con, sweet sadists, you don't stop the eternal loin from speaking its ocean to be. I can barely see you mixed up to be chopped like so many valentine hearts by the fierce blades that I roll out of the black star!

Beat of the interior fleet, I unveil your head grown from the four children of Horus. The Lion driven out of Heliopolis, the masquerades of the apocalypse, the whispering vision and other conferences of the children of light shall be noted once here along with my return to Kohl Castle and the rock where I raped the sea. The mirrors recorded everything. They wear the flesh of the Lion's cage, he's freed from the object and his lair sacred, the only shrine I find, but thee, marvelous child wearing out your torturers under the shade of blinding water IT FALLS

rolls over on its ear. I would spit on the foam and drive it INTO THE CRASHES!

POEMS 1970–1980

A Little Washington DC Dream

The Duc D'Aumal's cannonballs
Are being marshmellowed 370 years from their masonic inception
Now lie on the Potomac
The Duc D'Aumal's balls cannonaded
Split
Through mirror teeth Washington D.C.
Black City of white rectangular bits of fear
Blown fluff of fear
O the Duke of Aumal's balls are raging
Yellow vermin white houses of fear
And beautiful funky people
Diamond heart *D'Afrique*
Human blood human need
Black booming emotional vibes of life
White geometry of abstract cerebral death
I really saw at Fort McNair
In front of American General's mansion
A fir-tree *tied down* to a black coffiny box
Jefferson's phantom always rides tonight
There's a *solar splendor* burst from Eighteenth-Century Cannon of the Duc D'Aumal
I'm sure Citizen Lafayette was no dixiecrat

3 POEMS

. . .

On the plain
of the angels

the forked ribs
are sinuously
capering
the milk of their entrails floods a city

and the arachnids are dancing
out of our lives
the meat-eating shadows are riding
into your eyes

Blasted with rainbows
your agates are flying
and stilled on the black opal beak

about to tear down the sky

■ ■ ■

A gorgon of the language cabal
steps forth
as if an illusive nymph
of the pavement

but it's really a metallic dragon

As I hum over the bruised cloud city
the rainbow streaks
its fang of light
genius molds the footstool
where the giant's paths
are strewn on your foreheads
o marble kingdoms
thrashed from the jungle's thigh

■ ■ ■

Flying beasts
are riveted on the air's toiling
crystalization
where lutes are hung
on a field between blue and whispering gold

Here's Merlin's moulting cage
also emblazoned
in the crevices of boiling minerals

The philosophic hand is certainly
a glass reflecting makers

Here the grasslined face
gulps a liquid pearl from the gutter

Here heady garbage glitters
through the sand its own perfection
between minute star-specks

and the infinite calling the grains . . .

■ ■ ■

The Hand Moves the Word Flies

Charred on its river
Baked in a snake's riddle
Before the wind draped its buttered flanks
Maple dew crossed the street
As a conniving jungle
Even if ten suits wagged their tails of men
The lost egret smiles and strangles the lamp-post
Meridians of wolfbane stretch mottled feathers
Plainclothesmen denude the blackened window of their geyser
Speed punctures the wheel of chance
With solitude

Liberty

Going down like the sun smoking a guitar
Like the sun coming up bandaged with positivistic swine reinterpreting the
    mechanics of a woman's smile
At the cleavage of priests' manacles redeeming syphilis the bureaucrat pilloried by
    the sunflower tribe
The first tooth to escape from a match box speeds my victim by its vine-dinner
    testicles between the Ebers Papyrus and the everglowing termite that is poetry
    emasculated by a fingernail of cookie shadows
The indwelling mirage plastered through every crystalline tobacco herd inside us
    vanishes by *the back door* fumbling with its sidereal zipper at the penultimate

veil reincarnating mankind as a set of genuflecting planets *mistaken*—in their
   wheeling-down sneeze addictions—*for symphony conductors* growing two heads
   from their backsides
I meet you on that sea-wave in a postcard dissecting out of its indivisible ray gun
   style of life the masterless master who sempiternally creates light with each whisk
   and thrust of a churning forest

And who carves
emitting
         the call
                     from the ice knot in the vascular furniture of his blood's cowhide
overthrowing all preceding stupidity

Luminous Lady

I begin to dream of you held in the whyfor of my fingernail
zooming the balcony searchlighted by femur glands
a new comet of chance catapulting morbid legends
Are you a glass stocking?
Is your name Azoth's poison?

We join
in the happy primal dance by forgetting music
Only the volatile image will do
as we go through the kaleidoscope castle raking together Paracelsus seering into
   Marx

Not only the Star Woman luminous within convulsions at the apex of your
   cascading dress
but the Crab imitating the baying dog
drink from these cups of your cigarette ash
At my snowbound leap to you from the table gardenias subsume hungry wood
Is this galaxy pummeled by heroic gestures foreign to your mythic mystery?

Your thirst for me wolf-spun from Antares (my clothes)
seems to flash back from the future of contracting *personae* the worm on the tide no
   longer beckons

Only Creative Violence Reveals the Beauty of the Marvelous

Why do you sit hurling metal monsters
When the sediment of human sidewalks croons under the sea

The fisheyed pyramid of lust
Is sprinkled with fumigation oil
The beast kept at bay is today's motto
Tomorrow's can't be read even by the seers (they're so furious)

Ready to halt the globules of sperm
That snake through sunlight on a wet crow
The kind the porpoise strikes from its cigarette case at the coming of our beloved
    heretics
Only they make sense this vaulted night I hate

We go out of corpses as dust shakes the canopies loose
Better another life than this corrugated barnyard
Better crocodiles chewing the transmuting lotus off the Nile than this nausea of
    prosaic noise
Nietzsche my friend how much you resemble *The Mountain Lion* in the kachina
    symbolique

So angry I summon something scuttling down below
How hard to hail this clanging rhythm
(the knife-drawn sulphurs of unitist vision)
One moment gulps the next heart-beat
Two wigwams siphon their variable sledgehammers
A shadow beckons to oblivion before the mother-cow of lingual serenity

To scream "light!" "light!" from my cradle you must admit Heraclitus I am one
    with you in the mysterious law governing the fist out of a rose bush

Only erotic love that stamen to sublime confusion
And the heartshaped tongue on the escalators of detached corneas
Only this look creating by osmosis

Only this girl I drink
Drink and eat for eternity

Only this castle built between our pyramidic paths shall make it

Only creative violence reveals the beauty of the marvelous

Panty Hose Stamped with the Head of the Medusa

Her thigh of succulent fruit and carnivorous gold
Through the tunnel of her flagellated ass deflecting midnight blue ink
A crocus in her mouth
I'm doing the Sun Dance in Iowa
Traveling by Iron Horse made of her petticoats of the Nineties
Buffalo Bill loquaciously sits beside me in a green conch seat
Out the window prairie fires in her vulva
And violet apparitions of suicidal Indians
These last days of the Ghost Dance Religion

We dream the goddess of gaslit back rooms
Her eyes of coral sand
Her plaster-of-Paris lips
Her art nouveau hair washed by pelican juice
Her purple cow hips
The jungle that's her vulva
Klondike snow sliding off her buttocks
The weather-vane rooster on her tit
Mother of darwinian apemen
Sister of frock-coated fish
American spinster fingering her lover dead a year in her bloomers
Plum-faced girl of the midwest

While the muse Evelyn Nesbit on her trapeze over Niagara Falls
A young satanic beauty fans herself with rich brocade of mother-of-pearl
Cameo images of her taking a bath
Slither through the mirrors of our millionaire minds
I'm dancing with her at the first private performance of Ravel's *La Valse*
She's an 18-year-old virgin
Sweating dew all over the world's most gigantic ballroom
The morning after I kick her father down an open elevator shaft
We're married a year later in Paris
We frequent Black Masses
Our grandchildren to be devoured by living buddhas

Between Sleep and Waking

If I give you my thirst
what I retain is your radiance from a carrot's foot
its mineral parabolas moaning
on the moon's trajectory
This way the garden's ego foils
the ogres of innocence
the wind in its light of gargoyle
mauve the flute of leaves
tangled at the mutating crater I call my muse
Through cascades of thundering snow
with giant fires on saucers the earth left hanging
from its last general orchestration
what I give you with my eye of solitudinous matter
you return with your left hand of laughter
as it gathers ocular pitches
scattered by black needles
over the storm of wooden eggs

Tobacco of Harar

for Penelope and Franklin Rosemont

Elected by the marvelous
whose beam shatters the culpable mirror
and rolling an aureate field of yesterdays
sirens wake up
dazzled by the mandible of vengeance
its thorn rushing to sight a tower ruined by battle-fires

The machines in the elemental garden vibrate the feathers of treasonable frontal lobes
where Stamboul was decreed exterminated by sadness
Octopus purple
slenderiffically combines mimetic birds coming out of a toy-house
with the scent of slightly burnished leather

burnished with the eye-flame
and the yawn of a desert

Nostalgia on its thighs
raids the park for hummingbirds
when I suddenly meet you, dispossessed,
acquiring exotic markets between the vertical branches of X

Weight

Rushing to hide you my death
from horns at the ice-cap
and fill you with plentiful thunder

   radiant spider
meets a cow encircling the earth
through its nautical ear

Knuckle-headed river
I operate you
with a pelican's bulldozer
   at the chant of a secret constellation (rigor
put back to its spontaneous kettle)
and smooth you out from the milking tooth of my death

BECOMING VISIBLE

1981

Redwood Highway

From the great laughter
This cage with the phlogistic eye of Bruno
With escape hatch of Ibn 'Arabi
Uncle Tom and silver wolves underneath amethyst
Doubled by acrobatic redwood trees sailing an ancient horn
Straddling wheat fields of your ear o mediums
The great laughter eternally turns crystal rays

The salt mines of Amon
Come to the jade fingernails
Grown from a branch of sodom's repeater pistol
Horns of the great laughter
From the prehensile tail of the harmonian future
The sleeping armors of Gilles de Rais pick locks
From the green corn dancing the abalone shells

The powers from out there on the western horizon of Walpi
The San Francisco Peaks blowing their tops
Runners from the Chumash sprayed
Teleported
Over sierras hot lands deserts
    To the dancers
At the blazing mirrors the great laughter treads
With volcano of feverish diamond
Across the sleeping beauty
Morsels of luna embedded to dream

To desire
Desire's seashell dream
Far from this groveling host fidgeting poisonous grates
Shamans at Mount Diablo touched by antlers of light
Invisible bears crowding the coast of almond shell vestments
I'm at the owl haunts of the sacral redwood grove

    A slice of Oregon
To be there
When the cave's luminescence is fraught with killer fangs
Curling stalagmites for a dinner of giants
Porous cadavers lean from turrets
Splash asian waters

Trapped here in Lemuria
The pink hoofs snarl
And part the sediments of a million years
Onto the ceiling the mole's absence
Inside the mountain's look of terror
The whirlpool entices to furious salt
Behind the trickling of sonorous bats
Murmuring minerals parade the air with magnets
Above the singular flight of toads
                              The meadow

Through crystals of lava circuiting thought
Whose harpoon burst battle
Are the wandering ciphers
Revealed solely in their own mystery
As if the air could blind us and yet the word assault
From three pillars *a landscape blown away*

Jet of sorcery
In the incendiary inflammatory night
Cocooned as if the jitters foamed three baseballs
Each tearing a mite's fire
From foxes marveling your eyesockets
Terror
Fear
That words succumb to the flaming pool
Black as love is without death
Deciphered after the highland jigs of the mind summit the scape
To the rigorous multiplication the one from which we spring
Rose
Fire of sex
On the subterranean trunk
Water
        Woman's diamond fire
Whose center is the high beauty of her sleeping truth
Whose shape explodes to open
And cover the night effulgence of lumens from whence we came
But for which she does not dance ALL to the secret roads
Each of us in the other
Weighted comically fearful

Until you
      Sirena Intaglio
Until you
      Iron Sylph
The *mor* thrashed by winds of her seashell intelligence
Until the fay returns
. And more still until the horizon is coupled
And walking toward you Medusa turning into crystal
In which is written the seven pure words
On the black fire
            Of violent velvet eyes of Amor

      ∎

With the caracole sluicely forming
So delicate careless
The alembic sleeve to the ladder
Climbing your *rig-ridge*
            rigorous nose
With an iron cloud
Plunging in a molten *phallicular*
With the molding sweathouses of the people above
To keep memory of you Yurok of the north
Albino deer dancers dream over Mount Shasta
On these Ohlone shores of the central dream
Moon dancing the sun
Owl clothes wave from the weathers of your ear
With the grizzly instudded in its mirror
The fasting forest obsidian
And concrete dream roads
Dissolve against the grain

Chance to dream wide awake
With the antelope-necked tom-toms
Whose sinews of silence project
The perfect Edenic Reunion
Parapet
To the crystal obscurities
The sea-witch glamour undulates

At the transmigration of the tropics
To the Manitou's ionization
Of the aurora borealis
Swallowing solar winds
And floating magnetically down your streets

Antelope dream hoofs
Vermillion sight
Through waves of lemonade seas ah Charles Fourier
The oneiric ear of the seer
By golden numbers from tongues of silence
Peels the electric seashell tonic
Dazzling with Mythos Rising
Grandeur of the black spectrum
Of the sunset's cloven renewal
And heart to heart
This crypt sets free the hysterical vampire
Whose laughter confounds all the deities

    ■

There are those inner circles of gloom
The skein of ancient revived virus
The awesome tail of windows strapped to the cellular history
This glance destroying walls
With a bow to the veil of phantoms
Depressive daughters of vanity
Stooped in revealable mysteries
Freud Paracelsus and cycles of gnostic suns
Parallel to the mechanical usages
And the coming of cursive script on the Micmac barks

Here in old Lemuria
The Oregonian stalagmites
Climb the ocean's ceiling over the Bay Area
My dream identical to Coit Tower
As Chirico's Rose to you
Whose kitchen in the garden recites the blazing legend

To the Great Transparent in Sothis
At the myth of the winds
To the red winged mermaid
On the wintry sea of magnetic clouds
The shamanic vertebrae tilt the golden filigree
With the runoff of sacred vowels
The consonants reverberate resinous spines
At this glance of resonance
Processional of sudden stag
With the snow queen of the northern lights
The look of haunted beasts
Slaughtered long ago through crystal flakes
Shimmers from the imaginal tropic
To a star field of birds
Whose cries paint the sonorous language

■

Siren
Sphinx
Winged Melusine
Under the whorl of the rock
Succulently firing lenticular clouds over Mount Shasta
The insect confabulations
Around the spinning web
Overlook desire
Sparkling the abalone shells

Gulf of a face through the lunar Cascades
And faces at Angel Island seen on Samoa
Branches of ocean
                    Tusk of eruption
Sea-bright by Venus
On the crest of the wavering look
Through Medusa's feathery dance
Before time emptied this vista of Monte Alban
        Stone temples the area of Los Angeles
I write on crumbling borders of salt and sea
With gong of tides across the Carib

Belching watery thunder
As if an Invisible put out the spirit lamp at dawn
Sleep-
        Flaking
To the hinterland
In a circle bound by shooting stars
Ears beneath the sands of sable dreams

.

            The running sores of black magic
            The wounds of white magic

A slow volcanic ash
Superimposes plumes of marrow
Within the window a crimson Coyote shows
To turn visible mysteries into webfooted mirrors

Deep into the erasures of glyphs
The mind leaps to quadratic foliage
Words silenced by glowworms
And visages of dim perception
Crashing to the rhythm of spermatic horses

The first glimpse recovers the lost siphon
From the zygote's ash tray
In the operational fire at the world's womb
The tempests define you and me
Tasting the solace of mint

Closed eyelids through the eternity behind us
This vast ring of the rising crystal
To swim into manta rays
Mentation of the vowel
To the sonatal leap
Hidden on the verge of the verbal jungle
A tarantula
Quaintly with a diffidence of speed
Retreats back into its hollow

On this road flexing muscular sinews
The stoned expressions of buddhas crack in their sediments
The anteater ways I stumble on
A panther lady on the fleeting disk
Words tumble
On the stretcher bearer's static muse

■

Red mechano-morphis
Slides across the path of wolverines
High grass over the sleeping factories
Night blooms beyond the plagues of day
Gnostic ideations pin point the Hegelian dawn
Minerva's arms beneath the streets
 Logo-machia the vital spark renews
Drizzle of vision
Behind the celestial masquerade
Solar catastrophes and the lunatica of wind
We reach the temple

 The sylvan whisper nightfall carves to raven thoughts
 Am I really of the butterfly clan?

To dream of you acorn wheel
The lean-to takes a breath of burning cedar chips
The old tobacco traveling the directions of space
 Air earth fire
And the wings of scopolamine
 Washo peyote *yana Cora*
Even to the crystal web of central dreaming among the Californias

Lemuria is a shade pink on green
The myth a hundred years old
Rolling out of the fog to the voices
Found divining "the lost land" in a Wintun grove
Transparent Shastine
Air holes at Castle Lake
The fruit towers of golden noctambules
Through layers of wavy snakes grown from the rocks

Shadows of chaos
Ride roughshod over the sinewy ways
Thorny the Great Iguana stares to the stone portals at Nayar
Where the moon closes the oven door
Of black oranges
Crypto-maniacally falling
Over the gangrene of the world

The Romantic Movement

to Nancy

The boat tilts on your image on the waves between a fire of foam and the flower of moon rays, these the flags of your dreaming lips. I'm watching Venus on the ogred sky and a continent in cocoons.

Soon all the butterflies of desire shall manifest o prescience of life becoming poetic . . . and poetry the incense of the dream. A street and a forest interchange their clothing, *that* tree of telephones, *this* television of nuts and berries—the air edible music.

King Analogue
Queen Image
Prince Liberty . . .
. . . Garden of imperious images, life is a poem someday to be lived: the feast of our hearts on fire, the nerves supplying spice, blood coursing a glow of insects, our eyes the dahlias of torrential ignition.

The whisper of the inter-voice to wrap you in the mantle of marvelous power, with the secret protection of the forest that falls asleep in fire whose ores become transmined only for love—all your steps will lead to the inner sanctum none but you behold, your shadow putting on the body of metaphoric light.

The stone I have tossed into the air of chance shall come to you one great day and exfoliate the original scarab, the carbuncle of delights, the pomegranate inviolate, the sonorous handkerchief of the Comte de Saint-Germain, all the reinvented perfumes of ancient Egypt, the map of the earth in the Age of Libra when the air shall distribute our foods, the sempiternal spectrum of sundown at Segovia (the stork carrying the golden egg from the Templar's tower), Chief Seattle's lost medicine pouch, our simultaneous presence in all the capitals of Europe while traveling Asia and listening to the million-throated choir of tropical birds, your lost candlewax empire, a madrone forest to live inside of, which we can wrap up in a set of "secret bags" and open on our wanderlust, the turbulent cry beneath the oceans, the extinct bird calls in a magical vessel Christian Rosenkreutz dropped on his way out of Damcar, beads of coral dissolving the last motors, the redolent eyes of first born seers, the key to the bank of sanity, the ship of honey at the height of storms through which we sail to new islands rising from the sunken continents and the bridge between sleep and waking we will traverse in constant possession of "the great secret" become transparent as a tear drop—*with no other work but the genius of present life.*

Bed of Sphinxes

A light opens as a street closes
against the bedrock of insistent glimmers
and your face talking to its cloud
Always the rinsings of milky flowers cry on the crest
where I'm a magnet gamboling with a drunken adept
There's a cloth of wine beneath us
the sugar of precipitous birds hands out rectangles of light
Racing out of town
the nerve veined hair swallows the road

•

The verb cunningly made
traverses the shattered lamp
on the stockings' shimmering key
The plate over the doorway
swoons with miniature flames
impersonating what I'm handed out of shadows

The day heaving straw giants
if you can see them
expects me in a wet mirror
With the middling haste of quest
and further questions
rumbling at breakneck speed
the cortex of history looks through
the tubes of its material horizon

•

The hand and spoon
gather themselves into a turbulent cloudburst
before the latch key from the advancing storm
takes leave of its gullies
with purple screams charging the table of water become
the ocean I hand you from an antelope beating
the stream of flies diagonal
to the fall of an empire and perpendicular
to the truss on fire with scimitars of breath

A war in the clothes closet is worth a panda on the moon
I am fluorescent
And you are a teardrop of infinite agate

Primavera

It is the oaken village that falls, splintered through a dust of visage where I gallop, no more flint than air, to think of cabalist hope: a universal alteration in the germination of planets.

But, the mystagogic chairs smashed in seed wars, I'm conceived again by the imponderables of total conjunction—even my shadow with another's that left its organs (sex-ploding suns) some distance from the translations of matter into an image.

This way the poem becomes an open sluice for darkness. Only the most obscure body is the brightest unity.

I catch hold of a train inside an iris.

Time at the window of maternal cosmetic, the high-heeled foot garlanded by a silken phallus spectates the forest where the uterine furnishings sink into drawers at bay from that twilight flashing in a mirror of dressing and undressing.

The preternatural identities beat the clouds from their barks, a child's chance look at the raging smolder of roses. Nearing sleep, this same wind rustles the void of blood-stained horses (my first cabals) whose galaxy dissolves *with a kiss* the victorious rescue of the palpable shadow streaming stars, her face: this bed, the undulant phantom: her hips.

We ride wooden horses
Always a desert marries the boiling water.

Becoming Visible

A whorl of happy eyes and devilish faces
struck out of antique sensuous paintings
twinkle from the knees and calves
moving slower than dream women

the hands are gesturing with violet blood
come from floating feathers
their sea anemone fingernails opening tropical fruits
(mango skins over snow)
and quickly rising to summer I meet you
walking in sateen boots over jewels of ice we spread for you

        ▪

With the fox to see by
subterranean rivers advance
from under an asphalt sky
Auroras you exhale
the scorpion poem between our bellies
the mint's pebble trickles down the three-thousand-year-old flute
washed up on a lemon-leaf bed
the way your look born of mollusc tears
mirrors the fins of memory in a dolphin's eye

        ▪

Ah that taste of liquid spoon
magnified from the forest's apple
and where your odors lie unfurling
comets' toes fire into orioles
(on their steps leave no traces)
twining my marrow's light
from your turning head of nervous lips
The stars dress up their furrows
whose divers sign you bathing
a torch of musk awakening my spark of fruit

Visibilities

Through the cotton balls of sleep
a table from my stomach
walled on the precipice by gossamer veils
the anvil hungry for its metabolic secret lights up the bobbing motors (apparitions
your fingertips silhouette the sky with)

There is a voice to your singing glance
There's a coriander leaf with a spiked foot
as the terrace sleepily descends to the water
I pick up embittered mica
rolling from a bed confused with your castle of hair-spun riddles
You are behind me as I rip up the pavement
palpitant as a squid on a roulette table
The black lines lead the white however you see the invisible tendril burrowing out
    of a cyclone
Deeply sacked below
a tulip raves among the murmuring metals
whose ravines reconstruct my life
from the flight of vegetable-crows

In Yerba Buena

The brush is not the mortar

Red fog in the night

Across the valleys neon materializes
into shouts and descries the ogre in the manor house
(occulted though he is)
and the house in sweet flames
The flying parapet
has winced
three times the jolly crimes

Tomorrow
the black village will rise
with turrets of jimpson weed
engraved on a mockingbird's geometry

Beauty a great invisible
walks between luminous slabs
the better to blacken them
for the powers of the manticore
and the village which awaits him

It is the night and dawn of Robin Hood and Marian

The remains of sicilian flutes have docked
the archivists are pleased
Metallic brains alive!
lutes smashed on pavements of chicory
the climbing witnesses bang their heads
on far-flung empires of rain

Those natives called Ohlone
in the peculiar humors of the weather
and those who danced
to placate "The Great Invisible"
in the bay of Yerba Buena
              "dance on the brink of the world"

No reprieve for the ghost-catchers

Here the basaltic hieroglyphics of Sir Francis Drake
stream the lumens of California *"la maravillosa"*
Sequoia sempervirens
russet red
              vampire of wood
in you we have our being and move
who tolerate hardly a bird insect or other tree
but the woodpecker *darting rattle of the air*

Oraibi

What I mean when I say the key of the future is written now when it's seen
in the air of your great visage
an emblematic key
roaring
and with a wolf's expression
dashed on the ocean's knee

bear of lightning
in a black lanterned bay
smiling with the teeth of conch shells

What I'm saying when I tell you there's an orchard around my head
sprouting twenty-two engines of what will be
turning the blinding crystal
sightreading waves of fire
around the acentrical isle

What I'm doing now peering from invisible windows
and they also on fire
the wind masked as a moon
a hundred eighty letters volatilize into a forest of ocular organs

To read the green fire of lazy letters
truly of the metaphor's metaphor
the cabala rides through on a helmet
at the sight of the mountain
looking back at me
waving stones over a field of sleeping eyes

Obelisk at dawn
          obelisk at the crepuscular dawn
green corn makes a white butterfly
into an obelisk traveling at night
magnetic leaves of aurist fingers

What's written on the obelisk's petticoat
ventricles of wind hide
and reveal
          at the sovereignty of turquoise
intercepting great impossible cities
becoming visible
through the roads of the turquoise sun

Bile Nature

Available as a turquoise ice pick
changing the head of a butterfly into a *Bookwus*
(enchantment
    differing in every talismanic aspect from the
    otherwise inter-alluvial totemic usages)
the lure of a sky-speck garners hidden vortical ellipses
    by which photons fan out contrary to the normal
    retinal gobbling

imprisoned with cold fever
to emerge
parallel to arrows
seductively prancing from violet shadows
the rainbow leaps onto the gorge of daydreaming be it
    ever the sandy castles
fleeting as mental blowtorches
into the crashing water
quicker than a chipmunk's chess game
reverses the coyote's invisible dart

      the jungle lianas are sated with stalagmites

Further on
the medicines march
to meet before me this woman within a tree
the creek of automatic music
sputtering bluejays and a thousand rivers
caught by the bileferous heart I love
yours
to crystallize
dialectically
a lattice of tooth marks from the Gnome King's terraplane
arriving with the velocity of squirrel tails
carving tunnels into our radiant osteo-paths

stalactites leer to an alabaster woman
               the cave I kiss
and your look that seizes a branch of sidereal poison
from the hind parts of night balloons

            Union Creek, Oregon. 1974

Drama Set

Beneath the moss of eyesockets
the tower vanishes into the golden night
   spoon of raspberry
      chocolate flight

The blooming vitriol of May
kneads autumn's honeysuckle

The city sprung open like a bird cage
becomes a rainbow of mule feathers
sailing through the jail bars of the earth

Ultima Thule

The hoofs of sleep rattle from the blue whisper
of a crow plunged for sediment
gone beyond the frame whose disk flaunts the night's dawn

I fly into that marsh of brilliant gallop
the wheel within my hand
this glance of rain
sleep of sleep turning over stones the Lilliputians wake

Illusions of space vanish
where alone
        there are bodies only

Mask of Geometry

The path newly swathed swims from the horizon
like a clover caught with a pearl rose

bannister cupped in wind
railroad from the Milky Way

my vampire of words this body of light
I surpass the blossoms
cantering over the hole
branched by soothing flames

Beyond This Trail of Crystal Rails

If I travel the leaves
planes of circling light cloy the branches
to skip by twigs and charge
like rhapsodes of pain
                            into sleep

gargantuan boulder harbinger
where the pen dips only brazen
and tails of solvent grace . . .
. . . The prismatic apple explodes
from this long sought night
at the sight of you found on the limit
    of the returning forest
visibly crossing invisible dew

Poe-Baudelaire, one echo-in-two

Home is
            "the domain of Arnheim"
as it slips out of gear
falling through entangled metals
of its sublime view
from all the winged forests
the window sills of an old house
at the bottom of
            "anywhere out of this world"

Dissolving Lead

Carry me head with the rudder of your wings
for the dark fires are humming
and the murmer of cliffs is borne
to the kiss that seals water
Pulled by the vanishing trail
infinity flies the gales of the frolicking bed

> •

By my hand weak with coercion
to the basaltic neck of the tree
at the light's ignition the river's pain
break bracken of hallucinated eyes
only you have the ease of water

> •

Tantamount to the hurtling glen
to sleep over the rapids

The Erotic Limned

As a cataract gesticulates an abyss flares

On the lookout for the glass-lined tarsier
gnarled with oceanic spooks
dormant volcanos ply wounds

A mole's dream irradiates cephalic beds of atropine
Africa the hubris of life ignites my finger play

Swept on by the marigold of memory
sutures love left open close the abyss we scaled

A dream thirst animates the world
as a cataleptic wind turns around in your eyes

Vibration

There is a wind torturing bats
there are the scorched feet of dead suns
the city spun into the sea
where the gulfs of the pterodactyl beckon
there is a whorl of terror livening my mind
there's the hum-whirr of the skeleton of solitude
where angry corpses flower in a bottle
and red weapons vanish into mirrors

I look back by the blade of my double
there flies—through its eye—*The Hanged Man*
where a pyramid of water hovers in the dark victuals of the inner life

Below the Surface

If you catch the spring of the horse *gallo-potential*
whatever you mean
the absolute is there
raining green and supine
Foam arrives by the mantle soaked at rose dew

   Magnificent

Criminal sisters sever their parents' gullets with knives of savory
columns rush down to the sea
in various frocks the ladies pillaged
from the scented elevator I travel your head by
gardens wash the night
like sheep melded for music
other centuries
the human cabinets sing the sloth of horror
and wash the night with pumice
which scampers in bread as wives undone
wear hats of knees
and banshees vibrate
the shadows of mistletoe through the v-shaped capes
at the handshake of the *fata morgana*

Again I return as if the door had gone skating
and the lions at the gate took off for a cup of coffee
diced for sugar
and came back dangling the seafoam of venusian fame

Master of the dew always you
always another basket of flowers
to weave at your oppositional funeral
(which must cease *definitively*)
at the break of Eden fast cycle
of the remembered black rays

Oneiric Reversal

I implore the raven of dust to drop his signet, water-drawn, fury's flower, dawn's
bucket, that reconnoiters the winding terrace to the absolute tuber.

The Night in her golden lancet sings over the skyscraper I hunt, my doorway adrift
to the heat the child's mind leaps.

A room of spiked faces replaced by the shredded lake-at-arms where she walks the
street of floating sparks . . . and I, medused . . . What sleeps away returns an entrance
kicked back by the shadow opening the great flower of Night . . .

Sun-down
the evening side up
black lipstick and corolla of thirst
all the children are necrophiles at bay

The river, peeling dust, salutes this walking prey: cobbled limestone of a glance more
dangerous than clover's sighing foot.

The road to the pit in the sky: to see a dog typing into a cat's liver. No breakfast for
the flying spider. The dream of a labyrinth is *the shark's love for humanity* leaning to
the unknown the geometric wave's scorpion biting on a window pane of sodomized
glass.

Openers

The prunehook speaking the child's hillside secured by malignant diving bells was the first day of the goon's smile embracing a multitude of cascades, though by other leaping roads. The goon was born, as all others, in a hood's wink—frosted into a fire hydrant on the expanding pit of nail-jammers. A flourishing trade in nineteenth century bottomless lakes celebrated his geometry of excremental flights designing over oak branches chewing the elemental bankers who officiated funereal rites at the suspicious mirror by which the merry musicians charmed the newly-bracketed closing his fist destroyed by helium.

The claptrap of insomnia was awaiting its oven. Fury ran uneasily around the pseudo-grecian stone eyelids standing up as bamboo stalks ransacking the several vascular systems of the family group: the relaxed lard within dripped dogs seeking the proverbial paradise where threads were twined with the material cries of slit beavers.

Iridescence, the goon grew to observe, was triangulated to this lemonade party by a metal rod clothed in hieroglyphic emblems. The genuflections of opaque plumbing stirred the multiplying intoxicants no more liquid than brine but wretched in the form of white and blue thorns.

incubation by paraplegia and variable signs of
obsolescence

Gretta the hawk, the hawk's fancy and the milk of mired nights tempted the goon's playmate (whose name was lost in orgies and was never found again) to catapult toward the sanctimonious bannister pulverizing feathers; but to no avail, the ginger-flayed girl hid from the closets of doom.

the aerolith tossed to the "Happiness Cafe"

A stoke of headlines feeds the crypt inscribed with hatcheting yawns; whispering tars ensorcell the fields of bulbuls; rain-tooth cacti and phantom dirigibles carry off the sanguinary invaders at the very moment the sphinxian mechanism of the *iguana giganticus* portends the mass migration of the Coras from their "mountains of the full moon" mediating a potential cross-fertilization of the *pithaya*, erotism's crimson fruit, with the sand's most desolate cedar wing.

Violet Star

While I continue to rave
over the dissimilar modes
molding
excessively finite
transmutable
at the coming of serpentine volition
son of the daughters of sleep
the absolute at every street corner with a braided cap
the hair-lined tongue
disagreeably spills *the indeterminate* over the mirror of the world

The avalanche of anti-gravity machines
a tight rein to these vehicles
sometimes seen with the word "seer" spelled backwards
the fire-coated heroic
dances over the sparkling ruins
bird beaks
luminously
at the grating of historical jungles
the cities continually sink into mirages
the oil of tombs and frontal lobotomies "treasures" of the ruling classes
the evening salvo of "the serpentine flag"
my last glimpse into the card of *The Exploding Tower*
galvanic
to the ignition of the levitated glance

2

The truth is to see the mounted zephyr mutilate itself in a bowl of chick peas
The pastors of iniquity dance
on the night before crumbling cement in the beeswax of torment
the moment to transpire cities
What if the road is dizzy from the clashing tubs?
Alcohol venison sunlight like a steel fist
floodgates will open
invisible powers through the cataclysm at hand
a necklace of human heads
the sibilant voices cracked on a rock of *techne*

The cars fold obsidian men into the stale marshes
The open almond of rust invents the glare of high noon
Beware the teeth of numbers
but the lunar feel of steel going limp
another world
flight of the tamarind trees in the Mozartian sky
the shrouded catastrophes staring from the monoliths
the way the curve of planets escapes into view
beyond all the blind revelations
the fortunate thunder writes out the changes on the headdress of cured feathers
opening the old Amerindian tonic
the timeless in time and the regional compass

This Moment Eternal Medusa

from a wounded terrain   among the derailed fountains
love's erotic enigma
to stare
into the red germination
from whose interior
—veiled with vagina of window
death's head and boiling mucus
all set to fly from crevices of bat guano—
the flight justifies castration's pickle
of rainbowed light
through cups whose gold is a moment
   meeting the cabal
of the nightmare's eye

like the great beasts on their highway smashing bolts
the door swings inward
to the ouroboric baby doll
and banners of names dipped in a bloody Shangri-La
upon an ever widening vista
cuddling entrails in the void
"a nasty piece of goods"
—but let the climbing begin over there
with the sword
no

that saw
thrown to your ear's reindeer
this road to the egyptian miracle
putting the enemies to sleep with charred sexual organs
mixed up
in the amphibious graveyard of the dangling man

what went on here
cataloging watery carnivals
at the sight of the running forest
Rama-pithecus heartbeats
on the way to the slumbering palace
twilight reddens the harbor
with rebel fists at the dawn of revolt
a song to the sirens
from the shuttered room of black blood
raising spiked flags of longing
the ruins prance into view

what vegetable stones
what stacks of zebra and medical poisons leak through the camel's eye
what florid bequest tomorrow
scales the tropic transmigration
from here to there
when
you hide inside a redwood tree

Precipitous Oracle

Upon the current vaster than coal
minute as the weather's eggplant
of an athanor

between a star's gleaming shadow
and its great coat of morning stilts
thrown on a grave like a glove of drenched eyeballs

there is a splinter of green dust
luminously taking off for the hurried horizon

an ember to be
waving to a leaf of raining music
where the quiltwork of aura
salutes the hoof beat of a dream-forked kiss

Modular Prey

Orchid burns to the tilt of the house
inflames the socket memory seizes

With a cat's talon
dogs eat through couches

A finger is rent by falling shale

The steel rim of the world is sucked by venison

Weak statues of ignition
vent their ribcages of oxygen

■ ■ ■

Pulsate with stoppages
I periscope
Lazed out
Retrieving echoes
My eyes of clangor
With Taliesin's ear at crows landing

Radiant Opal

The languorous hurdle
    through the thicket
        the humming glen
    sights
the raven of the rainbow

To Begin *Then* Not Now

The skylight drowns
as you walk into my voice
carrying a box of flames
entirely secretive
you tap open by the charmed hairpin
of the mysteries of sleep

Life Sciences

Open the mirage that calls you

The wind's embalming fluid
and the deserted shadow
    originating the flaw at outposts
    dovetailed
    into the transparent substance
      the absence of water
turned around in the mirrors

   ■

My foot in the hair of spinning stars
    those curdles which limp through the shadows
In spite of the ducky corrals
stilettos wake up
and write out your names on the raving bark
which flows as water of fire
to blot out the animal checkers computing your brows

The Curtain of Magic Turns over Motors of Sleep

Commemoration of the *World Surrealist Exhibition*
Chicago, 1976

The purity of the dream-rivulet crosses the depth of day
    permanent witness from the source of things
    draped: a forest of fiery signs

From the heartbeat of electric pages, salamanders scintillate Black Hawk swathed in beechnut. Walking and falling asleep at once, talons form flames and magi—traveled by light beams—redden the gulping rim.

    There *and* here: Dawn.

The lock of hair pursues the bone's stalk of wisteria shadow while Galloping Forelock looms no less than Bugs Bunny over the castle's warlock.

Footsteps afar. The returning helmets rear up by lightning. Are you there, combing waves of air to the crystal blind,—*ourselves?*

There's a secret treasure on the run.

The ineluctable sleepwalker doubles knees to charm a murmur from the fleece-moving crowd translated out of dormancy and looked at by dragons.

The Fulcrum Loaded

With the serenity of goats copulating in a volcano of street corners
Curves of thought turn over the silver avalanche dreamt from the ocean's brain
The word Nothing carves a street draped with guts
A pelican's breakfast food hosting history
Hysteria of flea-mites out to farm the giants
Triumphant evolution irrupts "the ring of fire"
Human commodities open the mummy wrappings of another species
Voluptuaries sow the earth's hiatus
The noonday sun sucking the diamond pebbled night
Glue chambers fall apart
Gone through the boxes of mental mouths your head travels with the dragonfly
    casting words of meat-eating flowers

The "end of *Umor*" you say
New worlds come forth every minute from your ingrained bed of lumber
The complete history of man chiseled on a sunbeam
There's the turgid churning of the grate within
Hold out your root systems
Haul them and husk them
Freebooted slave on the computer printout erasing reality
From the bar stool of busting and mending
Wacky Wolf!
Severe hard with daylight chunks of concrete
There's the shadow to hand you light
Black suns that rivet space
Immediate coherence in a waterfall of echoes
Remember
To stick out your zodiac of the earth on fire
Paranormal windmills gallop the skyway
Your head steaming the space between a fallout of engines and florid beaks
I put the thunder of reindeer over the Kwakiutl mask of the most green-headed taboo
The angle cloven
Perhaps to see tomorrow twelve skulls on a shaman's brow
Meanwhile
There's nothing but audible tension
Hags of war
And the brainy bubbling buckets of sons and fathers
Shrouded by a portrait series of american presidents
Interruptions
Of the horned cadaver *The Hulk* and *Swamp Thing*
Wing-tipped feet slyly turning the corners of our brain

At the Emu's Domain

for Franklin Rosemont

Like the open grave radiating a laughing rutabaga
and the carrot tearing the arena to shreds
somewhat like a tree stamping its foot on a square-
    eyed leopard
moons and bread vie for favor among the diamond-hearted

Across the lake of being the wind is smoking tubular flames
Chains are braiding cormorants
The placentas refracted at the uninhabited tower in
    the squall
replace the Street of Marvels submerged again to its hidden exit
while the city wakes up as a flower of loving knights

The Jewels of the Vatican Board the Atlantic Cipher

Wandering
at the hour daubed in wax
love escapes the frame's ventricular ear
to kick over cupolas the grey fathers ploughed with their wings
Where did the rat from the monstrance take its ease?
Gilles de Rais coughs through the veil of the centuries
he who mistook a cutlass for the discovery of Patagonia
Choking encyclopedists was a swine's game
and a blow to the temple erupts the catacombs flying
    the iron brassiere Dolly Madison's painted feet
    joined to the beaver kingdom's wake
which is why money is printed in braille
across the faucets slid with formica on buffalo hides

The Days Fall Asleep with Riddles

Why ride around with the chains of the tortured
bleeding from your cars?

Grapes are livid with corpses
the regal dead are passing out knockout candy

The seas are a hailstorm of flint and oranges
Over the land the floating eggshell
Under the rocks the tobaccos are squealing

If I know the way down the seashell's luxuriant city
why does your feline marrow reverse the human alphabet?

The Uncertain Sciences

1	The monoliths fly from the central desert
1.1	Smelling of monkshood
1.11	And disgorging smoke of iron and wheezing flax
1.12	Raining hair of oyster and typewriter of split pea.
1.13	The visages: one part, President/Secretary of State
1.2	The other, a composite of Mona Lisas laced with spider grease
1.21	That exude fur and tickertape
2	Wag tinsel wings
2.01	And flex muscles of liquefying prairie grass.
2.012	Yes, it's the pontifical moment the robot armies
2.0122	Loaded on wave mattresses
2.0123	(Charged by the multi-leveled systemic universities)
2.01231	Unleash metallic rats who prance, scream and
2.0124	Limn over the coprophagic tendons
2.013	Of the sacred heart rinds
2.0131	Whose petomaniacal distension
2.0122	Of red white and blue vapor
2.0123	Wafts into a bucket of pate, Jesus Hamadryad
2.01231	Rejoining its gang of Dravidian cuttlefish
2.0124	To shine (drooped) from a silver nitrate window
2.013	Of the Pure Conceptual Behavior Maze
2.0131	Which conditions the smoldering fleas of law and order
2.014	For their "exuberancies" of entropic resuscitation.

Green Lion

At the street of caves where the four-headed gnomes
Arrive in pairs followed by arrows
Gliding on our footsteps
The flowers basking behind the chandeliers
Have thrown buckets of dragon paint
To overflow into the suburbs
Keyless windows open to the touch of meteorites
Which are nonetheless hallucinatory shadows
Wherever I live at the raging scabbard's signpost
We march through the swamp of the moments

With the gilt tongue of grail venom
With the venom of adamant ferment
We shall find the talons of the three-colored process
As our eyes close to the checkerboard
And the night rushes through her own envelopes
Interspersed with salacious lakes
At the coming to be of militant swans
The odoriferous stream of ocular telephones
Connecting the vial bearing a watery armor
To the geomantic tablets exalting revolution
No one but the crimson bed-calmer deciphers

Oblique and Direct

The trellis of the night opens
   head hunters askew
to magnetize the soap bubbles of the heart

The cataract of dentalic window wears a concrete glove
and juggles the wind-bone a carbuncle of derision
a flock of sandy planets
hatched from dew drops of my brain

The tub-boat beckons the lemon rind
to a party of delirious guillotines
magnifying automatic tarot cards

     The Female Pope with fish nostrils
     The Emperor plowed into an egg garden
     The Tower in a squall eating a bed of lava

Hypochondriac Weather

The cavernous overhead opens millipedes of submarine postcards I cannot count to nail where the rhombus lamb fondles the brain of roseate grails. The sleight-of-hand wisdom v-necks the humming hair which grips the mastodon of oil that scrutinizes with the glass of Bedlam the beds flying in half across the blindfolded barricades.

A Slice of the Atmosphere

The hanging tomato plays the echo's cocoon
Auspicious pies shoot the rapids
and you fling a bridge at the cow manure's thigh
Let this be no lesson
less than the wigwam's pit of reason
delicious arsenal of a vampire at noon

With your hand in your head
your shadow questions the meta-window's glance of the bellicose
Time and the timeless go hand in fist
My shadow dressed in birds
You'll know me
when I put you at the beginning of the indigenous house

The Element You Love

I can see you from the headgears navigating the beach lined with cement,
  motioning the fallen arch of a comet that pelts a falcon's river, unheard of
  jostling submerging the lamp posts.

A waylaid victor at his flying pyramid, *ochre is the window of the salutory eye* . . . and
  a blast of doorways eludes a lion here and there nonchalantly signaling *sudden
  ladies* about to vanish through the rain's escutcheon where the civilized lusts
  plumed with anti-cephalic inanities bid their guests go up in flames.

No less than a burnished chicken machineguns the greasy light of preachers sinking
  into the docks the woman sets free by water, combing a vitreous dress out of
  which fall foxes-in-hand and a macaw whose beak *softens* to become her cachet
  of liquid poetry.

Time Traveler's Potlatch

For Simon Rodia: The sudden appearance, at once, of a million Americans in Watts, in order to be in close proximity to his Towers.

For Charlie Parker: The materialization of his old green jacket re-forming the flag of the future republic of desire and dreams.

For Edgar Allan Poe: Upon awakening, an original copy of the *Manifeste du Surréalisme*.

For Charlie Chaplin: His wrench of *Modern Times* reconstituted as Merlin's magic wand.

For Bela Lugosi: A chance meeting with Morgan le Fay at the observation roof of the Empire State Building.

For William Collins: His "Ode to Fear" engraved in vanishing letters on the Scottish Highlands between the bleeding milk of night and the death wish of the coming day.

For Clément Magloire-Saint-Aude: The cinematic projection from a hummingbird's eye of Charlie Parker's spontaneous musical session at Bop City, San Francisco in 1954, fixed in an order of black, white and red crystallizations volatilizing the the human brain on the brink of an evolutionary mutation through a circle of blazing rum.

Notes

Redwood Highway

Giordano Bruno (1548–1600)—philosopher and poet, the first significant dialectical and materialist thinker of post-medieval Europe. Burned at the stake in Rome by the Inquisition.

Ibn 'Arabi (1165–1240)—Andalucian gnostic, theorist of the "autonomous imagination."

Gilles de Rais (1404–1444)—companion-in-arms of Joan of Arc, hero of the Siege of Orleans, and Marshal of France at age twenty-five. Later accused of sorcery and of violating and murdering hundreds of children, he was hanged and burned. He has entered legend, euphemistically, as Bluebeard.

Walpi—one of the Hopi villages in Arizona where I witnessed the surpassing poetic beauty of the Kachina dances. The San Francisco Peaks are the home of over two hundred kachinas, powers and forces of nature, ritually represented by masked dancers in annual ceremonies.

Chumash—the indigenous people of the Santa Barbara area, whose resplendent imagination was expressed, from the year 1000, in polychrome cave and rock paintings, still extant.

Yurok—the original inhabitants of the Klamath River and northwest coastal regions of California. The costume worn in their Albino Deerskin Dance included a headband of fifty scarlet woodpecker scalps and an apron of civet-cat skin.

Ohlone—a group of tribes who lived in the San Francisco Bay Area (also called Costanoans). The name Ohlone derived from that of a tribelet once located on the Pacific Coast midway between San Francisco and Santa Cruz. These people are known to have honored redwood trees and owls as sacred species. As with other Amerindians, dreaming was a vital determinate of their way of life.

Charles Fourier (1772–1837)—French utopian socialist whose detailed vision of a future "harmonian" society revealed, according to Marx and Engels, "a true vein of poetry." He conjectured innumerable transformational possibilities, using images of extravagant desire (e.g., "a sea of lemonade") that suggest how the imagined might be realized on the plane of objective reality.

Washo—a tribe whose original territory lay in the verdant area of Lake Tahoe, on both sides of the California and Nevada border. Their peyote rite "The Tipi Way" in which I participated in the early 1950s has been a constant source of poetic inspiration.

Cora—the indomitable people of the Sierra of Nayarit in Mexico. Ritual use of peyote among the Coras was first mentioned by a Spanish observer in 1754. In the spring of 1955 during an extended stay in their village of Jesus-Maria, I joined the Coras in a night-ritual celebrating *yana* (the Cora name for tobacco). On the lintel above the entrance to the temple in which the tobacco rite took place, there was a representation, carved in stone, of two iguanas facing each other. Every day I watched a gigantic real iguana, reputed to be over a hundred years old, moving over the rocks beyond the village by the river of Nayar, which flows through a valley enclosed by high mountains.

Wintun— to the nineteenth century observer Stephen Powers, "a beautiful valley" of the Wintun, where ritual ceremonies took place, seemed a "Mecca of the mind" to other tribes living below Mount Shasta in northern California.

In Yerba Buena

Yerba Buena—Spanish "good herb," for the white-flowered wild mint. This was the name of the pueblo, settled in 1835, that was to become the city of San Francisco.

"Dancing on the brink of the world"—line from a Costanoan dance song.

Oraibi

Oraibi—literally "high rock," Hopi Indian village, Arizona, founded in the 12th century, the oldest continuously-inhabited settlement in what is now the United States.

Cabala—the term *cabala* has been elucidated by the twentieth century alchemist Fulcanelli in *Les Demeures Philosophales* where he explains its derivation from the Latin, *caballus*, for *horse*, but signifying the transmission of knowledge and "revealing the source of all sciences"; the universal "unspoken language," yet easily understood by all, is, according to Cyrano de Bergerac, "the *instinct* or *voice of nature*." The figurative image of the *cabala* as spiritual vehicle is the Pegasus of the Hellenic poets which derives from the Greek word for *source*: "to know the *cabala* is to speak *the language of the horse*." Fulcanelli mentions, among the many carriers of this knowledge, the poet-initiates: Homer, Virgil, Ovid, Dante and Goethe; the chivalric poets of the Middle Ages, the recorders of the

Round Table and Grail cycles, Cyrano de Bergerac, Cervantes *(Don Quixote)*, and Swift *(Gulliver's Travels)*. In the English translation of Fulcanelli's other major text, *Le Mystère des Cathédrales*, Eugene Canseliet's preface distinguishes between the two words *cabala* and *kabbala* "in order to use them knowledgeably" since "the Hebrew word *Kabbalah* means *tradition* ... full of transpositions, inversions, substitutions, and calculations, as arbitrary as they are abstruse," in contrast to *cabala* in the sense illuminated by Fulcanelli as the source of the whole of ancient esoteric knowledge.

Bile Nature

Bookwus—legendary Kwakiutl Indian forest spirit and "wild man of the woods," superbly demonic.

Poe-Baudelaire, one echo-in-two

The Domain of Arnheim—tale by Edgar Allan Poe, a prototype of the luxurious transformation of the physical world into a garden of the poetic marvelous. Charles Baudelaire found in Poe's writings the English title he gave his intransigent prose-poem *Anywhere Out of the World*.

Time Traveler's Potlatch

Time Traveler's Potlatch—a game invented by surrealist friends in Chicago. As in the Northwest Amerindian potlatch tradition of sumptuousness and excess, gifts are offered to those who attract the imagination of the giver.

POEMS 1981–1985

Willow Wand

Juniper tree slashed by obsidian

In my hand cupping sun assassins
lines of mercury and unknown stars
    pure poetry of Pomo night
        shades of Mount Konocti giants
the almost invisible mites of chiromancy among the tanoak vibes
stream of lapping water-transportations
in an oak grove the secret name immortal
    through the wind of a paranoid dream
O supreme idol
from a druid long ago
to these puritan shores of the face to be
sylvan presences seep with mist
    obsidian-flanged to Venus
and deep within the boat on the five-fingered lake
    flight of fanged lights of gore
        beneath fingernail creations Coyote intersects
beyond the ticky-tack gloss of sirens
(computer-spent at contemporary pores)
sweet williams on the cuspidors

terrace to the graveyard of valleys of diehard hummingbirds
ravens in their cups of sky descending horse
is humankind more than the mite's mandible of chance?
Are you higher than the stony insects at the windows of thunder?

Take down veil of dim vision
and find through acres of iridescent goblins
perchance the meadowlark's mimicry of all the tongues of space
and there's *little*
for Boulder Brother on a limb of tanoak
    with the grebe's desire for mental grandeur
beneath: a coot's bill
foraging the invisibles through the ancient water

Meadowlark West

Choppers in the night husk the brilliants of thought
Beyond the cities of patina grow caves of thought
Coyote Hummingbird Owl are rivers of thought
The lumens the pumpkins dance: pits of correspondence over the land
Birds the dream tongues warble Iroquois Mojave Ohlone
Market Street of "The Mad Doctor" via the occult centers
A gang of fox spirits at the crossroads
Bandoleros set between the obliteration of grizzly bears painted by an Arcimboldist
    and the monstrance of bleeding chains
Montezuma's feathery headdress torn up in the boondocks of the Rosy Cross

Coyote girls in myth-time
At the central dream of edenic treasures
The irrevocable annihilation of christian civilization is taking shape with
    carnivorous flowers of volcanic thought

Sentiment for the Cordials of Scorpions

The heart never grows old
it grows stilettos, thorns, rays,
it is the cup of knowledge
it grows to the gnosis of becoming the gate of streamlets
    and jungles of power
it contracts, growls, spits,
    scratches—eagle talons
    are its outcroppings
The Divine de Sade is the heart's dilation
and the heart dies, never to grow old
the heart lives and makes love to the brain

Birder's Lament

Robin, rare Robin at my window
below the introduced tree, pecking black seeds
Blessed be, this
otherwise difficult day
gracious vision, Robin, of your mandibles
to counterbalance the Killdeer birds crushed
on their nests by giant tractors at Crissy Field

Poetics by Pluto

The dendrophobe across the way just demolished nests
    of finches sparrows other possible birds

Wild in the city with green teeth up through the pavements Phoenix is that bird
From ashes of the kali-yuga
            another root in the great tradition
through caves of animal fetishes Cernunos in the lap of Diana
            A wee chance
            Better falconry
than the definitive end Better the poetry of the birds
Up from salty deeps, Dianas, to rule us and reweave a scallop shell sacred to Venus
            There's a cleavage possible
Mother Shipton's prophecy that the end of the cycle is not foretold
but only the end of insane mankind
                            Read it here before amnesia
the superior salt maneuver
in the language of chirping finches

            is that bird, Diana

In a late Goethean mode happiness ignites its grand illusion
Timeless all that old cant about the hermetic art
opens a poetic fundament deep into the pyramid The processional colors
of finches repeat ritual doorways in aura of instant death
the poet No Name by chance seering open pavements of Ol Frisco
the Barbary Coast from carpets of brown dust to Twenty-ninth and Courtland
    Avenue

a crustaceous wind from ancient oaks off the *E-chi-lat* River
        near a minor fault line but active in the nineties
off the semi-wild park which will have a monument to Isadora Duncan
        where I ran and danced with youths of frenetic romance
lash of the bay below
curving geology with two-thirds of a whole number
to tip the dragon of summer
into transfigured space of thin peninsula
        Costanoan tribelets from San Bruno to San Juan Bautista
Mockingbirds are returning to Frisco
to lift the ancient taboo
hummingbirds by the milliards at the feeder stations
Meanwhile empires are vomiting
not some nineteenth-century phano-sphere of coming blight (trotting castles) but
sudden death for a whole continent of forest here & everywhere
        sparrows strangled in midair with the last condors
situate Acid Rain and the Green House Effect
        plague-lined trees oil-slick birds
There's little time left for geographic enclaves to form Aquarian islands
(from them only could I be reading you)
If (as Hegel proved) poetry is a rare assemblage
a Watts Tower transmuting junk
how over-quantified to vanishing the prosaic is

        "I always thought there was something funny about
        our generation, now I know why, it's the last one"

Violent flashes to each other words become cancerous with meaning
The hood of horror has actually come back those mornings insane
mankind signs all the prose of the world
The gods first craze those they decide to destroy
Think *nous, ment*, ithyphallic Min
to project sensibility
How do I feel? rotten, misnamed 'hysterical' who calls freely for the Annulment of
    Nuclear Physics
as if technē were the issue and
not a cosmic catastrophe
Ask those who put the sacred animals in niches at Altamira
and those who call up the beasts in islands of new forest

Now there's mostly monolithic media noise
            on the inner cliff a shadowy figure who announces
the Admonition, again
but certainly some attempt at statement, flying wild to the polis, is proportional to
        our destruction as a species
When does the winged bridge appear on this terrified earth?

Somewhere between Walpi and New York as they are Another world Whether
        others see it or not is aleatory
but the emerald vision persists, a bygone reformed off serpentine rocky shores
transmitting abalone shells at midnight all the way from New Ireland
'Dances of the Pheasant and Quail societies are generally attended'

Pluto retrograde five degrees into Scorpio
            Radioactive rain days
Will dejection ever end for incantators
once the mysteries of falconry join the old art of an inner dance?
            Frisco was like that
There are thirty species of birds feeding Telegraph Hill
                        Site of appearance
                        visible light
                                    The Invisible Light
                        and the night of gold: imaginable
                        origin of language
                        Quotidian humming
                        gradations of vocables transmitted
                        among the very few

Dripping pine needles generate geometric thought Is there any other?
On this language island night's my day
Empires are still rotting A Sandpiper trapt in oil slick

Itinerary of Drift Bane

Give me the thread of the trance over the rocky apertures of the wandering
siphon, poetry's gale; a titmouse immense beyond the shrieking cells, microbes of
wormwood where Orion pitches his tent in vibraphones through arteries beneath
the zephyrs at Cape Arago whose iris decodes the breath of motion: monsters of the
auroch's brain of trepidation.

Ambulation of roadless names out of crevices, the white clitoris of divine breath. At the mental plume, morbid delight inundates to succulence and windy maps; animals extant and reborn in "the next *kalpa*": geodes of vomiting acephaloids, genius with the itch of dolphin teeth.

The match of telepathic hair vibrates the row of lights at Crescent City, outpost of the antediluvian seahorse, the bungling sandy vision when eyes search the zenith at the boat-speckled careen of the butterfly's path.

Doomsday eats the moment before the massacre of Indians on the Oregon reef, Capo Blanco silenced between the doorway shutting down on the watchers and the floodstream of shadowy sheep dogs.

Mexico City Central Moon

The humid chemic from lobotomized trees
drinking coffee dust off the Alameda
the funereal peoples ringing the solar gong
buried at the magnets of the Street of the Lost Child
your blood-cries from earth of cosmic humans after volcanos running
    to the mists below

Symplegades of roving balustrades and turned around
straightened out worm-wooded with the earthshaking news at the
    labyrinth's eye a *Pulque* dive at dawn Osirian as Quetzelcoatl
all the ancient dramas piled into one / solar divinities
    and solar birds
concretes of lunar city dreaming jaguar spooks of the south
leaping gulfs
in a sea of fruits
windows to the maze of stuffed hummingbirds in the witch's market
    luminous death-hangar to the superstitious mental blades

1950 *Calle de Garcia Lorca*

the Empedoclean suicide in a volcano a green sigil There were the
    fountains of hate in the womb of obsidian clothing
the iridescent descent to Toluca exploding the Presidential Plazas
dimly Pancho Villa in Sonoran desert the very thought of mirage
alligator, iguana, armadillo
here too it's prohibited to dream

monks, lamps, vampiric final rasp Cactus leather stretched to sky
ease to earth;
a sugary throat sends up the steely sand, moon
dust, the twinkle at the zelicon's run
to your hoary rim, Mexico

They call you "the sixth world"

Bird: Apparition of Charlie Parker

Our poet of music
      lyric windup
at glove's edges
        green grey eyes
        Bird's and mine with the phoenix-band

the perfect pitch clashing
        mute mnemonics of "dulcet
          tones"
our Lady Sphinx
and you melancholy awe
triumph at 3 or 4 in the morning
the salt shakers wobbled / on the counter / frozen / at Jimbo's dream
                        palaces of musical civilization
every step to halt nuclear self-destruction / 1948
I'm writing this 1984
the Vegetable Stone fragile on a fraction of—

Elegy on the Migrating Nightingales
Massacred by Nuclear Physics at Chernobyl

il usignuolo
el ruiseñor
filomela
luscinia megarhynchos

Ah living bird I've yet to hear fullview in ancestral haunts
        chook—chook—chook
        pui—pui—pui

the latter phonemes rising crescendo to the gods within
(for they ain't anywhere else)
They were on their way
                          navigating photo-
synthetic air
                from mystery to mystery
It's gonna be Gaia's turn soon for the integral destruction of
all corruption
                  Though these words burn
who deciphers who reads archives of their ashes
shall remember Keats and long before Latin
at the turn of the Great Year
PHILOMELA from Atlantean groves to the remaining Trinarcian shore
dimly you see but more brightly then
when you may hear me in the new count of islands

reformed glyphs carry all the birds, not least the HONEY THROATED
of which we are but mirror specks since poet's song
is but a crooked chip from the perfect Flying Heart
and this annunciation but an ancient image to be clawed
to presence down that dung-heap-science (infamous physics
radiant tool of Sethian fools)
for which there should be a miracle of tears out of occult caves
    to wash away iron ages and flow ambrosia from countless islands
until the sole nightingale appears in the final west I see
and sweet with me now if chance opens the crystal with the confidence
    of wild birds
the supreme symbolic raptor's downward gesture
                such speed, precision none other has
whose name is Mental Light
from the beginning to this end over Chernobyl

what glass reflects
                          a minute before midnight
suddenly down drift
zinging air
                not to speak your real name, bird
but those tombs over Chernobyl make visible your name
that has never ceased to signal the harmony of the world

MEADOWLARK WEST

1986

Isn't Poetry the Dream of Weapons?

The impossible is easy to reach
Who knows the way out of the labyrinth?
These are not rhetorical questions
the heart has its reasons though reasons not
                 Imaginary
the postmodern world has faded today
tomorrow, well shucks, it's here
a wedding calmly observed between heart and head
Relax the slow confusion flows until
the tooth of it
forgotten on a summer beach in Southern California
the way it's drawled to death in Southern California where death is cozy and Lemurian
Today I had my *tamasic* enlightenment the federation of anarchs was conspiratorially
    formed in Albania
the news came by indirect means the lines were jammed but I think I got it straight
here in the Far West you know how hard of hearing we are You've heard tell Ah'm sure
the clay hands looking a little moldy of Joaquin San Joaquin
the lazy simple status
nowhere to
and
always AND
Can this be the surprise statement
    Nuub
        nuub
              with high rhetoric back from bright death
what else to say of it?
No luck a metaphysical symbol
There's soaring even among the tortured minerals
These are the gilds of free verse
Doesn't the horror of writing Am I reading?
Better not to repeat you Sovereign Powers
the astral too plain at noon black with engines slipping again
five times
the secret hoarded afresh
Look at the basket now, my friend, *where* the fruits among the froth?
Between the ecstasy and the secret
I've touched bottom I want to be lost
the glow is bathing me in pain
the master would say, *souffrance*

Cosmic recurrence of the light of the old
its youth becoming
planting Dada on the trees
The within is without at once
no sooner dead than living
the unique perspective dangles the motion
it was called the boat of Ra
and the golden night hermetically sealed
          pure rollicking play
hands are glowing the last look back
lighted shadows like video
the words you see
pomegranate of idea
a pile of rust
Poetry knows in the unknowing
but *Kemi* is the moment to send up the aroma of dragons
beyond the limits salt of the sun
the deliberate anomaly willed by nexus
covers the filings I remember to forget dead to the sun
                    Nescience
the sandpiper's ignition
Illuminate manuscripts explode through glass
your behemoth or mine
the salty bowels of Satan no less a shadow
the aquarian *pied-à-terre* this crocus of glittering mud island,
    the grebe's look, diving
. transmutational obsidian
between Mount Konocti and Shasta
          across the boat of the sky people

But for love
there were new forms to birth
life was not
but for life only begun
among the various gleamings, light bearers, I met one and there are others at the
    heart of the mineral subject
It's the irrational factor
unraveling out of sight Joan Crawford at the heights the snarl
    of Dorian Gray *Comedia* of sleight of hand the velvet tissues
Watch the bean
          the Marvellous

in the wisp of wind rounding the corner at Carabeo where the magician had set up
    his rectangular table, hand and eye in the other
Today tropic birds in winter overhead as if I knew something
cubicles of wandering sound
wild parakeets to the lighthouse on the hill
This is the dream of the supernatural land
from rocking to it, what was once pain
is the bliss of it
The green demons with silvery genitalia rain down the flags of omnivorous pines
                dilating light

Native Medicine

Forty years ago I was born from a crumpled tower of immaculates that twist like
    the fleeting damaged bridge torrential rain on a road nearing Chehalis
                love driving through her native land the beauty of all I've
  received from her
the tears of an erotic Amonite sail Puget Sound to exalt the forest spirits we for
    whom all was Coyote made
the moments at Daladano our home in transfigured space
When I say love of the land I begin with native Amerindia:
Ohlones, Miwuk, Pomo, Ramytush, Salinan
with the Washo peyotlists from the morning prayer in the bowl of dawn
none shall ever steal from me our sixty eyes to the smoke hole at the Tipi flue
embers of sacred earth—the myth has not lied—
a poor man like they—old in the vision of the floating tipi over the hideous towns
    below—once with the gods they say—but I'm no metaphysician, stop short at the
    crumble of dogmas—
the objects are prefigures of omniscient dew
the slash of cosmic jokery
corpses of the doomed sciences light the way against the rhetoric of anti-rhetoric
    and human misery true fault line of Birdy Dick 'Old Grandmother'
I send up the song I could not sing this land my stony prayer people of human misery
Repetition shall not make it less than our hearts entwined
I am your mystery as you are there among the Pleiades
Ancient ones only you shall see us through
Serpent of suffering
they say there is nothing higher in the black grackle sounds at nightfall

    Spumes

Tree

The slab of secrecy Wordsworth rays with remembered light
    the luminous forest of wakened subjects birds weaving his words
the voice of *El Señor* the cape in the umbrella of voices
exchange of crowns on the watery steps Never Before intricate
      movements of subliminal audiation, fade-outs in the fabric of words
    the laryngeal vibrations of the crow of thought
fading steps to language
a few sparrow notes in the dense fog
a heraldic demon of the moment
Exactly perhaps perhaps exactly
it rains horse pearls of *anglais* from Alert Bay
the seething pit on the cubicle to strain the bit
Old pony
from the antediluvian age has carried man from the beginning
    to the end if only a shadow now
the eyes of ka-ka
                  in the circle, their ten eyes glowing
with the clay figure
the old ones on the polished abalone shell

Surrealism in the Middle Ages

I'm eight years older than Artaud when he died
For thirty years I've looked on the world he said consolidated in 1946
It's still consolidated, but denser. 'Enough, you charlatan, you hangnail vampire, the
    phantom above all
only the phantom, I don't want any doppelgängers in my stadium'
The mountain ridge extends the eating and the metabolic metaphors why not
    rhyme?
obscene photographs are burning like lava from Mount Rainier
'Surrealist? . . . Man, we don't like those labels, yeh don't have to label poetry . . . it *is*,
    man . . .'
Me, I'm preromantic. I'd as lief roll up a leaf to Lady Day as anybody
the blessed clichés in sight of the tower
'a': the winter scape ghost eggs in the pan
the material image static on the Ohio River

the breasts of mounds nearing prison
pit of the world cycle sudden illumination
the coiled dream door
hungry snow cycling the land of earth's horizon
an afternoon with Osiris in the *stellae*, scorpion at hand
Masterless, the enigmas seep out of the air
on a roundout without memoirs
to red ribbons the wind-scrivener wheels to ancient storms
medusae in an optic dance
metallic blue hats across the bar
loup-garous back from the tropics
Scott Joplin's ragtime and a faraway land to the Natchez Trace
murder as only euro-americans can sing it
a slice of wigeon's tail against the timbers waiting at the bend of the river
great flyway of ineffable seasons
Mississippi echoic spangle there's the sea it can only be the Columbia or the Klamath
loon loon I see the pelican clear
Violent Ocean (another name) Pacific never

pulverable dunes of the Least Sandpiper

West

So the atomic apocalypse has re-arrived this time borne on a scalding iron with
    curlicues of *musique*
the Age of Bronze is the whole future-dream rainbowed with festoons of resurrection
south by deepest west impales the nuclear holy of holies besotted with dust and oil
    lesions rancid beetles black among the reds
coherent waterfall
the best is lunacy stress points humanity spores in ringlets of anxiety
random mystery at some black hole
chalk-lined figures run and dance through dunes of birth
an erosion of worlds
the cosmos in a nutshell of dreams that attack
at high velocity with plain chant Barbizon school of art 1930's Big Band Jazz and
slides out of view 'Mutilation Baby' the birth of the light

∎

Salt survival glistens in raindrop third eye Polyphemous-thoughts graze Whether
    the head clears off this field of key-lined space
the torpors of harmonia
the joker leaps at the hole
from which werewolf unknown the speeding frozen fire tropics travel

At the Cafe Paradiso the glass of mineral water on the oldest rock

■

There's no worship in the temple
the hermetic secret floats elegantly among the muddy images
'I hear you diamond, drum, beat on the hill of stormy stone faces
with the end of *technē*'
The mind is a black hole of beautiful chance encounters
as with André Breton *the* André Breton in whom Jacques Vaché *is* the seminal gesture
Birth of the revolutionary rose
Sirens at doorways on rocks in place of gutted rooms
All the beauty of woman implied by the secret gnosis
Imagination at touch of silver flasks as they open the forest traveling the stony
    river's need

■

The vilified mathematic
foam current rolling oceanic lips
eternity's veil intricates of fading geometry
To imagine Luis de Góngora y Argote advancing on the Segovian plain with all the
    horns of his third eye
the poet of *Soledades, Polifemo y Galatea* at the storefronts of
    El Duque de Albuquerque
Oraibi of the next ten thousand years

■

Crab gore To give capitalism its due duck-cracker the head of a christian fart
graveyard of sanctimonious filth
Overkill, the throat of the gipper the chief of the team loaded with scrotums of
    black babies
Neptunian highways of dungeons etched from the colorados to the shithouses of
    their gory southlands
Reverse gear, I'd balloon evaporate on the raging horns of the

Marvellous the engine's vulcanization of the clerks of reason,
the forced sodomies rammed with a sauce of fried bankers into
the vast brilliants of the social liquidation

■

It's transparent sense: goblins gallop rills
Beneath, mankind prepares its suicide
Since 1910 the signature of angels O demons promised only Death as in the tarot deck
Morta-doom fleshed out on the morbid sky
leathers of psychonic enigma spelt out under the draining Ocean
drained to scarlet wood
the millenarian nightmare from which humankind, the above-man, the flowering
    of higher man, within, beyond the Nietzschean a-rhythm
Dionysian mandrakes coeval with the transforming sea, the serene eyes of Pelé in
    waters of the West
Oneiric Ocean, there's a sense through Cimmerian clashing gates
a chance in the golden sluices
above on the marshlands of being succotash and flying wormwood
spliced out on the apocalyptic nuclear wastelands
But the becoming of humankind lodges frozen limousines—1930 scissorbacks—to
    Freud's dream book
the mote in the real shaking the dust of coattails Madrids of Gothic dust whose
    sinister cities re-open the superchargers turned in under the seat of Toltecs and
    human pits
as if the Ranters, at perilous roosters perigrinating fields, tuned the transforming
    card's magnet west
to the Lemurian crest
                    Anna Anáhuac
Antillean to the coracles in seas of Dream Raven Pele
Hypnos belly the leviathan-squirrel jumps in the grass of the dead humus-machines
    of the marvellous Rosicrucian Heidelberg in front of the Thirty Years' War

■

This infinite reference to the external world
laid out bare bottom from Vasco da Gama
to the Mississippi slung on a wheat loaf in Kansas

1) the articulate wonder hanging over gretchen woods woven in
    pretzel of pop dreams
    spun of the lost seasons

2) the turbulent West always receding dream more than vision's
   damask
3) the baroque madness of Columbus from the ropes of Thomaar
   glistening in Shaman's burnt fetish
4) the fire stone knit with the waters of the West

   ∎

The ring-tail of an Arcimboldist
and the genital history of this wrench
                    the clove's dive peanut of
the wing-tail of an Arcimboldist
even then the deluge myth universalized the fanciful lore of bat enclaves a sauce
    of thunder and bluebearded photons curl on the tanoak sidereal convulsions of
    Molino's 'disentanglement' of the pneumatic sponge
webfoot out of gear on the lake's rudderless voice *over there* in lands of ancient
    chiclé, mouths but mouths the bizarre traits that lead back to the
hangnails of an Arcimboldist
like parapsychic semblance homunculi of Absent Life
morbid delights
angle of quotidian flying glass framed up in a core of magma

Talking antlers gesticulate the coming on waves of the King of the Western Isle
his tree-lined face seen from a beach at Fort Bragg

Ship of Seers

The dust of intolerable social conditions packed like melting bombs floats the grease
of the human condition. The crystal tones form your face, Lady Urticaria, waking up
in a dream of yellow jacket hives. Fixed explosive in a clash of bull horns . . . recurring
portraits of the dream work gleefully watch the cannibals eating the Europeans. But
for your exits of shattered glass, the stage magician's hand turns up the joker tuning
the valves of twentieth-century wars. Political torture machines fornicate over the
frozen mire, electrical beds rain down engraved stones siphoned by arks on the waves,
luminous shadows of the invisibles. There's the glint of plural worlds in the play of
matter, 666, horsepower to veil and rend the putrid walls.

Pluto in Scorpio—the devachanic sheen on the perceptible plane—green gloves on
the trees of the Calafian summer are the minced cuckoos to end the slaughter of the
beautiful beasts.

Only eyes will be horns as antlers touch in a deer dance. The mounting collage, *The Sacrileges of Jesus*, indwells an age and scores holes the death squads shall not pass.

Only man and the bird are divine. Coasting on folds of air, the White-tailed Kite meets its mate, the great sun of love, between the paint of feathers—touch in rigorous thought. The vision situates who we are like an oracle of another world. Whoever meets the sudden revel seers the earth's renewal. From the powders of Pele: the return of real life. The primordial ferns wrap memory's rotosphere.

The prince of birds thought himself the intelligence of wild pride, forefront of the flying objects, hoof-marked with victory through granites of language, on paths only woods in agony spare to flight—this, the raptor's alchemic sight, oppositions of delicate harmony—harpoon of the Inuit shaman, at hand. In an ash of words, the hanging mask floats over all the fires

Oceania

Oceanic west, the husks were sculpted in your caves like the maverick
Grackle

      Oceania oceanic.

Haven Root

Ichabod, Jonathan Pressgang,
lutenists populate the land
firing Poe on Fort Sumter
Malacca canes replace the tobacco of the Mississippi culture
O great Chickasaw the fox clan I invent subverts gonorrheas of language
the sublime Marvellous at Burney Falls in the life and times of Teddy Roosevelt
time to plant the magnetic spheres
at the heart of the mystery the lalops in Crater Lake
the phantom boat approaching the green beams
the man writing in the masks of Lemuria
destruction of species corruption
green speech from a green stone
the green wind of green winter
the mimetic forms
on a tongue boat of lung
sun of the bottomfish beneath the dip
where water rushed the faces in the rocks
years of green reformation

green grace
and a farflung season outside *Sol y Sombra*
America is a Transylvanian outpost occulted
but sometimes visible down a lane of trees by the ghost of Netzahualcoyotl
Sandman from the north always the pure aroma of pine resin electric to the Great
    Tetons
the rollicking maypoles of imaginary Canaans forgotten in redwood dust
Out of gather silence gathers
like snare drums gushing the golden articles
federating anarchs
the jiffy solution at the unity of opposites
the rush of Shakespeare in the oblivions of Atlantis
'this rock, sir, a blind set of blinkers'

final 'em out

the black pounded face
'vut the nazis did vuz wrong'
There's too much Aleister Crowley and the vaudevilles of,
anti-visceral campaigns are waged
no quarter in the dream desert, heraldic
       ORNITHOS
             the planet Venus
penultimatics coverge
the muscular ignitions sleep Better sleep but awaken awaken then as 'before'
an eagle dim on the horizon
         the Great Year revolves
between the close view of
THE WHITE CROWNED

Invincible Birth

The glaciers of cities, pits, the abysmal mysteries of Baudelaire's labyrinth, one can
    say, breast of the city
tufts of avian mystery in the sun's eye
the old street gleaming with lizard paint
to drink ecstatic
as with, ectoplasm
the first sea-wash stain
with wind sonatas scratched from an old bore's heaven

It's in this city the supreme magic is enacted
The ballplayers appear under illusionary catapults
wood impact to wood graven images scooping invisible graves the solemn moment
    of sunlight
The afternoon habits destructions of Annapolis
morbid freaks à la P.T. Barnum
Aristocratic slaves siphon the nectars of poison
I catch a fish or let it flow
hone a jigger of gin lemons sighting birds
The deep feelings are fumbling a screwtop of the heart chakra
the death of love in youth Poisons are scarves presaged by heraldic kites
the marsh in a tide pool of seers

the owl occulted
the kestrel darted
poised to bridge the white eagle's tilt
to the magenta tree in a heron's eye

Two meters from Golgotha spanking Mohammed
spyglass of an ancient falconer on the *parvis* of the Temple
a human esoterist secret

harbinger of erotism
wonder of thrones
the last remnants at Klamath Falls mobbed by flickers
distant loon more distant loon

In my frenzy mantic mania whatever poisons surround me
from where to where death answers with blank disdain
Ministries of wonder are death's unknown
It's marvellous the unknown spins this pen
pure monad from the dyad
the pyramid side-glance abyssed crack
echo by owls rolled in an arbor of timeless time

The celestial dome in the sleep of eternal revolt
flowers in a couplet's eye jade horses anything will do to tread in every sense the
    psychonic oracle
It must be you Ghetto City
the drizzle of grizzlies before the flood
the electric guitar on the lugubrious slopes
On hills of popping silver
city of valleys at haven's gate

Frisco before the bucks went down the leaden towns
five thousand Indigenes under Mission Dolores
Wind tube of hordes belches the stone of silence gemmed in a series of ecliptic yore
passing the Shakespeare seal 'it never dies' through the happenstance Frisco crunch
the spinner of all violence is dove
spangled floor of vision cliché after cliché
a rerun to Gallic springs on the boat to language
the glitter of green fossil sphincters of worn pages aglow
all the animal treasures and poetry goes on swelling the tides squandered with dew
jonquil and juniper-flung subaqueous Sausalito
the red-winged hawk from ink spots in a knot of lore
The silver curtains of the Asterean Eden flow all the fuses at the pine forest
    decembered with infamous solar radiations
the world federation of anarchs
the myth of the South American Brilliant returned from the shoals
Perishing star systems Enough of a raid on the tsetse-fly

The kestrel's armor is a woman hunting a site beside a man becoming bird
Donna prima the wind in their sights
                red skylarks of escape rare seeds in a covey of quails

Black Window

                        typewriter heap
    point point the external world a sublime slice of superfice
standing like a star over the slaughter house
the garbled language a garlic sausage to Shiva itself a texture desire herself all the
    beauty of the world in the clashing bodies, sur-objective poetry, the letter 'a' in
    folds of obscure light from the dream forehead of sexual sleep lost to the highest
    splendor
the rocks crumble
this trance with or without you
white shadow rifting the tidal chamber of children's cruelty
papyrus dust to one side
on the other, the hungry hounds of nostalgia
orchard of her mouth of peaches
on her wrist the Arcimboldist medallion of tobacco deities in the crocodile mimic
    river whose symbol outshines all the others

on the brink of indigenous dawn
clear in the autochthonic remnant
the blazing shadows on the rocks at Hopi
the lords of life rising in the age of regeneration
the *orgia* of the first corn from hollows of earth
In the desert the Sentinel embosses lucidity with geodes of geomantic frenzy

Everything is in the tortoise shell
I plant the foot of Crow
symphonies of squirrel magnets thrown with disdain
Past? future? the matter matters little in sight of *nigredo*
                          and the oils of ointment
putrefaction to the bridge of purification
like new wave in the arid land stymied with sphinxes

Indwelling the calcination of words
'misanthropy forever!'
a passerby in the Pythagorean legend Dracula old friend the wheels of your revolt
    from the grave have undergone torments through the antibiotic bardo plane
Star War syndromes hang like purple flowers and the smack of sorcery
tiny crabs of tidepool gather all the optical rainbows for the apertures stigmatizing
    the subatomic into a calm sea
When you hear my words you will see them after coming home they leave me
these palpable shadows that sparkle
show their sides
dance
blow out candles
grapple
diced in sand
Just now a magnet of living juice has been whirling the mental plume
and death's sacrifice on the stone below traveling the lingual stalactites
Only verbs glow on the absolute rim
Discourses of the doctors of death are the poet's chorus
                  'September in the Rain'
Turkish quarter of raspberry ice in the gloom
of immaculate restaurants a spoonbill between her thighs

America in the Age of Gold

This one gives out he thinks poetry's at his beck and call
magic though proves it otherwise
even if adhered 'spiritually'
soul whoppers gleam like solar rain
swift beaks of spring
golden automobiles in the muse's eye
the only darkness set in the distance
back to spectral Demo rotten mythologies stifle the air
thunders of the external world internalize
'and pay them no heed'
laying out the cards of triplicate dreams
always the future ruins of Coit Tower Manhattan African cities

From this north my head is full of you, Sur America
Sor Juana sailing the cloud her back to us from Mexico *real*
meeting John Donne in Arizona nearby the Penitentes are active
the massacres at Humboldt Bay later in the nineteenth century
recall now to memory
under the ruins of Brasilia
the red obsidian light of Church's *Cotopoxi*
siphon from the black marvellous swan in glass
the way trees revolve cosmic beauty
                         Pine of diamond crest
                         warblers of dew
Oak on the swollen breath at ocean
ancient wood my native land all this that vanishes

It's Blue Jay the doctor bird under cover of the silent machines
waits in the wind of Crow Raven Blackbird
ways the language leagues to bridge the polis
                 sugar of the secessional forest city
the last utopia a mimesis like the tree monkey of Borneo
given to Mallard 'the most beautiful of the Bird People'
for the Pomo there below Mount Konocti the home of Obsidian Man
to the whisper in the waterfall
There are many centers of mystic geography
but the great Black V of gold flashing in the meadow Bird unknown
opening the air like all the lore of the chants
                 this may serve as shield
for the companions of the kestrel

At the green bowls green the revels of time
to step into orbs of the before time
wake up where the glyphs are lit within
with purest golden light
the Dawn-Bringer Meadowlark
the inner temple the forest temple
the American destiny line carries us to the Klamath meeting the ocean the river
    salmon spawn
Karuk of my dreams who dance the world renewal
the pentagonic flower of spring
legends of pine warblers
Junco of the most elegant suit
in a song of dynamic black and white
                        alternate tones
harmonic wholes
           alcohols of
              the secondary powers

In the last wilderness of the mind
the chatter of world destruction below above the telepathic line
the minor key to the weather
the landscapes of Volney's ruins of empire
the expanding luminosity of Cole's Catskill paintings
I think of Cole at Burney Falls
Quidor at the Rogue River Rapids
the anonymous painter of *Meditation by the Sea* at Cape Arago on the secessionist
    coast
South channel to the riparian woods
all over Northern California still the end day imaginary land
lupines and poppies vegetable craters volcanic whispers
Wind ancient wind has hatched these Calafian landscapes
the sublime in the old sense
in the last days optic revolutions open the definitive end a forest to be
the irrational on a hindstone
Fata Morgana of the desolate strait
a hundred-mile wind and waves of violent ocean
There you drown send the death and with lumens belabor the straits surfaced to
    Shiva
She angelic tongue or not We're coming from the east to Celtic shores across the
    golden belt hanging the sights the flare of sand in the sea of dreams
wave of constant death the way red by chance comes forth

Antique language diagonal to intersections of time
south by northeast one with serpentine rock
warblers off nets the cliff hanger's spell
birds so caped the skies in the time of the Karkins
to walk a living bridge of salmon
what was once joy with the supernatural beings
Gilak in the Pomo legend
That these spirits are here now with the clunk of material letters
the yellow-billed Magpie in the dry wind

Old nights of Bisbee the parades rolling back to Frisco
the Huachuca mountains inflected in a grossbeak
Copper blue rim of the rambling planet
across the *collini lombardini*

> 1985 a number of antique
> printout somewhere primitive
> countryside of
> imaginary birds

Who can knit you in a closet?
The onrush of the western mythic image minute luminist transcription subverts the
    language the Canadian octophagic sails out of sight

The leader of a band of criminals
old Murrel It's good enough to skewer the waters
of the Natchez Trace There's sympathetic survival
early nineteenth-century outlaw of the wilderness
'Murrel's the finest'—'a wit of the wilds'—'a poet of predatory powers'

There's nary a Wilson but the warblers send cascades that wing
    the ears of Choctaws
Poetry magic love liberty
the unequivocally mediocre is an anti-meditation on bird houses
golden ringlets rare afternoons
the glade of theoric ornithic hermetica
a talon of deva dravidian bird
dæmon of legend
plucking the string
a diagonal of dew for the finches red-streaked
for the blush of the sun
the fifth note

Wilderness Sacred Wilderness

It's cozy to be a poet in a bed, on a copse, knoll, in a room
It's terrible to be a poet dragons around to bite off your wings and dream of the
    Standing One
as Nietzsche turns into Victor Emmanuel Re di Italia
Helen Ennoia looks up into the eternal pools of the eyes of Simon Magus
and all the botched lies of mythic ties kick open the corpse
    a bag of museum dust
                    manikin
in the manner of Simon Rodia, Buffalo Bill, like P.T. Barnum like
    Alka Seltzer
              goes against it
burnt pork eaters
El Dorado is the flashback to pancake mornings 'home is where you
    hang yourself'
              signed Bill
The games of golf on the misogynist wastes
centuries multiply metaphysical field notes
There's the sleep of Ra in the West
a blurred photo of purple and lumens
on a windy hilltop in the manner of Man Ray
luminous sky my own poetry chimes at the horrid hour of hideous chimes
Poe's Appalachia in the far western sea where the forest saves us the forest hides us
    telepathenes in a circle of friends
salacious hour of shadows regions of the undead
hangnails of the Gilak an infinite crystalline substance spun all the traditions
moored in nine powers the gurgling carburetors
the video cassettes the people are coming we're at
the communion on the mountaintop it's true but
the wheel turns the beaver chews the pole holding up the world
It's coming back home like a dream-memoir at the death of day in the poetical
    pastiche framing a mask of postcard view from the dawn of Ra
it's the moment of Maldoror
the collage objects of the end days conjunct the plutonic week a roadshow of
    nineteenth-century bison
as the Buffalo Bill Follies autodestruct by 1916

Sweetbrier

No time like the present to damage the brain
at the hoodwink of nuclear physics a lamentable science
the red-faced cormorant on the rocks through the filaments of original creations at
    Fort Bragg

Precipice of a lost floating object of deciduous funnel
sighting the common merganser
From the prevailing temple a xylophonic rendition of concordant Symplegades
triangulated to the harmelodic pentagram
seven disks of seven depths
with a mirror transcribing Mount Hood
the erosion of redwood graves
the sufite mysteries multiple worlds (you've heard it before)
a majestic earthquake Los Angeles-style the forefront cranial thrust
It's 1879 I'm crossing the Rhineland
laughter in a glass of bilge water
the crust of the frolicking wood
hands off the waterfowls!
a little creep noise obeisance of slave enigma
oyster catchers with orange tourniquets
(cut the nonsense—no—emphatic yore of lore—bring it about, Burgundians!)
with a clip of Edward Lear
my fork of splintereens
gull ladies on the fleeting deck
macho voices flail lambs at gurgle obscenity

the gulch rococo pinnacles
there the birds land
a violent tradition glides by the heart of those rocks I live
the last time round a spore war

nowhere to go to see to be to crimp

    ■

It's nighttime in the wigwams of the West
(there never were any)
There were tree houses and lean-tos
the link to the antique esoterist oak
millions of Squirrel Girls in manzanita
only the lucids of luciferian dew

Yeh-ho-wosh-ohey-yah
the astral interludes
motorific cyclones a bridge of garnet almost granite
the prediluvian sand
no more infinity
a sulphuric sun of cement
no more time
mirror that reads me
turtles and the *roi du monde* to garner waves womb and Anglo-Norman relations
power of dream sonnets Piccolo above the powers
rites of the mechanical man
the green restaurants of his slow-motion grace
leaven to the Celtica renewed Martin de Pasqually to Saint-Martin two hundred
    years
from the reintegration of man
You've got it I am Mount Shasta Also acid rains

    ■

At tungite
oil beams coiling Lombard Street
the medieval tomtit rare sighting
a coracle of repellent forces a snipe
There's the grand sentence
oriole wrappings over the hound dog mouth of *poesis*
It's time for frickle frackle
glut of virus
the voice of klunkies in the street
my friends the Blue Jays of *paradesh*
the juggler veins of jungles
beached out the entrance to the dream curtain
imperishable myth and the slip out of dream figures in an irony
Close-fisted volcano
slow reams of clashing bodies
harmonias of silt
fog monsters the quadruped renewals of lark
we live in the north of the Gilak's Land
It's the solar magic of the place
swifts starlings cabal on a plane of pitfalls plots the polis-pears and a hocus-pocus
    hand tears from a Twenties poster generating the rose of the winds
pale cloth of reformation on the far western shore

Treasuries of hummingbird preserves sequestered against the vegetable ogres
perishing dolmens
silt of gold gulches
the wind-spread of velocity's gale
vulcans of Ocean far western rookeries and phantom birds

The Romantist

Western winds from Oceania and the dream of sighting the great singing thrush
wings dart the sword in hand on the crest of the Duke of Calabria
all of this which confounds 'cabala' with 'gabalis' and the Immortal Cagliostro
the power of *Chi'i*
erotism denuded of its chalks
off into morbid matter the flung dozen puncture the Smokies
eagle heart swallowed on the Rockies of icy dreams

Ornithos looms

with sunlit shafts of western isles
whale challengers over the driftwood gales
dreaming the birds of Borneo and the great
vulvic breast of Mount Rainier

              rituals worked by material substances
the powers of bedrock across the lichen-headed toads
of powers, dimly they say, the massive unnecessary pain heightens the White-tailed
    Kite and favors Aurora
the pith in the crack of the secret lore
      a Punjabi more or less sacrosanct
          bilge in a faun
Elemental animists mount the surrealist card of Pancho Villa and the supreme
    independencia of Simon Bolívar

but the hideous chimes
children we dreamed the bells of Edgar Allan Poe in the school bells the trajectory
    to nightmare the broken curl of day dream
            waterfall of jugular veins nazi hips and the lichen-frenzy of church bells
the cloud of Poe's poem seeded in the present clutter
of revivals of Lovecraft's
seer of the sepulchres of bells the flocks of reason mimic the gongs of all the bells
Enter the Queen thigh bones wet with moons

Fleeting dizzy with death
the lugubrious pianos dim out the song of star wars
the fleeting regenerative revolutions to the source
the Great Blue Heron intersects humankind on the path to the stellar *obscurum*
Forever is a day forceps of mind
melted glacier churning truth the lies on time
sudden eclipses
the rent run of national bejaysus gabble history
a strand of ritual teeth the author of *Maldoror* precurses the swift's mandible at the
    close of the century the blooming trace of Robbie Burns vindicating woman
the rite around the oval, planes air
a crowd of anarchs
liebe Silvanus love and mysteries
a glade, deciduous temple-scape
junk food spit loggerhead to Merlin's maze
                seeds
of funny cataleptic electronicals nudge the licorice ball a female of the lunar species
    the black
sun of dreams that swallows all

I'm back from *Kemi*

there's an edge with wings solstice calm bracts of ashen rectangular dew
the hanging ovals the cream of oasis
May peppers popping Whittier-scapes through Chicago's brown dust
sentinel of wind at Surrealist Street
white houses crumbling Manhattan
and the ranches thereof

The smoky snow of me nostrils the lame deer hung with sunrise
silver snake up the rib of the Pawnee prairie at the discovery of black holes
    Chippendale with scrumptuous barracudas

                muse of the day
all the pleasures *à la Fourier*
                the spinning rose of eglantine
            terraces of cherry-passing rites of cedar waxwings
in communal regeneration with the forest of cities
    a twig crystalized to scavenger birds
black-horned suns in the glen

The bird landed the flower spoke
poetry is for birds

all voices clamor now lightly
a broken tool, spadixed, mumble at the torn edges
to dream awake
porous rocket of roving
members of our band
old-fashioned chloroform sends up the theater of new cities

Embarcadero trance-conductors a slip of hip

the wavering bunch angulate their eyes move in morbid costumes

ash tomb of light
romantists reap the swirls between the glances of robots
this time of sibilant rhyme

Revery Has Its Reasons

'Operis processio multum Naturae placet'
'Nature takes great pleasure in the processions of the colors'
this thought from the book *King Hercules* illuminates *la noche oscura*
at the time of dangerous catastrophes tipping the scales by tortuous labyrinths
    traversed by misspelled messiahs the christian communist descent to the final
    pit and only then the chance operation another species transmuted to the quick
    conversion of liquid to the Age of Gold
'The Oak and I are one' said Taliesen
(the oriflamme will not work, ogre of washed-out valves)
to go off the traveled road
the cells leaves birds frankincense tour the corners of the glyphed theater of the
    walking feather river
Heat the secret longer moot point
leaving the livid solarity at the beehive's mouth
the sap explosions of honey enthuse the wood
intervals of the durational image
suckerpit of illusion taking up the reins of magic
horsing around the sacred whiskey, *'Yo soy marihuano'* wrote Barba-Jacob
There's a laugh confounds the door to assimilate husks boiled up from crystal
ice links the sirens in a glass of soma

There are no antinomies, *Masau*, in your secret room
From the fissures of Walpi you can clearly read the age of the colored corn
species variant lingual upon the forms

the secret thought of an ancient site
Golden Gates speeding the Pele-lined warble Igneous Polynesia
Always I see the three-horned head to count thirteen cones rainbowed
    to stalagmites off Captain Cook the fetishes of elephantine animals crossed by
    libation and pleasure at the roots
It's the skin of shadows, ornithic rites
a pulchritude Raven approves Coyote frolics
        madrone berries, miraculous *convivio*
            the final sublime on the carnivorous floor
'The right to be lazy' continues all thought
Only then the pure dream
scallop shell intricacies
singing up the spring migrations a telepathy wandering before returning White Crow
Night and day your head in a tumble spin of circulation

Virgo Noir

burning heart of love
open wound of being
through the crystal palace under the waters of Madumda

go the light body
at Mount Shasta
a sprinkle of fools
with spiritual fascisti
General Ballard into the golden Tetons
semen dripping the teeth of Saint-Germain
in his role as the abbot of atheism
Human waves of Cairo meet the ponderous faces at the Calafian coast
She's in their mouths
    a house like a pyramid
    built with rectangulars
perfect pear of a diagonal
down to the stars picked from photic jargon
The hand that writes is worth an empire on the moon
elbows on infinite plastic counters
a crashout to impressionism
flute in the mingled feet—a way out of Dolores Hidalgo
'El Español' at the end of the road visions

the sky of black patches
Twelve blazing candles
on the road to Dolores Hidalgo
Corpses with bloody worms on the road to Dolores Hidalgo
They say there's a world outside me but I know better
Enlightenment in the *kali yuga* is a daily recurrence
shubahdu it's over taking a long trip to the stars
waves of *ta-meri*
gums up to it—shaky—dracula—up under it
the beauty of it tilts the aromas beyond the gargoyle of spume unknown in the still
    sea of years aeons before in the after time
beautiful evil only you are beautiful
in a potsherd
falling through embers of sleep
to spell out the pit without mouths
but a tongue salty lepers sibilate the false bards pontificate Elysian dust off Mission
    Street
In the Far West all the birds fall *sinistre*
rise of triple towers
solely the ancients
the blue gash of manzanita
joy of the revelers passkey to Neptunian depths no surface baboon can smother
orbit of faery spirits on the green scum
    silvanus erectus
the phalloi swung like a boomerang in groves of clitoral ferns
green in thunder
woven neat over the glossological floor

Irrational

> On a hill in Frisco
> the gothic spread of the mantle
> Pelican fragments
> through the black port
> of a species speaking stones

It will be another earth, parallel earth, in ancient states of becoming—igneous,
    mineral boiling seas of other earthen worlds

But this one, once called 'the new world' is again the old world of ancient earth, all
the more living from the neural feet of vision, *Vesta* the giver of forms

The return of the ancient earth is America in the gothic art of its name, *Armorica*—
Hy-Brazil—ancient Americas rising like hieratic light in Thomas Cole's Hudson
River painting

as in the Hopi cosmos and the alchemical visitation
the earth within the crust we tend
to the sidereal maps of its seas, luminous shell over the sun belt of sky for those who
fly to the sun
This old earth this old America is beginning to smoke the *krita-yugic* paradise, the
Age of Gold

As poetry is wedded to silence
the last word heard is the gold of silence the ancient earth is weaving
      the humanisphere is turning
      landing dead on arrival
      the seances of poets Poe Blake Whitman
      Emily Dickinson Samuel Greenberg
            Jones Very above all

Game's the Right Title

In all the mermaid taverns of the world
his master's cap was tipped to the dregs,
the wayward leer of seers
draped another drudge, Beelzebub's bracken horde.
The floating gentlemen souped her briny breasts.
To the west from the west the ships knelled at heart's DisEase.
Knocked with frenzy
the lintel's song and the scent phoenix
piebald on a bait's long scallion—formed.
Let it go, the brangled leap,
le grand pas on a moonlit eidolon
the ricochet between pinball mouths,
rerun to Reason
digging the dank stone rizzled with reason.
Flayed on a corpulent bed of the irrational,
the open diphthongs dust the scholar

but the hated voice, become lovable with skeletal horn
to tear up the debris.
That's the light, the hand that writes
quicker than the eye, no escape from the triple stone.
Angel risen, beaten from the streets
optical illusions are my meat.
The grindstones of reality are crept with learnèd gnats,
but out on the tundra
the first-sung sparrow's song:
     a painting that windows the coming dawn
in a past so present the future tumbles to the lattice
platforms of dew. Spaced with fluorescent modules
the fact is, hate has molded love to be free
which coils around the sighted tree:
Fair Child or none. 'Cut the tree!'
the hawker's shriek. In a bobcat's dream,
Egregores from the North meet casually
at the foot of Mount Shasta
that mysterious scape of fading newspaper headlines.

Words I Dream

A gem with a head
a life on the brink
falling like a lute
through endless space
heart strings are felt
the wonderous look of invisible fish
drunk as sober is
the street a dream
no dreams in death
the outside inside
and the tediums of insufferable labor
Captain Stalin in Generalissimo Franco
believe me 'the turn of things'
nightmare in a glass eye
smooth and simple as Milton's dictum
Sensuous spirit

the Babels of violence
I'll say it with sputniks and spuds of desire
on the loamy earth of the heart's desire
for the grandeurs of absolute equality
There's permission of persimmon
lore of my time

the gravitational pull of passionate wavelengths
a crack on the horizon
The fireworks of nostalgic festivals in Mexican villages
soothe the footsteps
up the city beneath the sea

Phi

'mystery of every day'
nothing has been written over nothing there's the title for the
    swan's game
there will be written never spoken in the horniest glade
forces are moving It was never done
There's the foam of its nothing that was never written heard in a gong without lips
    to speak it a horn it was peeking through X
the matter at hand
on the fire of the expanding cortex
there will be death there's no death in salt the lovers coalesce
never known how not to conceal
and yet light grows to a fifth seal
the rumpling waves of what is written
the pure blind beacons are the focus to the dream forest
to be read that has never been written

The Marco Polo Zone

the way vital power dances the old hills the fabled
rivers of gold
seeping to summer eruption of gullies like phalloi in a windy city future ruins pucker
lost languages reborn on a crystal drop of lingual bliss

The sage-outlaw brain of heroic powers tosses the metallic labyrinth chewing
    Methuselan myths mixing alcohol pepper haunches a deliberate scheme to
    saunter the avian anarchia
I shall outlive insanity and mark the spectrum
zoomlens to the treasure
pennant-cults among barrels of squid
                  electric odes
Belladonna of Atlantides
Die dreams of death and pain
die forever 'glorious militarism!'
The red-shafted flicker flames redolent fungus delirious stones
phi-tonic
let poisons thrive elixirs to be

all mouse of thigh bone
flexing pleasure pharyngeal automatism watches
Violinic triumph, *du temps,* the midgeon-eaters swimp the muffets of glee flayed by
    cotton mill workers on strike the burning cathedrals of ten thousand years smile
    on Pan
ligni-neo-logo 'permission granted'
I am lore bundled of crow dew finger of pine eaglet bone of my bone soaring
    thought
It was the witch of Endor
faeries like rock clusters
key of putrefaction of all possible worlds
feet below concrete terra bones crunch underground
the green solarities phanic masks
    pituitary phallus
          walls of tumbling history tiny hands waving from windows

this is no wind but hails of the West
silence the true luxury
against an auger of pain like a screaming root
linking vegetal man to Ithypallic Min from the navel returned to upper air of gem-
    lined dream of imaginable space the tooth of omnispheres at passions of granite
    and lace

Tum

my eyes are yours Great Blue Heron
the pleasures of writing you invisible telegraph of nature
a spent *dea* on the turning cycles
oak powers renewing the mythopoeia

Fez from the Atlantic waves of Tingis
the city that waves
donkey on the ocean
closing gates of Osirian disk
in a wandering rerun to the far western
serpentine light
muddy river at the wispy beams
the night fog comes to dream

the bulging orbs the bunches goey-oey
        cherries winging suckle dew
my tree haunch grape glow of spark nails
hot hills of hair
down the forelock
of the rumpled explosions of Shiva
the gist diadem
lost like swan eternities in an epiphany ending the worlds
Paroxysm of Coyote's manzanita berries
        all that is lost/fugitive/maddened by drugs
turns to prose, but poetry annulled ciphers another voice
the gilded deck chair in a rodent's transvex corridor publishing aerian copperlinks
dissolving Arizona *alchemiste*

Zanoni   A Western Border Town

    sits like a gesture
        moment by moment between the afflatus tinctures
Vel Vel the grimoires are leaking
not to know the lianas interject the plausible metaphysical bridge to the Great
    Adventure
as the sands converge their colors
        scintillate the bronze morning
let the tears blacken
the fertile acids deliver the branches making a lingual fruit for the so-called 'gods'
which is not what I meant
fall this way or that it's the same
'That's the last you'll hear of it, de Chirico'
        the Head Man *Testa di oro*

the heave of the ropes as we sight the great unknown land

Unachieved in winter a visit to
the fault lines of earth
        my right to leave the wheel with the horned ones of the hills

pelagic birds in oilslick
at hermaphroditic play no more tray to the intermediate world

Phantoms of the mind there's nothing to it
the mediumistic bridge left open by Helene Smith continually opens the way 'From
    India to the Planet Mars'
the cacadoo of vedic dust kicks up the Silurian script
the head in the Mug sphinxed out as a choir the warm feel
    of *vox humana*
as silence ennobles you diamond darkness through the terraces of being marvellous
    subtle Spring of livid rocks
the merganser's tones climb to escape cerebral comprehension
the green gorgon sights the scalpel of disjunction and the instant of re-conjunction
Return to the forest is arduous ritual
the serpentine forms, indivisible, irreversible
Mercury
Quick
and your dumpling burned to ashes There's the lighted passage to the glossy-plate
    photos of ancient Egypt the Sphinx the temples of Karnak Luxor there is
no explaining it away
Luxor of the mental gesture of light
'There's nothing outside *Kemi*'
the secret seals the way it comes back to me
                Downtown Philadelphia the angular sunset
sensorial particles
from the tip of the pyramid
at nineteen taking a sleepwalker's trip into that abyss—the abyss of certain poets
    like Lautréamont
there's a tunnel to the past that left the future
tunnel to taking hold of it
as if it were a pile of clean shirts
                in the spirit of misanthropy

Buncombe

the wounds gape out of the green cape of flimsy steel
on the hill the European tourists
are cannibalizing the gas-guzzlers of 1965
beautiful wrecks
the entry of rosy-eyed grace
tasting the juicy art of chassis-makers of the old school
back there and front chrome-goddesses and the hoods thereof
fakers of dash

put your head through this block of gores cold gores
I am swept among the trees

Death Jets

three of them have terrorized my apollo finger
most hideous
of human existence
for the umpteenth time, sans life

commentary   3/10/84

These lines respond to the omnipresent threat of species suicide, to an 'eternal' moment of decision, since it is certain that the sentence of death is passed unless there arise a conscious revolt against the forces of death—a mutational movement in opposition to all the moribund political powers who continue to sanction 'Blue Angels,' whereas, thrills vaster than the poetry of Ausias March await us if, by the next century, Betelgeuse
always Betelgeuse
pervades the skyscapes a sudden sensuous freedom to sweetly ask for *chi'i* in all
    moments

Are there any toxic beasts? Is Klamath Falls the origin?
Lemuria awaits its Tungsten mines florid with great masters
    Finally the gorge is redeemed
    with a sight worth revealing
accent on the plutonian age
your cipher in the markets of gloom
I'm over the borderline there are no barriers Accipiter ferries take us to the final
    solution

Are there end days in the ruins? The scandals of Cagliostro still ripple the curtain
    the Heraclitean wind effects Orbs rolling over Silence before dusk
Even here there's the *symbolique* of the birds Infinite tonal convolutions
the immense coil of the *Neter*—better the blur
than illucid light—better the talons will grow
as in the vegetable stone
It's prohibited to censor
A dream of birding the ancient Presidio
October when the warblers are caught in visual nets beyond the replica of Rodin's
    'Thinker'
on the headlands
the red-shafted flicker feathers are ancient Pomo fetishes
for the Stage Magician (trees
clamoring the rosebudded chest)
soars among the mental acrobatics the Venus Torso whisked away at the mysteries
    of Anarchy
at the mysteries of Anarchy, they will deny them, the thinking Heads are
    rethinking 'the Idea' in the commune of Anarchs

I have loved only the fleeting riches
                luxury before you
shiva, unknown, a forest power
shakti and I are one among the Anarchs

Fading Letters

a certain attention to detail
sight of forgotten life on the wheel
                Ebony finger tip
to water the lip of Osirian dinner
China of the ten thousand dishes
To write frantically madly fanatically
like those idols the old men sold in the ancient turn of the Age
harmony winters the octaves of the shell seduced by mineral salts
glinting from spores of being
objects dart as far as I receive them
shadows of despair coil in every urban eye
rural congresses retire
dance of the Rogue River at the clashing points in the rocks

When I took off I was going to the land of poetry but I didn't know it
for a few moments I saw the enigmatic castles suited without a tie
the glow of sight
never to fade
all that divides me from it Porous lava
no one says 'boiled' with sweet vengeance the forestation of Tübingen
On the arthritic river
swallows are languorous divinities
                messages in the chipped stones
Ave caesar
pure bird
Swainson's Thrush last movements of sensorial freedom
Werewolf or not
meat must be eaten
                shiva
suture on a flyway
dampening the peppers dancing at Half Moon Bay
copper hills eating crabs eating microscopic fungi a lemon of mites of eyelids
the way harmony is revealed across a room night has veiled with high noon
I think there will be a cowboy poet at the end of the cycle
the Kid in all the Tombstones, imaginary sludge over Bisbee
nostrils on the lunar crater dying in it collectively
                the dwellers Copper, on you, dwell
something miraculous as thirst in the desert How to handle it without magic
the bleeding head of some nineteenth-century North American poet Canadian
    maybe French-Canadian
There's no town like Vancouver British Columbia
Poe and Whitman to the people of Raven Whale Thunderbird and the supernatural
    beings whose names
ring the ether O to see the Karuk dance Irrepressible Geograph
children laughing down a green hillock in a Spring painting
to Quidor's imaginary travel-look tails
the disintegration of the bullet aimed at the miraculous Pigeon
Robin in the aerial time of the rotten borough
the task at hand I can barely burrow but the hyacinth of the season
    A Poetic Instant
in Hegel's bacchanalian revery
back there in the old spleen chamber
modest or not Death maudlin with spring clothes
the winter sun has always been my favorite
Yes the dying sun sons of the weed to its dying madness

sparrows in the rocks of the lookouts after Prophetic Famine
all was Ra in the West
from the reeds in the transient room Mid-Earth black orbs the oars of the fishing boats
swarming the insects craven with red streams of ornithic talk
the Sombers were blazing lights Hummingbird octangulates summer with all its
    chiaroscuro doublets of dew
in the morning of Ra

The Mysteries of Writing in the West

Tellus old earth whose houses are perched like 'the language of the birds'
giants of genocide slice the shadows to species suicide
the air of the message in the old sun
volcanic oil of lime at the edge of the flame rearranging forests
the priests have rioted in the last prison
Mark Plug Stone and the radiant cliffs at Hopi
the bronze raindrop
the churning rasps of the *bohanna* strips
the legends are silent
huff out at end of the century
millenarian shuffleboard diagonal to the cybernetic cipher
hawk-eyed tambourine in a glade in Spenser's liquifying glass
    of gremlins
spoofs of the waters of Renaissance Grace
the long cut of Gypsy garb in the cigarette century
the perishing republics blown up regenerate roses in honey dip time

In the monastic life of Jack the Ripper harpoon of subarctic glaciers between the
    teoria volcanica and the array of forms
the ultimate species suicide by nuclear bombardment
to the slobbering emptiness
of the gyrating generals with exploded testicles
the sly crisscrosses
precessional processional
in the night wind of solar implosions
Nicolas Flamel at his cafe row
the rats of christianity void the gates west
we go
of all nights the solar spectrum is most redolent black with gold

To the fly-plinth of death
the dogmas of Clementine shackle and shit centaurs
morbid the seasalt spark
breaks in a heart-mogopolis
the windshield wiper's gamin grimace
and grimoires of
flouted flute of your embrains Lagolith a portion of the Grail
mauvey the lung-eh
          a smithy
            to flake
the formal gargoyle sucks in its sweater
sails in pockets are shells
a dream far away in crystalline shells
beggared with lichen and wind-jambs
with dentalium of worm whippers
the sooth sculptural flywheel gasconade on the destruction of socket-scrapers
prisons plagued to an empty card deck on the horizons of Hopland
syringes balanced by elixir poisons
goggle-grinders from livers of imaginary volition

                fly bottle on the crimson sea

   •

Fawn of granulate stone
It's Marco Polo time in the Far West
down by the bunkers of thunder
'Move the prisms north
           the south direction is not propitious
follow the star . . . '
Invisible visible the hobgoblins of light saunter past bricks falling over Krazy Kat
in a summer of fogs
the earth my marrow
the sponge of nothingness gluing the atmospheres
legend winds over the window of natural devices plunged in a flask of green venom
legends go down the drain in old salty warbles
duck farms cut up by elemental decretals
forty buckets of thorn apples
dew to the ramble in neutral
Flavius Josephus rolling the bolts to the shippers
and dim messages from Easter Island

Buenos Aires in a silver bullet fondling the diamond black hair the longest in the
    world weaving home the swan of Montevideo in the year 1926
the dust of Patagonia is world enough calling the spiked aureoles of water, cave of
    mental geomant, at the zodiac at the Cliff House
a little gulf of spectral sediment
home free in a bug's eye
let alone the mite's zygote of marvels
the little cone of light hardly noticed on the brink of delivery final matrix of sex and
    thunder
stand up for Reason The Sun of Darkness
all the opposites dimmed to existent chaos
the splendid wart of incipient conundrums
and the poet is born on the chance wonders of the next century Tubalcain returns
    the metals on catcalls of wandering rivers
of *poesis*

This is a land I once lost myself where the mountains cast spells
flame throwers signal their conferees below who hatch the fire-stone
A doubling of myth
the bodies roll over on the northern roads with spectral mist 'the little cloud'

Moana at the scorpion's lair with aureoles of corn powder
the seven years in the seven salt shakers
in the green altars of the selvas of Manzanilla
the statues become pebbles
decrying the iron-clad man truncated by thunder soaped in stony eclipses
the *zocolo* of will-of-the-wisps
the first night of fireworks
the sleeping loaves of terraced corn

To look into the mirror black sun in the clouds of Magonia

Even as I meditate on an ocean of mastery, the sacred herb ensorcels until the words
    of its presence concretize the momentary short circuit of daylight as if it were
    nighttime
and suddenly all is flight
little warbles of shivaite fingers cross the sea of Enigma the way of Inspired Gull,
    despised bird of deities
words on the marrow actual wing dissecting dream worlds
    the only truth

Dell flowers on rampage of graceful solutions
the morbido-suit in porcupine pleasures are man's teeth
Only the feminine unspeakable Nun bled on all the pornographs of noise great snot
    rag of the gods
their metallic heels snapt to the rhythm of the labyrinth

Spring

In the meadow waiting for the plane to San Juan Peyotán
on the mule to Jesus María El Nayár
eyebrows of the mountain cliffs simulate the western sun
crossing *el rio de los Nayeri*
the dolmenic rocks glisten at high noon
going down the mountain to the valley of the *Nayeri*
to drink cool *jamaica* water in the warm night
dreaming of the rites that will be they were and they are knitting the
    tobacco pouch by *luna*
        carving the bowl by *sol*

the aesthetic harpoon vista
           vine
a layaway
       fleeting feet
Andromeda of the birds

Paris at the beginning of the Heroic Age in the Twenties making the round of cafes
    with surrealist friends the young Breton Soupault Péret Artaud
time of the Surrealist Research Bureau
Amber liquors
'modern style' at the metro station
vision of another world
'end of the christian era'
before holocaust and nuclear war
nymphs and the horned men of the harvest
the winged heart which is bird
Spring on the boulevards with the phantoms at high noon
Here in Calafia Spring has returned
the Chanty Bird sings in amber street light predawn song the automatistic weaving
    worthy of Neith the ancient Egyptian Neter She Who Weaves the World

There's the perfection of harmony from Hölderlin's heart sailing the Bois de Boulogne
stalinist betrayals dim gargoyles in the hypnotic glance between Chirico's masked men
even in 1936 the Lone Ranger ravaged the old oaks to Southern California
the brick hit Officer Pup Krazy Kat overtook the American loneliness
the irrational smiled in Spring
the crazed war came later
We're at the foreplay of liberty
the void expands the warm heart of surrealist spring

The young poet died in Mexico taking the wrong road to Dolores Hidalgo
where a mysterious plague raged for months unknown to the rest of the world

An American Place

To have heard Moon Dog on a corner in Manhattan visage and sounds of Moon Dog
    in a video of the imaginary assault on 'reasonable solutions'
awakens the fool-proof diagram of antique script defying computer printouts
fungi eroding metal Hope the Glimmer Goddess at the platform of hieratic beings
    moving in the landscape
handing the fruits back and forth into primeval gold
all that the triumvirate exalts
milking the Babylonian computer games
shreds of lowgrade dipthongs
shady political pits only the doggerel mongers eat
reversing gear
an encyclopedia of Swiftian solutions
                           per force
the mall people conjecture
'Are there are other lives?'
In the myth of Rimbaud the living live on in the living
sons of Arto
and the companions, navigate, navigator—gold!
Oh the paling Pounds and Eliots
when I think of you, seers, Poe Whitman Breton Rimbaud Blake
Do I dare mention their names? Thelonious Monk Charlie Parker
Magritte Oelze who smokes all the old world charms
              into the woods with binoculars
              five minutes before oblivion

A dance a sacral dance a blend of harmonies baked by igniting redwood trees little
    mystery theater when it was nothing a boogie a wandering minstrel show of the
    Plague Victims
how the old got new
Before the eighteenth century
there's a furnace coiling at Ypres On the Natchez Trace there's the spirit of the
    beatific Chickasaw
to listen with my left side No only the bridge to the right brain
there's a beckoning of the roads meeting
above the plain

Fourth of July

Resin Man turned the corner of his faery palace
Decaying politick Infinite buccolics
dim boat of crossing warbler messages
bats the dawn at Rubber City whales conifered with black bears
the chief of the Karkins and friends attack the prison of indigenes that was Mission
    Dolores
like no other the art of dreaming rattles the unknown factor
morning dew from temples of compost
all that is sacred in nature
after death poetry shall have its morning of birds
whose shimmering green light baffles and prates precisely as
germinating vessels
what escapes pulses the earth's cascade
that falls upward in a multiverse of shattered shells
overhead the flesh-hangers hiding the secret of regeneration
Chang the Invincible up from the trap doors the author of Hiawatha with his head
    in his hand
This path leads to manzanita in bloom
the vulture above Daladano signs six times the avian mystery
before the berries were Squirrel Girls
the acorn giant at Squaw Rock
the Black Cat Cafe
                Sun Assassins

Shadows turn sediments ancient hills speak in the green wind

The Geometric Hallucination

ten the shadow dual infinite pathfinder autodestruct the flint
    rotospheres Amon's secret room you all know
beaver the strews auerhahnded Hölderlin
anything transmitted at the floodgate an opal object
like a bridal suite on a stack of burning
a cosmic heap blown on a feather raping all the images of god
Delirium will brush your teeth and glue the foods away

meta-man ithyphallic shakti

there'll be gold or never be
bone the fissure intrepid with silk suckers the morbid atoms reconverge to open
    lodges encamped with a native torch
rain, her image, to berry the desert floor
flow like language in a drop of water
there's no turning back explosive blackness subverts the
pseudo-marvellous at the knell of Capital
walk-on parts of a decaying hole
The tungite given Doctor Satan veils all the flaky colors and lords of whimp
the baseball lost to the Pleiades the gory military buttons auger the time
brown wind clichés   pneumatic metals
there's the viral hook and cranny crammed up fissures of church steeples hosting
    dead matter in the Vatican's exploding tomb vampire monks ascend
the vedic crispies drip from burnt flesh
poets in flames to earth theories gulp nibelungs deranging Vesta contained
    biometrically in the shadow's shadow
the orange object spins the dusky shells and the mystic peppers
                                dance rivers of the true marvellous
bone of echo the solidified mask of the poet mummies fatuous prisons of the
    afterlife

Murmuring but faster
Maneuverable sidereal flow

the dark solar membrane famish the morbido stone

Reached the Turn

like the opening of a door
to another land a wisp of cloud the seed reels
In the ambrosial air of the cafe across from La Scala
the *visione noblissima*
                    Tameri
marvellous contortion of the *milanesa siciliana*
morbifies the nostalgic exotic
to pare to wood the ray of carnal love
space emptied of three visions in one
This way the Isisac force expands the havens
where immortal beings move
through the computer rooms to spatial mentality

things alone are happening
legends touched with regeneration
further along the end days we appear neat/clean/whistling through
                    the bones of the old indians
even to Calafia
for there was an oceanic continent or two
secrets walked the winds of Market Street
and the lost paradise a black hole

calling on the invisibles very carefully
that a signal from Mercury is a chance

                A wind and a rain may come
                another crack in time brings
                the oaken feel of an ancient
                wind at least twenty centuries old
Mother Shipton in 1991 wistful archaic
                frenetic the very arcane cant
                shredded in the commonweal

Exorcist Exercises

With all that winds her with wiffets of glory
beneath the sloth's gaze putrid honey of the Benedictine Brother
Woman at the antipodes
feathers of dust and perfume
island of exploding beds you pucker the ingots to glow water
of the cherry hung streets
the black mud sun on your brow ignites a rhomboid cascade
the heat-won symbols gamble on your knees of eternal marble
sly locks of leukocytes
floating billboards your thighs the flocculent seashells in all that spins the luminous
    stone of sphinxian matter
the plains rising from pink columns fiery ghosts liquify
Mirror of bad taste 'sent up' by the Deadwood Dick of spectral lips
the card of Blazing Star in the slow drawers of the Far West
The loss of pleasure in the nicotine heights
straddles the dragon of omnipotent pleasure
primordial self
succulent stone
the raisins of your timorous flesh magnolia of night of day
architrave of the future
my spigot my nomenclature against the orthodox
morphomatic revolution by the lyrical swarm
the blinding sun dissolved between
Greece and Portugal

Other States

Everything tilts and falls in the molochian void
a pitch of curled fingers serrates water verbs latent bowels of concrete explosions the
    sleep of metals in the 'thousand year reich'
logos Sogol another 'god'
                and Amor
Stretched out love underground
a horde of monsters cross floors beings frozen with cold fire
draped interstices of 'the flat earth theory'
Tellurian thought turns with a gem in a baboon's hand
        Impenetrable land
           dreams beyond the walls in time

Laughter walks as a three-piece suit and *baba au rhum*
down to the tip of Aquarian hail
the lugger in the spindle Tamerlane and haruspex divine
the third cheese from the left at the splatter of Doges
a seascape spliced with alcohol and *khat* from Timbuctu eros again
a thousand gamelan orchestras the tree's ear any tree any ear
In the madrone forest emblems petrify green footsteps at the red solar disk
time, the perfume of will-o-the-wisps
The mad eye rolling across the gulch
There's nothing
the empiric fortunes by snagged processionals
and the undoing of knots by head winds circling from lightless machines
putrid air in the nose of the Pope
the imams nailed on a gaping face of djinns
the starving bodhisattvas stranded on a dessicating leaf swollen with
    Bon's bones
the bubu elixir swarmed by rotting refrigerators
It's the eclipse of reason
the magnet ray gun lash at the apex splashed on granites in a green sleep and awake
    with metallic grape leaves lemons of computer tech detecting granular orations
    the first chance net the golden forest of Elphane
sounds of lingual gorges
and water's sound as the city gorges it

The movement is spent hide-and-seek between the hedges
the words the hedges
'demon in the angeloy' (as they say)
the provisional steps of quick change
world destruction in a pluriverse
infinite perspectives in the space between forks of leaves and the turgid marmoset
    in a whisky glass
the fumbling of symbolist scapes

Excreta of writing
quick! a displacement of mobs on the throat's columbiads
blooming deserts on the rough grade to Laytonville
woodpecker shamans saunter through firs of owl mechanics
the rapid growth of horse whips against the flanks
the flanks voyaged with pearl studs
the last look back and the trays of light afar
a shake up of shoveling death
a ray of regenerative death

matchless pain on the snow-banked summer
poured out from a cascade into a jar assuming the ocean

deep in shell's castles
the lemon leaf balloon tears up hundreds of steps to Coit Tower

>Bear's paw
>river of imaginary rain
>mite's bridge
>the forest diminishes
>a turn edenic at the end

wandering in a morsel of graves
flowering manures volatile with smelting ores raining away
>under *Huracán*

A great struggle to widen the gap
Another chalice of drifting metal
the flocculent chance of onyx leaves
the dark of lights between the islands secret suns in the fires of the night toward the
>Kwakiutl dawn
'Siempre Norte'
Bear Power travels streams of paper ocean
Phantoms of light scissor the scapes to drink nine rivers beyond the Modoc of
>raging woodpeckers

At world's end the jay opens the water at Burney Falls
the spinning beaks music the green phones in a gull's speed
to tip the tree with nuggets
stillness and silence behind the egret's map of vision

Saunter a paradise between the bent rods Just so the goatherds
>of menace mandibled from Pennsylvanian hills into spore wars at
>Thunder's Place
the sheep have lunged from their star paths over Alhambra and the curvature of
>convolvulus in summer gone to the brisk of the wind gnarled with the smoke of
>mummy fat irrigating membranes of overturned earth of the hundred varieties of
>Peruvian potato
the jacknapes of surprise line my vision with orchidian trumpets
the mountain ridges of cigarette paper send up the six directions of Mary Austin's
>desert informants
leaving Los Angeles stranded on a rock's erosive ocean

The patch of summer fogs screws the ears of the forest city
through the absence of bells lacerated by the onslaught on all the world's religions

Reversing Year

> Swifter than hunger
> Raybolt a shift of the hand
> Slight out of gear
> And a ringlet of buzzing sound
> Speed of starlings
> The Frisco of scorpions rare mirror
> Of Nineteen Eighty Four
> The multifarious spin out of graves and pyres
> Of a wipe out by water and the golden powers

There

on that chain of Ohlone mountains
shafts of light on a bobcat
through the thick madrones
first seen emblems that endure cupped my nine years
the great booming voice of nature
in the red bark's sloping labyrinth
who called my name
fetishes of pebbles and tabac in a redwood pouch
secret house of bark between the branches
these lights never die whose'embers glow wilder
than wilderness at the beginning of words
to catch the ring of stars
                              at the still point
of infinite sur-rational flight
all was bathed in red
according to the perfection of temporal mirrors
elastic time in the gape of memory
visionary recitals in the exultant spring oblivious to the sea

Shasta

Against the current words came looking for me, the spark which evolves from *luz:*
   youth in the wind, tugboat in the bay, pollen lashes the gulfs of earthquake—
   laughing pilot, lingual lip sopping mineral waves—lost Aton hurtling forests
   down the atomic flue.

Steady the age, moon-signed zero minus zero year. Alexander Pope sabred the
   floxgloves. Whirlpool of Ys, the churning of divulgent scapes, everywhere the
   locus of dream. A jolly pencil in the void spins the tissue of stone. Graveyards of
   redwood root systems flavor salt systems going up river; the sparrows of summer
   launch pyres of rain.

Shasta great Shasta
Lemurian dream island, perhaps Atlantis, scallop on the sierras, Hopi sovereign of
   animate dream, oceanic claw: Alta California climbs into view.
Shasta great Shasta
geography in a mystic state later pruned by seers.

The return of the mad child molester, talking to him unravels the secrets of the
   Second World War. In the alchemical legends, there's a certain star seen at the
   completion of the Work, appears on the silver horizon through the trail in the
   grove. The languorous green dew strokes the burning red beam. The succulent
   pine resin writes kaleidoscopes between seasons.

The roads are closed by fire. The roads end, darken. Omens thicken, the psychic
   pain of being born. Only the blue vapor endures like sidereal weaving at the black
   seed, decay in the waters of the equestrian sea.

From the spiritualist masses of the nineteenth century, the flicker feather collectors
   were defeated in rampant raids by inhuman hordes. Our ancestors born of
   the fruit fly are delusionary landscapes founded by autochthonal forces yet
   unknown. Wisps of *tankan* containing subatomic particles in the Azoth, the
   climbers mask the daemons where all was created . . . Transparent does lighten
   the prisms, ochres and green winds converge to interject the crossroads to the
   hooded figure . . . Apertures open to the Red Pepper Shaker . . . Silken inner
   tube—dream voice—is it you? Toxic filaments orison the radiant ebony idol.

Like a poet of the Phantom Empire, the roofer is tarring plutonian bones. By the
   melting computer stations, the power that was called up in the Fortean Society
   on Union Street drifts powders over the Lombard Steps. Hidden Marin to
   Mount Diablo in the east, first greetings from Blue Jay.

Rock power to the evanescent tabu-city sunlit on the leafy leather lizard of my
hands—the madrone berry-lovers unfurl. Heat unravels the paradigm of a
unique climatology of minds and few summer days auger the flame of Grip, a
rider of rhododendrons to the north. I see chthonic man, and it's the wheel—
the hated wheel—sending up a sliver of lucent dawn arched on a sunbeam
serrating the vegetable stone: the light of her going by, a superior earth being, her
clothes blued as a tissue of incandescent gold, something like an appearance of
words—seen.

The fox spirits screech a pentacle for the fields drenched with flamboyant flagons,
the baroque from all times, and flamenco barocco, as I leave you, Albion, gore of
song: sempiternal dream curled in clouds of seashell, putrid cupids and the Black
Fathers raping the wood nymphs of Nouvelle Bretagne.

The masked poets rise from the crumpled floor. The last aperture, reseen, glitters
like a tortured cat. The flaming madrones are projecting the ballrooms of
old Bisbee Arizona with Frisco *haut cuisine,* around the horns of unknown
catastrophes for the Ohlones . . . The point is, the point is, the external Frisco
scene is beginning to look like a 1928 *National Geographic* pinpointing Atlantic
City, the European tourists wearing 1984 American-style, the marriage of Europe
and North America, a locus of imminent sedition: Shasta from Suisun Bay north
to the Rogue River; Frisco: diplomatic zone between IT and southern empires of
regrettable memory

and LA-ba
           a special *là-bas* policy will prevail.

POEMS 1986–1993

from No Closure

Yes, those "arts," poetry and music rhytmos eurythmos
the leap to pentacular time being here, duration to starve you for images
Notices on the return of an "immortal" Cagliostro a poet who published
    miraculous cures
to the final entrapment of the Great Magus laved & reverenced by the people and
    the few
For this "the powers that be" schemed until he was tricked into the hands of the
    Church Militant dying, some say, in a dungeon in Rome
They confuse him with his "double," Saint-Germain, credited entirely with
    longevity
But it's a story too short a myth too long
There are those who see in the martyrdom of Cagliostro the definitive
                 sign of his Power to so upset the Papal Inquisition—
    but the Virgin state of harmonic proportion is that of the net of
        birdsongs melodic to the last moments of day the true four
        times true
    Visionary Concordium—
    the green language—
    whose green life of birds
    becomes the language to
    receive the heraldic sign bearers
There's a foot movement Again the glyphic representation of a surrealist event
In that case harmonic proportion is a word cluster
Life would be pleasant—harmonic enuf—if the green world would re-forest all
    urban centers

Re-forest first my native Frisco

   ▪

True to four streams of wanting to fly turned into a
vocation for winged words
whether here or there the motors churn to an invisible interior
For I have, as the poet Cowper, known 3 cycles of "depression" cursed by my own
    line:
". . . fallen into the goblet of suicide . . ."

Principle / triad of a glimpse of the Mozartian Kant whose synesthesial
    imagination plastic surprises and the postcard a friend showed me of Arthur
    Rimbaud hieroglyphically coming through old walls of Paris apocalyptically
    collages what *photographie* suggests
Stuck here as poor Cowper, I keep writing simulacra of those long riverine pauses in
    memory's exhibitionist edge the cult music overrides

∎

Hail, Wagner again, whose musics move a symbolic sublime to those steps where
    Les vampires de Paris ride
Here the honeydewed verbal message into a gesture with *phi*
let these icy heights funnel the nomenclature
there's a fine wing to these measures of an avian species
that's in my, ours, to the invisible window
I have the spectral last words before
there's no poet left, for without words I could not bridge you
Bewildered sophic
the phosphorescence
birth & death of deities galore, like in the myth: writing logomantic to
all the infinite light splendor solar   blast   winds off sudden moments when
    death's Revealed
        This long stretch of road ahead a road to Phainopepla: sulfur's red eyes

∎

Found again
There—it flew!—what is lost—coming back to me, Schelling's unified field theory
is to writing this what
art without science is dead is to
poesie and music are one
and words are that cement to borrow the term from hell
here as the revived nightmare riding our eyes to the significant *caballeria*
Yes, there's another world seen so clearly it's immediately invisible
summoning
the ice again is held like a crystal stone
Is this the Divine Cacophony?
All this studied bungling of post-18th-century Science
These tecknical applications lead to Auto-Destruction—

Here each of the two or so thousand groups of the
Beginning at the coming Confederation of Decentralized Bio-Regions the
    Consensus is herein possible
otherwise the usual carnage revives until the inevitable Catastrophe
I'm writing this, not you, It's time to give and not merely receivable

    ■

Those clusters of vampiric time to be surmounted
technical facts of practical poetry
to have an Aquarian conflict with a Piscian inversion Full moon on this thorny
    cusp
This kind of day
is a cosmic conflict
to go with the flow To throw in the sponge is not enough
    The beginning of Forms in Motion to move like Ubu into Reality
not on the way to Albania
but with gusto as
in the Italian model
    to be hailed here in Francis d'Assisi Town
    actually OHLONIA
Today I didn't go birding on the Palo Alto Baylands to look with despair for the
    long sought Clapper Rail
But who can forget its call once heard?
    in the *res*
Taking a pinch of risk powder there's the way to the future, the past we're written on
Here come the ghosts of some of the better known sages
make your own list
very "american"
A place where we shall again and for the last time apply spiritual force
I can see plainly a thousand years hence It's gone Long Gone
Blues of the world
    those crystals of night we dipped fingers into
    the god of Rivers like so many others from the Levee

Haiku for Satie

On a dance in light
You run and play
There are none there—but stars

Once in a Lifetime Starry Scape

From this being, from her, we have our breathing, green
There's another, other message through the air
at last, where she chose to shudder and quake
from the San Andreas Fault, scraping mineral life
What was distant is suddenly closer
We see deeper into nature's chaos and yet there's a stony sense
of Gaia's arrangements around the central hearth
Magma curls
water licks fire
ignitions of boiling balls
reminds me of the dance of Shiva:
a doorway turned sinuous with wood and glass,
buckling high-rises out there over the landfill
                    la bahia de los Ohlones
I dream a moat between this Bear Hill I inhabit
and those buildings of monolithic glass
a stone bridge to this new island of three thousand,
later less than five hundred humans on it,
but before contact, brown bears, owls, oaks, bobcats
and lost bird species—now only fifty or so, resident to rare
It could be, again: Avian Hill, a new Ys in reverse
outlasting earthquakes from its Franciscan stone formation
a true Frisco, "haven in a storm at sea"
to seed a coming cycle . . . Ah, brief optimum!—what if it doesn't be?
Yet, this city's night *is* marvelous when there's a general electric breakdown
The stars come down to us, I see Orion's belt close up in the eastern sky
With three-quarter waning moon
this second big one happened a little after Five in the Afternoon

"time to sacrifice one or two heads? half the human race?"
Looking into the Shulamite's, there's Morgana, the fey Morgana's eyes
till these cross-cultural correspondences form a necklace of whispers

> We are living myth
> Earth Terra Gaia speaking
speaking always, a signal from there
> into the body
> into our bodies
become a secret passage to Osiris

> *Who* lives, *who* dies, *who* resurrects?

> *Midnight of the second-greatest San Francisco Earthquake 1989*

from Triads

It's Stanley Willis playing *Wild Man Blues*
on an ocean of sidereal pianos
the web through the tonic whole tones
slip out a little geometry harmonics and Debussyian riffs

"I'm international" you said hip 1948

from BED OF SPHINXES:
NEW AND SELECTED POEMS

1997

Poem for André Breton

When we met for the last time by chance, you were with Yves Tanguy whose blue
eyes were the myth for all time, in the autumn of 1944
Daylight tubes stretched to masonry on Fifth and Fifty-Seventh in the logos of
onomatopoeic languages of autochthonic peoples
Never have I beheld the Everglades less dimly than today dreaming the Ode to
André Breton, you who surpassed all in the tasty knowables of Charles Fourier
Only the great calumet pipe for both of you We are hidden by stars and tars of this
time
No one had glimpsed you great poet of my time But the look of your eyes in the
horizon of northern fires turning verbal at Strawberry California
the Sierra Nevada seen from Mount Diablo on the rare clear day is enough of a gift
to hold up over the rivers of noise
Metallic salt flies free
that "the state of grace" is never fallen
that the psychonic entities are oak leaves burnished with mysteries of marvelous
love whose powers wake you with the glyph of geometric odors flaring in the
siroccos about to return to Africa
Mousterian flint stones caress the airs of Timbuctu as I turn a corner of volcanic
sunsets from the latest eruption of Mount Saint Helens

Ex Cathedra

To weave garter belts with chaos and snakes, the nun's toenail of crimson phallus,
her breast of alligator, her tail, crow's buttocks. Steel pricks of the ciborium
dovetail her white pantaloons—snake oil on a eucharistic tongue.

In crystal movies: an owl's path beneath slumbers of the woods that died to bolster
the miserable stations of the cross, instead of Bugs Bunny laminating the
hedgerows through the pews, stench gathers power in censers of the debasing
perfumes.

Time of frostbites laid over crumbs of bile-soaked christies, famines roasted with
divinity, allah jacks up his "prisons within prisons," the flayed kaaba-stone
pitched to the solar gobbling machine.

After the Great Dusting, this Pope exhibits his toes in carnivals sure to spring up
in sideshows of enigma, hot flints of the anti-christ, my brother, in lesions of the
darkening space, Revolution the Star in the West springs the play of foam on the
rocks below....

Field mice from the mouths of "the hell sermon," I lop off the head of the oldest
nun with a fragment of the reforgeable brassy metallic cross; this priest whipping
Sister Matilda with guts spilled from the monstrance his tongue laps up at her
feet. Oh, junkyards of eternity fester in leads of clock time, but Humankind
invents the bomb I hurl to *The Box of Infanticides,* Black-hearted children flee
gehenna, pissing through mountains of priestly corpses, those burnt hams in the
tree of winds.

Schools of fish move in the night, plagues of scripture blown to smithereens.
Secret rooms fly open absolutely by stealth.
The star card bestows the charm of new rivers, this word tomorrow, Andromeda,
and with you, Amor.

With the skull splendors of the imperium romanum, the alchemical pope skewers a
host of puffers on the backsides of saints.
Cardinals butcher in the market day for clerics.
Inside the chalice of battered gums, the vengeance of witches, salmons to spawn the
invisible eruption in the Street of the Five Rats.
Talismanic, the marigold's not a wing-feather less!

From the stone bubbles of Mother Angelica a herd of corpses rides to the spider
compass of my bones: the blood of swans lace my handcuffs floating the altars,
the inebriate sickle quick to slice those melting emeralds inlaid with scripted shit
the great unknown rages to fruition on the flanks of Carthago.

The absolute pulverization of all the churches will be the grace of love's freedom!
On that day black holes of thought radiate the wind's lost word, this death that is
not death: that day is magic is love.

Unachieved

Compared to the transcendental realm, the world under the roofed-in-cave is somber
but the colors, signatures
five senses and the sixth, their purifier
        touch by imagination's feather
     sight & sound of liquid flight from those waters the spirit scrys

Beauty comes to it at the heart's desire
to transmute out of pleasure's pleasure a distillation of birds into visionary symbols
the processional of variable coloration of finches, choral lights, *that* and the shadow
we brood

I, in the wild state, inner feelings soar

Transcendence the mental dance imagines, but for an instant, as the poet Bryant
   returning to stone
                              The starry sky, Pluto's mirror the way you could talk about
   your life, splinters off a carpenter's floor under a microscope, those perfect
   symmetries or better, visible shavings, but never the tool

Invisible something may strike through the black room of higher perfection

self-torture in the humanisphere a sure thing before a whole forest revolves to sign a
   bioregional imperative

consensus of the Hopi Way Separatist communes of no more than three thousand
   souls
         Dianas out of Gaia's caves

this window does not fade from view in the coming pre-industrial age

retrieved in a narrow shoal where a Gull Feather given in bliss turns the deranged
   corpse in ritual passes

healing prayers legitimize to exorcize the sick stain of being that death, die, at sight
   of the Androgynous Republic

Drums of magic, *salve,*
                        caught here

to return to the caesura, the interrupted fault line Frisco day which tunnels thought

Every time I think I'll turn off the main vein, quotidian concerns take over
   initiating script where you cut it, different than esoteric cant

but lingually deeper into it, like "cut it" in sacred science

... this flow of thought is different for the surrealist than for the rationalist diehard

Emotion signs this pain you're at the terminal syndrome Fabulous tunnels turn
   inner to bring up The Transcendent World Anew (it's never what you thought
   it was)

What I'm getting at is, why don't you examine with great care your entire body of
   death?
         and

reorient the auditor to a gnosis so mystical the tree bark from which it claws refuses
   to inscribe whiteness

One with the supreme ego
                              nothing more elegant on the avian plane

flicker mandibles arrange the dwelling

and from all the gifts of Gaia, head for their origin:

      In my dream, the Goddess in her heavenly palace on the earth
      a kind of Marienbad in lunar light
      She in her silver gown slightly décolleté

has me watch the Stellar Mirror
while stars of the Pleiades run in a rhythm of Eight
and do an astral dance, *tout court*

Thus begins it, Love, she and the avatar in the Bo-Tree Garden
and consider from where I'm situated here in the Far West

           green lightning at Thunder's coast
looking east to Pharaonic Egypt where the West began
          bonsai trees among the pines
a swan's luminous power in air of mist

         haunted redwood shadows
world immortal because AMOR wove a tissue clear to specular sight
Wings of this city
           an otherwise haunted hillscape
             ultimate Ys
Frisco once also covered with ancient waves
a kind of lost Atlantis several kalpas ago
its seven hills imagine old traditions of jazz

           Harmony is that secret
between the machines coming through Death is that machine
the wild wee drop
           snow to the solar radiant a fumbled perfected
  Rebus of mental luminoids
               music married to meaning when
    the orange
almost red-streaked crest
magnifies millet
         to mark off the duration:
Ornithos
      gold
      a parabola
           The treasure perch is you and me, love
a tiny winged fiery tongue through the green window
                   Forms are
    weddings
that spring trays of meaning between chirps
flutes garner ellipses of word
fork between eclipses of comet lore across lagoons

                              salt
from the Mediterranean Sea fixed here at Nova Albion
A boy painting earth colors above the valley town
my first poetry atop San Bruno Mountain was all power ekstasis
as if all tracks had left the last railway station
the sensation of sudden union with another attraction
to decipher no matter what suffering there's no pain at the taste that tells an epic
     begins
brown & red over the mental rainbow
not to close this grandeur beyond words?
War mental war and no other These the weapons on the highest nest Golden V sang
     to Violent Ocean
It was forbidden to know what the melting glyphs said over the horizon
the ways down in the valley flowed away like darkness painting poetry to light
At this stage of the great game you can assassinate all the stand-ins with cosmic
     disdain *El Poder del Niño Jesus*
In the dreams of the Philippine "master" late of Frisco gone to Alaska
"Joke's on you" The Plague reminds The Fluke
Grey cant explosions through cells
prisons rent to specular essence
where it counts . . . is it laughter?
The old necromancer calls 'em up every day faster than thought Ibis eye of the
     Sacred Geomant
Gaia doing this dance down on the plain
coming of the inland sea where once there was none
I begin to steal Gaia
but Gaia is another circle of the rose Pantheism of the moment
where all rivers meet from the mountaintop

Thunder for Gaia who's more than thunder
mysterious as in the beginning
Gaia the more I say you the seldom I leap through you
to my own ego
                    upon the bread your birds beak

Diana Green

Of that spider weaving reality I can't speak
to pink it up under paper
riding away on invisible webs stopped by specular turns
These tiny living things happen to the King in his Bath
digression to a strange unhealthy place the first seen Great-tailed Grackle signifies
    mandibles true north

                "Could he be serious about all those esoteric ideas?"
that resolve everything into dust whose remains are alkaline salt
Go read it with supernatural teeth muttering a winged language
What if it were the moment before the perfect whole?

Watching months of decadence go by
Pluto retrograde five degrees into Scorpio "It's nothing, just an appearance"
    Several hundred million humans
billions of birds
would have fried if a second space shuttle had been launched after the first
    auto-destructed
What is shows up   galloping the inner image   the finest mirror to the
    absolute clock across a sunlit room buttercup wild thistles reeds and fruity trees
    where once there was only Crissy Field
            From the femur bones of language there'll be nineteen varieties
of Oak to meet you any day of the week "The skeleton of solitude" once writ is writ
    again
and the temple of Luxor goes over it in a transparency to catch it before it goes
    A Vision of Synarchic Bioregions over Northern California's haunted scapes
          Redwood powers in those fires across the Bay
up river to Mount Shasta
             and below the Oregon Caves
I've become this sublimating hand attuned to a darkness of
sudden light on simulacra: the Great Green Faery Head thrust from redwood roots
    in the Humboldt Woods
          luminist sheen

with the wrap of words penetrating wood
I like the old legend: this paper writes me working from
    predetermined
      feathers
        a mancy of chance

delivered by Necessity
from the Mistress of the Birds
When we knew her under giant ferns Madumba's world from an ocean of her
crystal palace
This calls for an Ode a Dawn Feast
Red-faced Cormorant will be there Magnificent Frigate Bird and the Red-Crowned
of all species This imaginary avifauna suggests more terror before ritual indents a
world indeed
meditated from a bow string
to speak a visible language
when you began   where you'll end   to begin again   Preserving fire
What moves the aging man closing a car door going slowly up to a metal gate
The alchemic lesson after seeing what "Steal fire" means
Geometry is that key
older than Paleolithic
Attar's birds to the sun
I lean to that philosophic fire in caves   seashells   in the slow stalagmatic of
geologic light
Surface only is ours to see below Reason
reflect the Black Sun

Every autumn Nature has a way of showing that dragon-knot of
iridescent rot
Any forest sends up a message
clear   non-occulted   lux of darkness
green ogre of putrefactional life Poets are
speleologists at best
to see on rocks offshore The Language of the Birds

The clear-obscure of symbolical tropes
zings cosmic pleasures of laryngeal thought

Become my own cave? No easy matter   There's a reversal of those actions which
may turn into gestures "These things I'm talkin' about"
Why not dare the despised? No sooner done than asked

Precious stones dance in a ring to distinguish a redpoll's song from the local finches
(see to it, mercurial eminence, resolve it by contraries)
Fierce wild beings presage our transformation into salt—the whole past burnt into
a phoenix nest—and leave a way open even if the smallest   whatever great took
off long ago

The horizon's turned over to read the *medu-Neter*
The great crystal pool Starry Night breaks into caves
There's such a sky   instant colorations   green to
                              magenta
            harmonic doubles of ascending letters
                  dropped with leaf life
to the fogs of midsummer Doors expressionists slam An attempt to photoreal
    insomnia
There's no closure, sweetbrier Heightened teeth   for the vowel's intent from
    whence it situates
transmutable power

            a hand too languorous for drawing

this palm of oneiromancy can be read for thought, *if thought*, is diamond dust
"In harmless radioactive fallout"
on the way to the Rainbow Café
between the harmony of Clashing Rocks
there's a marsh and a meadow to call back the beasts
            "Your love affair with the birds"
Again the quintessential multicolored wild finches chirp 'round a tunnel an aerial
    way through the great game
Talking about divine emptiness (idiot-maniacal) I'm interlocking chips from
    memory's arcane shift to it
            Mirror specks devolve
to the Labyrinth Sacrifice seems sempiternal There's something about the ecstatic
    virgins of sacrifice that ties into our Subject when finches land swiftly
to fold out synesthetical displays at the brink of the world That
    tribelet's misnomer, "Ohlone"
                  mystery of holding a banner a stream of that next corner around
    a trail into redwood bark to imagine
bubbling beer of manzanita berries when Coyote made love to thousands of Dianas

Proportional to the salt of the myth
Orpheus has the ticket from Daladano to the unique Fern Forest fronting Violent
    Ocean

            Spirit of transfigured space
            perfect equipoise
from having traveled to find and to have found it Poor Medium
There's hard-headed search for it among pebbles
radishes of crooked streets

marbles with knickers a naturalist in English woods of the 1920s
        between vectors but dreaming
and isn't it with daydreams that poetry begins to dance?

        Over Land's End touch Terra with your toes

        Someday to hear poetry from a cave
as the poetry of caves ignites all centers of Gaea's embers of new light
Given that flutter of sparrow wings to the tree
        Isis
        Diana
other nameless names
crossing over dimly with portmanteau Down channel
the way so fogged meeting all that which opposes itself *Coagula* at Crystal Lake
   rock castles of green shadows and the flaming dragon completes a torment *That*
   was you, ISIS

in Diana's glass   the birds

Egypt

    In honor of R. A. Schwaller de Lubicz

Water   lustre of fire   this Hapy, this Nile
cobra skin dangles
from a crevice of a wall in the Apet Temple
stillness   soft sand   rustling breeze
Reading images around papyrus-fluted colonnades
—these moments wonder the world—
the hermetic secret   Plato   Pythagoras   Moses
finally, the Companions of Horus
come into view as the Resurrection Band
Music! perfumes! magic!

Risen, diagonally, from sun-bent water
to a green snake of trees, the Hoopoe bird
inflames gold-tinted air over the Nile
Each plumed locket on its redolent necklace
calls up spirits of the Libyan desert
I lay this baggage   to unravel   as this bird

that confounds us   You're the vowel "O"
of the higher *ka* looking to the flowers in Amenti
Kingfishers dive from the people's ferry boat

Over there, the green western bank of the Hapy,
wandering egrets scan the object
of Nut's function to carry us through the netherworld
Fire preserves its season
to become a green flame of the living face of Egypt,
sequence of a visioned recital memory's
framed revelation musics to sight
Seeds in water open the book of black silt
Hoopoe with bands of Geb's brown tones
black as Kemi is to those indwelled by light

Predawn, the fellaheen saunter to their gardens
from non-electric   amber-lit   red brick houses
so silent, slow, lifting wooden hoes over rustic *gallabeyas*
     it could be the Eighteenth Pharaonic Dynasty
Gemmed, caught up in the old ways, silver flesh
gleams between mandibles of the African Kingfisher
These moving realities appear on the Nile
as if a postcard view of it held up a hieratic bird
          silent tonalities   a secret passage   the beginning of language
crowns   caps   flight of Wagtails   Hoopoes
                         and the unknown at Karnak

Into the Dwat   gone into the Dwat
supernatural beings somewhere become vanished Horian light
          It's said   the Port
          driest of earth sand
          between powders of the Two Places
          as we come to them from a difficult crossing
          on to a way of practical harmony with the breath of virtual
          plants

Another day to write you out,
the second time round, forms pronounce
and gambol over to become phonic discretions
In the sepulchre of a sempiternal King
sometime between the Seventh and Eighth Hours
we view the circular intervals

double twelve on the stone ceiling
There was light at the end of the narrow passageway
to the Covered inner chambers of the Temple
At the invisible door of gold, Earth's lover
by a mirror seen   Better to go to the Dwat conscious
following dawn to dusk   joy   wind   and the branches thereof
Be calmed from the western horizon at Waset
The proof's in being there
Fourfold curtains drift dry to indigo
    nine blue herons on the horizon read from right to left
scent dimly recalls an unction savored in the Twenty-fifth Dynasty
      Interruptions will be solutions
      forfeiting the so-called fourth dimension
      and if this evil goes into particles:
return to the supine in serpentine form

There's an inhalation of dawn's dew
a boat furled to the Red Sun opening and closing
those horizons that are Egypt

It's easy to hallucinate Edgar Allan Poe
sipping Turkish coffee, *mazbout*, at Groppi's on the Talat Harb
Nineteenth-century Italianate masonry curling a corner
of endless newspapers of the world
The Oudj Eye multiplies invisibly
Horus visibly wears a Falcon's Head
become visible within crepuscular shadows at the nightfall of the world
whose matrix is Cairo

Reminiscing Heliopolis, ancient On of the North,
the winged shadow of the Sphinx
and all shadows between lit-up visuals
through the dream-veined streets
frame the great signature
that is eternal Egypt
       KMT Kemi the Black

    from which this and the Mirror ⚥ hath come . . .

From a sojourn on the Nile (Hapy), Autumn, 1989

Egypt II

Hi, Klingsor!
the vehicle through which Amfortas
poses the question to Perceval who doesn't know what's going on
this fixed state of infinite flight impossible from the right side crossed by the left
here in the diction everwidening to contract obliteration
a source of something and nothing
pours into the simultaneity
woof & web of
crackling wood
life & death the same
nothing's out of context
We who built the Sphinx to look at us with absolute discernment
conscious eye breath ear touch scent
the way we're annihilated by life
dissolved & coagulated in the mineral embrace
should I expand a desire to wear my heart over my dreaming hand?
a neck stiffness that changes to wood, to be in that wooded gold furnace secreted
    from the profane that lies on others?
Since I renew an ancient desire to see: Repetition of movable objects, becoming the
    risk itself   Is poesie less?
to dig diligently for the answer to the Three Vital Questions, to make a quick elixir,
    ride a horse with sinuous rhythm of neck movements
moments into monuments, Philosophia, whose secret is *that there's no secret* become
    an image of its being there
to take a look at the shadowed and phantomed outside from one's cave and tunnel
    of Ram-eyed origin
is my element
it's the perfect set of moments for this lifetime—Zervan—
Heraldic correspondences breathe where I'm fixed
eternity is elsewhere
to reach it
is an inward repetition
Nuut swallows a fiery solar disk through silver, indigo, these monuments of the
    Living King within me   this far the words regenerate beyond recall
recreate the silence to hear again White Crowned Sparrow's spring song
More precious since the Thirteenth Century, since Elizabethan times here in Frisco,
    Calafia, working on the green Androgyne

is it always the lot of the poet to be misunderstood?
who writes, re-writes? look deeply into your ashen self
in theory, transparent as glass—reds & blues—quick before the poison stops the
    Extension, flame of non-reason
synchronicity Zervan writes to keep seeking
come alive on the walls of Luxor
from the land of Punt south to Turn of the North
can I say more? since more has become the smallest in the thicket to communicate
with the Harmonic society to become a thousand years hence
Renewal from the resurrected aetheric body
fully awakened the second coming out of Kemit
This will be Joy in the true sense to play in matter
Rimbaud is a graffiti on
an outer court wall close to the Covered Temple
many more who are now the few   i'm gone
life a flying dove's mercuric shadow
to afternoon light this side of edenic illumination
working stiff-necked obstacles
still on the Road though there's preternatural fear Trigrams unresolved to the
    Quaternal One   this was not said before
though cycles of Zervan are metonymic form
spiral written records to the vanishing—cut the cliché

my apollo finger strained by writing
inscription into the salty secret of "it never dies"
the finger's infinity reminds me of one side of death
wonderful *baraka* "to die in Waset"
a rhyme and great reason   what's blackest? as climate alter
the water level rises around the Sphinx
to have been given deep science
the current of *maya Nil*
Hapi of the Hathy
diagonal trace of the Hoopoe Bird at Amenti
what's secret here is precisely known with certitude
from "the Palaces" beyond the Hoopoe vanished tree
furthermore there's an end
an invitation
the only one necessary to resee rehear recover retouch retaste

reveal glass
        to the chiaroscuro the
evident light that
gesture holding the garment with sleight of hand
of the African and American Peanut Man

Passionate Ornithology Is Another Kind of Yoga

      Thirty feisty finches at the window   FINCHDOM
Four or five double-tufted crowns
Midsummer   Spring-born
most daring of the lot   clumsy but quick
at our plastic feeder tray
Beata framed nude at a door
points her Jupiter finger: Rarely seen
a White-crowned sparrow gets blown away
by these non-Kropotkin red   yellow
silver   orange birds
            They're mean
never give any sparrow (though higher
on the taxonomic tree) even a mite's chance
to beak powder flecks finches drop
while scarfing up their hulled sunflower seeds

   ■

Glass shadows a suprasensual object
become a secret shuttle
down an escalator going simultaneously up
"the one and only god" found
from that dawn and night on the Nile
        space
where all ends in a beginning
        Amenti
mutating roseate to indigo tint
behind the darkening horizon
Over to the River's other side
my hidden eye of Horus sights

one old jazz record repeated
myriad nights & days
on a plane gathering Bird and Mozart
distant Vivaldi, wild music of
contrasting flowers whose tones
interject this Ohlonian Spring of
superfinches I love more than to become a star
Ah   visible angels of superior affectivity
with the most perfect language of sight
The chosen Red-plumed seeder
ritually feeding the Silver-lined
and a chorus of them form
an unpremeditated pentacle of erotic song

    ■

So few of us
if the seed be
become scythe, its own end
as wheaten being
germinates a songbird's form
We, too, were once avian
bridge—window—to another life
So they do know us
though now in terror
A few listen with attention—
instant Ornithos, rare
flashing cordial of communicating grace—
who see what I imagine they become
Their gestures speak with deep silence,
flying hearts, before they take off
and primordial gnosis takes flight
to carry seeded mandibles on the wind
who are clothed in primary colors
range, breadth and tones of what
red streamed from
Then, branching leaves envelop
perching forms beneath
a swathe of indigo

from SYMBOLON

1998–2001

⏺ ⏺ ▪

To be served continually with this platter of nothingness that nothing less than the graciousness of God could consume it—but, no, the ineffable transcendent is never known more distant the presence being obvious.

The next hit, the last, will display the endurance. Only a few moments give the illusion of hours . . . and if there's a secret it's a shift through the way out. The metaphor of getting tossed back together: a symbolon. Then here's this lurking thought: "The manic stance."

Ultimate Zone

> the most modern European is you Pope Pius X
> GUILLAUME APOLLINAIRE, *ZONE*

Also around 1910 Apollinaire wrote "The new spirit which will dominate the poetry of the entire world has nowhere come to light as it has in France."

It can not be said that you Pope John Paul II are the epitome of post-modernism
since for two decades you have been one of its most responsible critics
Now after so many changes so many revolutions so many end worlds
poetry itself pronounced dead in these disunited states
while you, head of quantitatively greatest of world religions
travel this world as its supreme nonconformist
announcing humanity's ultimate terrestrial hope
       "the civilization of love"
silently gathering a serene somehow impossible/possible miracle
to overcome "the culture of death"
I imagine the cosmic heart of Omega point
breaking against the cutting edge of all pseudo-paradises
whose technoscience conducts hedonic/euthanist man-unkind
to some final evil nihil
garbage chemistry/morbid physics
and on to the latest insane project
the slavocracy of biogenic clones
demons from the petri dish
recklessly to shore up a pseudo-future
at the service of hightech information machines
maintaining programmed nihilism in continuous global progression

against all possible/impossible resistance
sure to rise from the least heart of humanity against
the rule of mechanical phallus
invisible central transhumanic idol
perceived on altars of neopagan death

Memorial of St Pope Pius X
August 21, 2000 AD

Seraphim City

In the city of Saint Francis
at a grand choral Mass memorializing San Francesco di Assisi
in his new Shrine of radiant marvels
salt of his bone next to hers, his spiritual sister, Santa Clara

On this day like no other
two years since I first heard some Franciscan say
with a smile, over scented air:
    "First there was Christ
    then Saint Francis
    and since then
        a lot of Franciscans!"

So like when Francis wrote into the original Rule
that his brothers were "not to appear outwardly sad . . .
but let them show they are *joyful in the Lord*"
happy eternal moment, my heart sails out *over the gifts*
over the gifts of self with the whole Church open wide as the universe
we inside the Saviour's body
he in us we in him
for all power is in the seed of the Father
happy we, born from the spiritual womb of the Virgin Mother Mariam
prayer finally made within
from a heart cerebration can not write
yet unspoken song ripples spatially
over durational air
makes memory of what's given
    taken left/given right
begins lightening of matter, lifting spiritual weight

clear as mystery is
                  when fire caresses the given self
. . . and die to every word uttered not the word of God . . .
But no one loves except inspired by love
carnal, this side of the mystery
From atoms you come, into atoms you go
and who has ever seen, touched or even heard an atom swirling past you?

Mythos real, legends true
Resurrection invisibly visible
every bodily atom every still-to-be discovered subatomic
is good as God made it whose formal dream
is yesterday's spheric harmony
                        of clashing bodies

On the absent parvis hightech street illusion rules the day
the fact is
a TV movie was in the making as we came out of the Shrine
of Saint Francis in the very unheavenly city named for Saint Francis
Super-cool simulacra were standing around
almost robotic
as I looked back, before crossing Columbus Avenue
three tiny boats
two of them not more than a few times
the size of a classic Mediterranean fishing boat
apparitioned
                  suddenly
through the turquoise sunlight
of a timeless afternoon
I, wrapt by coat of invisible darkness
glide to embrace a whole cafe row
where postmodern unlovables ooze daylight nightmare
Love them? Not I alone, unless through, by
and with her, Creator love might
like the Saint who once repelled
was divinely moved to kiss a thirteenth-century leper
I would by love's miracle
hold those twenty-first century heads
of living death.

Saint Francis of Assisi Day
October 4, 2000

Theoria

light remember is a shadow
       casting images
       through primary colors

faster than thought
          poetry is
          slower than words

words are eidetic
perceptions of a synthesis
of symbolons—*"things"*
thrown together,
            these
            those
            under
            snaking by

Recall

      Fog be-numbed and stoned
on a cul-de-sac corner
enveloped by grey moist density
      to myself invisible
on that edge of
poised trance, hour
lasting a lifetime
      caught again as
          arrowed gift from
the next moment: these moving
points of ductile thought.

Pure Automatism

                        it seems
Prayer is quicker than thought
words coalesce: sudden seed
                        "thought"
            into
        trunk, branches, then, up a whole
solar splendiferic Tree!
                (diffusion)
effervescence   A quality of
        subsumed quantum—
        there's nothing harder to do
                        like true love
                        —like automatic
                                pilot.

          ▪ ▪ ▪

Not with the cerebrating head
but with the mind of the heart
there come to be ineffable
intellective tears of shafted light
circling the mystery core
of being from which love flows
back to you who is the
one and only source of it

Echo of St. Thérèse of the Child Jesus

Jack Kerouac praying to the Little Flower
a smile on the face of eternity
she who vowed to save
                    the likes of us

■ ■ ■

Facing branches of a flowering tree
Francis ornithic saint   flys with sufis
of ornithology   He who preached
to the birds
                read their songs of God
written in his heart
                "The language of the birds"
is never spoken

9.20.98

Hyper Sleep

> The poet extends God and poetry
> is nothing but the renewal of
> archaic divine thought.
> SAINT POL ROUX

            Undulant walls   Yellow moon
Imagination set free to do what she needs
just so two poets meet on a street corner
invisibly drinking each other's words
the coffeehouse tossed like a Chagall dreamscape
spilt milk of trauma
rises to join one to the other
we read through our lyric eyes
sounding the visible cafe secret
        public is private
Acceleration at pitch of melting steel
                        webbed and flown
images fuse improvising sound
Yesterday first telescopic sighting
of an ultimate astral anomaly
coming from the constellation of the Serpent
"A faint steady beam of light"

Hyper-somnia gives nothing but
states of awesome dreck

A poet's frenzy changing syntactics
Fourteen species of hummingbirds
at one site on a ledge in Arizona
watching the language of the birds
euphoria of their metabolic perfection
    kaleidoscopic plumages
primary colors
        gestures
                predawn language of God
heard in some ineffable bliss

With love at your side musical mornings lost to eternity
birds into ashes wait their phoenix time
what writes outside time two poets inhabit
an invisible place in the midst of everything
                        with hermetic affinity
the same frenzied eyes gaze at love
and sleep a visible daylight dream

involuntary, indolence emits black light
going through cycles of depressive windows
                the dread nothing
depth below depth to somnolent dark
become its complement/opposite
                a moderate heat maintained
                eating raw cooking
freed again from inner mantle fall

Precision
with which the sculptor
perfectly embodies
the Divine proportion
without knowing he did it
shared with the mystics

but I hallucinating on *the other side*
greater than any mescaline-visioned sky

came swiftly to a winged lion
listening for pure rhythms and
the oracular voice we must hear

two poets separate into the muggy afternoon

Humans Have Just a Few Genomes More Than Fruit Flies

Distract, to go off the text, forgotten clues to the
great game, enigmas of Cairo surveillances,
the Kuwaiti British chaos soup. Distraction like
a burst of electric flames.
Looking into the nation-face, the empire consolidates
Look away and it's rubble.
Die to poetry, live to pray and not be diverted
from—
          George the Third the abstract George
and the missing George.
Intention guides attention. Absence *is* presence.
Praise to suffering phylogenesis
discarded forest of biped arms and
opposable thumb: the furious Emperor
in his cups and asleep.
the multi-billion abstractions offer up
altars to technē out of control
Information bombs over Kabul.
Where the white shadow opens the door
Dame Perenelle and Nicholas
Flamel pray together at the athanor.
Distraction has become the intention
of praise, presence and raison d'être
of distraction, fruits of dilemma.
Steady gaze to the ineffable,
logos crossed by mythos.
Cry of crystal
               God is a surrealist
in the union of opposites, the great
proportional complements of
bipolar second raters.

This my dryness, depressive
          distance
of all the whos none I am
Totally invisible I see you clear
the simple way and the complex network

■ ■ ■

Today and yesterday are fusing
          granulate
                    to me
their reunion after sinuous painful journey
          my words fall upward
There is no vanishing reflection
          become
in this cobra skin high noon
          looking into eternity a breath
of mystical love
          Midnight
the King is Born
          still fire

Triple V: The Day Non-surrealism Became Surrealist

I: Unknown Mexico

Going the way of a Nepalese hill-tribe chieftain—Gautama Buddha— is for warriors, conquerors   who put their bodies on the line. Poets at most play with war. I have ridden horses in Mexico, but for the precipitous climb up around narrow bends of a winding trail in the Sierra Madre Mountain Range of midwestern Mexico, only a *Rey Mula* (King Mule) will do

          who
carried me eight hours to the Nayeri people
          who in their sacred (oral) text the *Majakuagy-Moukeia* were never conquered by Aztecs; nor later by seventeenth-century Spaniards nor even by Mexican regiments they beat off in the nineteenth century.

The mule knew it was sure death to round the bends unless perfectly attentive. Only once his eyes shot back rays of terror (head jerked sideways) with an infinite look of surpassing fear. I then heard sounds of tiny pebbles clicking under his slightly off-the-mark hoofs and the ruddy eye flashed while his body
tightened under me
and with the perfection of the other beauteous beasts, regained his footing, securing us from the sheer drop to the abyss below

. . .

and now: *above*

flocks of Canadian geese in their slow and perfect

round.

II: How I became a poet

for Garrett Caples

Re-volution
is simply a return
to the source. Sin is *amartia* (Greek) missing the mark.

Twelve years old: obsessed every afternoon with throwing darts a few months until one day i finally hit the bull's-eye one hundred successive times. Not long after, day came when three hundred successive throws attained their mark. In a paroxysm of ecstasy i decided to stop playing the game. About two years later the next "thing" i knew, a sudden raging wind rained autumn leaves on a clump of trees where i sat drinking a rare *licor* of music from an 1845 edition of Poe's "The Raven and Other Poems." he who had prefixed his *Poems* of 1831 with the idea "poetry should be a passion."

III:

Peace, and the sword
divides this from that:
law of Nature's eye
    descending volatile

he who catches up moving prey from the surface, putrid outcome rifts fertile crust with cyclic fruit.

Hidden Truth

for Nancy

what is site
              of the feminine but
a secret
hidden in the Virgin
                        to see this
your ankh-gestured arms
                              transmit to my right hemisphere
surely as the motoractive points in each of our two feet
cross covered rooms of the Temple at Luxor
                        on both sides
of the brain
                    taste of frankincense
                              golden musk and sacred herb

                        transmuting senses
I perceive you, chastely
                            is the divinized eros
                        metempsychosis of sexual joy the otherside
of unconditional love

                        at once the triadic crystal
when lovers first meet
                        to the second stage of erotic mind
and, this, beloved—*dilectio*—
                              I, purified,
              we find each other
                                    after a long darkness
                  on this side
                  of the mystical erotic

Selected Bibliography

Steven Fama

BOOKS

Erotic Poems. Berkeley: Bern Porter, 1946.

Ekstasis. San Francisco: Auerhahn, 1959.

Narcotica. San Francisco: Auerhahn, 1959.

Destroyed Works. San Francisco: Auerhahn, 1962.

Touch of the Marvelous. Berkeley: Oyez, 1966.

Selected Poems 1943–1966. San Francisco: City Lights, 1967.

Charles Bukowski, Philip Lamantia, Harold Norse. Penguin Modern Poets 13. Hammonds-worth, England: Penguin, 1969.

The Blood of the Air. San Francisco: Four Seasons, 1970.

Touch of the Marvelous: A New Edition. Bolinas: Four Seasons, 1974.

Becoming Visible. San Francisco: City Lights, 1981.

Meadowlark West. San Francisco: City Lights, 1986.

Bed of Sphinxes: New & Selected Poems 1943–1993. San Francisco: City Lights, 1997.

Crystals. Berkeley: Bancroft Library, 2001.

Philip Lamantia and John Hoffman. *Tau* and *Journey to the End.* San Francisco: City Lights, 2008.

FIRST APPEARANCES OF UNCOLLECTED POEMS

"Ages in The Wind." In *The Young West Sings: Anthology of California High School Poetry,* 43. Los Angeles: National High School Poetry Association, 1943.

"Symbols." *Contour Quarterly* 1, no. 1 (April 1947): 20.

"Another Autumn Coming." *The Ark* (Spring 1947): 51.

"The New Year." *Resistance* 6, no. 3 (July 1947): 11.

"Revelations of a New Order." *Contour* 4 (June 1949): 32–35.

"Scenes." *Beatitude* 9 (September 18, 1959).

"Cool Apocalypse." *Big Table* 1, no. 4 (Spring 1960): 105–7.

"Blank Poem for Poe." *Yugen* 6 (1960): 15.

"Apocalypses." *Provincetown Review* 3 (1960): 63.

"Visions." *Damascus Road* 1 (1961): 17–18.

"Last Days of San Francisco." *The Outsider* 1, no. 2 (Summer 1962): 66–67.

"Song for the Intellect." In *The New Orlando Poetry Anthology,* 44. New York: New Orlando, 1963.

"Mumbles." *Residu* 1, no. 1 (Spring 1965): 38–44.

"Ceylonese Tea Candor." *Damascus Road* 2 (1965): 36–38.

"Without Props" and "There is no death, only sempiternal change." *Once* 1, no. 1 [circa 1965].

"Thorn of the Air" and "The Flying Fix." *The Paris Review* 36 (Winter 1966): 96–97.

"For Real." *The Floating Bear* 33 (1967).

"Inscription for the Vanishing Republic," "Orphic Poem," "The Call," "Politics Poem," "Lava," and "That I burned by the screech owl castle in Berkeley Hills." *The Floating Bear* 35 (1967).

"Rest in Peace." *The Floating Bear* 34 (1967).

"At Random" and "She's Appeared and Disappeared at Once." *Anti-Narcissus,* special issue (Winter 1969–1970).

"On the plain / of the angels," "A gorgon of the language cabal," and "Flying beasts / are riveted on the air's toiling." *Caterpillar* 17 (1971): 3–5.

"New York Blank Poem New York." *The Intrepid-Bear Issue* [*Intrepid* 20 / *Floating Bear* 38] (Summer 1971): 24.

"The Hand Moves the Word Flies." *The Seventies* 1 (Spring 1972): 86–87.

"Willow Wand," "Meadowlark West," and "Sentiment for the Cordials of Scorpions." In *Free Spirits Annals of the Insurgent Imagination,* edited by Paul Buhle, 78–79. San Francisco: City Lights, 1982.

"Poetics by Pluto" and "Birder's Lament." *Exquisite Corpse* 4, nos. 9–10 (September/October 1986): 8–9.

"Poetics by Pluto," corrected version. *Exquisite Corpse* 4, nos. 11–12 (November/December 1986): 14.

"From *No Closure.*" *Caliban* 7 (1989): 19–21.

"Once in a Lifetime Starry Scape." *City Lights Review* 4 (1990): 13–14.

"Triads," excerpt. In *Purple Moonlight Pages.* [Berkeley]: Subterraneous Archives, [1993].

"Ultimate Zone" and "Seraphim City." In *Jubilation,* edited by Stephen Ronan. Berkeley: Beat Books, 2000.

"Triple V: The Day Non-surrealism Became Surrealist." *Untitled* 2 (2001): 3–4.

"Today and yesterday are fusing," printed broadside. San Francisco: Greenwood Press (December 2005).

"Haiku for Satie." In *Beat,* edited by Chris Felver, 174. San Francisco: Last Gasp, 2007.

"A Poem for John Wieners Written on His Paper" and "Jet Powered Suicide." *Cafe Review* (Summer 2012): 52–55.

"Time Is as Eternity Is: On the White Road: The Muse," "The Juggler in the Desert," "Poem for Indians," "34 Words Six Lines," "Panty Hose Stamped with the Head of the Medusa," "Babbel (is a language)," and "Babbel (Ali ben buri)." *Hambone* 20 (2012): 125–33.

Index of Titles

Note: Italics indicate the first lines of untitled poems.

Designer *Claudia Smelser*   Text and Display *Garamond Premier Pro*
Compositor *BookMatters, Berkeley*   Printer and binder *Maple Press*